Cultural Diversity, Indigenous Knowledge and Biodiversity Conservation

Cultural Diversity Indigenous Knowledge and Biodiversity Conservation

N. K. Das

SERIALS PUBLICATIONS
NEW DELHI (INDIA)

Edition: 2010

ISBN: 978-81-8387-316-1

Published by
SERIALS PUBLICATIONS
4830/24, Prahlad Street, Ansari Road
Darya Ganj, New Delhi-110002 (India)
Phone : 23245225. Fax : 91-11-23272135
E-mail: serials@sify.com

CONTENTS

INTRODUCTION

N. K. Das

Anthropology, literally the study of humanity, is a discipline which helps us to know each other more realistically. It also contributes significantly towards characterizing our identities. Given both our biological and cultural focus, anthropology often prompts us to expand our sense of humanity, of what it means to be human for both ourselves and others. In order to be compatible with the focal theme of "Humanity, Development and Cultural Diversity" of the 16th World Congress of the International Union of Anthropological and Ethnological Sciences (IUAES) 2009 Kunming, Yunnan, China- 27-31 July 2009, we have chosen the somewhat allied theme of Cultural Diversity, Indigenous Knowledge, and Biodiversity Conservation to bring together this special volume for release in Kunming, China, the venue of the 16th World Congress of IUAES. In doing so our prime purpose is to present before the Chinese and other delegates a fraction of our contributions towards understanding the larger visions of Humanity, Development and Cultural Diversity. There is no doubt that there exists one- real world anthropology, which addresses the common challenges faced by the humanity, in a universal vocabulary. Anthropologists are everywhere in unison with anthropology's basic tenets, concepts and perceptions. Nevertheless, there is one constraint. What about presence of local and regional trends in the academic world of anthropology? We still hear of the linguistic imperialism of the English language, and this term largely scaffolds the academic world of anthropologists. We also still hear of national anthropologies (American, British and the French schools etcetera) even in the era of globalisation ('New Trends in Anthropology: An Appraisal'- N. K. Das: Man in India 82:3-43-4, 295-305, 2002).

Anthropology: Scientific and Applied:
Renewed Focus on Ecological Anthropology

Anthropology has origins in the natural sciences, the humanities, and the social sciences. Holling has described "two streams" of science, one experimental, reductionist, and narrowly disciplinary, and the other interdisciplinary, integrative, historical, analytical, comparative, and experimental at appropriate scales (Holling C.S. 1998 - Two cultures of ecology, Conservation Ecology 2(2): *http://www.consecol.org/vol2/iss2/art4*). The second integrative stream is the science of complex systems. Anthropologists have had difficulty forcing their complex subject of study into the rigors of the traditional first stream of science. Case study comparisons are often our only choice. Historical peculiarities are unavoidable. Human ecosystems are vastly complex, and single dependent variables often lead to unconvincing explanations. The research in this special issue suggests a different direction. The context of our human experience is tremendously complex and endlessly evolving. An interdisciplinary science that addresses itself to evolving systems with determinant processes at multiple scales of space and time could be a better fit for anthropology. The long view in anthropology is the purview of archaeologists, cultural evolutionists, and biological anthropologists. Scholars have suggested that the prehistoric "environment" must be viewed not as a backdrop but as a "moving target" negotiated incessantly with humans and with other processes at both larger and smaller scales. The prehistoric and historic records of emergent structural diversification and economic intensification, studied and re-studied by cultural evolutionists and archaeologists for decades should be given a fresh look.History and symbol have undoubted causal force in any equation, but in complex human ecosystems they must be contextualized within multiple evolving scales of energy dissipation. Methods that can provide a complete environmental accounting can be applied to archaeological sites and their evaluation.

Anthropology originated in the West, and it has mainly developed as a field that studies other cultures, many of which are radically different from the West. Ethnography is both one of its primary methods, and the text that is written as a result of the practice of anthropology and its elements. Social anthropology has been distinguished from other social science disciplines by its emphasis on in-depth examination of context, cross-cultural comparisons (socio-cultural anthropology is by nature a comparative discipline), and the importance it places on long-term, experiential immersion in the area of research, often known as participant-observation. Cultural anthropology in particular has emphasized cultural relativity and the use of findings to frame cultural critiques. Social anthropology is, in the classic definition, dedicated to the study of distant cultures in their traditional and contemporary forms. But there is a larger aspiration: the comparative study of all human societies. Anthropology courts controversy and revels in critique, happily these days we have the bloggers produce a running commentary on events of every day. Often they come up with right visions which provide us the strength, perhaps even some authority, in offering critique that takes "common sense" and shakes it up, questioning common assumptions through cultural insights, cross-cultural data, and archaeological and evolutionary ideas.

Applied anthropology is simultaneously tied with four subfields of anthropology: ethnology (cultural), archeology, biology or physical, and linguistic, and finds ways to apply these subfields to societal problems in order to find possible solutions. Applied anthropologists are involved in government, corporate organizations, social, political and economic fields, including world business, creating public policy, law enforcement, the communication field, and medicine. These types of anthropologists provide anthropological perspective to areas not previously considered relevant to anthropology. Traditional anthropology focuses on tribal studies and extinct or dying peoples and cultures throughout. Applied anthropology remains valuable in these area. Applied anthropologists use anthropological methods and tools of research and data retrieval as professional consultants to solve real world problems and issues. Applied anthropology involves applying the study of human culture, behavior, language, and biology. Anthropologist's help humans using observation, ethnography, and collecting research and data. These tools of applied anthropology help people understand the "other", an individual or group of people that are different then the observer, and provide comparisons, differences, and evolutionary information to gain a holistic perspective on a different way of human life. Today the applied anthropology is the "scientific investigation of the principles controlling the relations of human beings to one another, and the encouragement of the wide application of these principles to practical problems " (Griffith, David, Jeffrey C. Johnson, Jeanne Simonelli, Bill Roberts, and James Wallace eds. "Mission statement". *Society for Applied Anthropology*, 2008. Retrieved on 3 February 2008 from *http://www.sfaa.net/*).

It is obvious that today anthropology and the other social sciences have embraced ecology as never before. An explosion of ecological-environmental specializations is now spreading through academic departments, including historical ecology, environmental history, political ecology, ecofeminism, environmentalism, environmental justice, symbolic ecology, ethnoecology, human ecology, evolutionary ecology, environmental anthropology, ecological anthropology, ecological economics, sustainable development, traditional ecological knowledge (TEK), conservation, environmental risk, and liberation ecology. It is pertinent here to turn to the interconnected themes of the current volume of Book of Social Anthropology –'Cultural Diversity', 'Indigenous Knowledge', and 'Biodiversity Conservation'.

Cultural Diversity

The term "cultural diversity" is perceived differently in varied contexts. It was first used, in reference to diversity of 'cultures' and 'languages'. Subsequently, it was used, in a context of the cohabitation of different cultural systems. Gradually, the diversity of cultural identities rapidly became a political argument. From the 1960s the attitude for a new vision of endogenous development and the need for a new link between culture and democracy which would lead to "the promotion of the cultural expressions of minorities in the context of cultural pluralism" are highlighted. 'Culture' indeed is core concept in the notion of cultural diversity. There is thus a focus on art and literature, which refers to the cultural expression of a community, which encompasses cultural creativity. Then, there are the ways of life, traditions and beliefs, value systems, which refer to a more sociological and anthropological vision of culture. Today the concept of cultural diversity, like that of biodiversity, envisages the multiplicity of cultures in a systemic perspective where each culture develops and evolves through contact with other cultures. UNESCO is currently elaborating a "Convention on the Protection and Promotion of the Diversity of Cultural Expressions". The protection of cultural diversity from a political and economic point of view in fact became pressing with globalization, which is characterized by the liberalization on a large scale of economic and commercial exchange, and thus, what has been called the commodification of culture. It has been noted, for instance, that over the past 20 years, trade in cultural goods has quadrupled and the new international rules (WTO, OECD) on trade are increasingly removing State support and protection measures in favour of national goods and services in the name of market freedom and free trade. New information and communication technologies are fast creating inequality and greater dependency of culture with respect to technology. This prevents the manifestation of cultural diversity that is so vital to the knowledge society. On the ethical level, the Unesco Universal Declaration on Cultural Diversity, adopted on November 2nd, 2004 [4] recognizes cultural diversity to be the "common heritage of humanity". The Civil Society Declaration to the World Summit on the Information Society in 2003 mentioned that every culture has dignity and value that must be respected and preserved. In this new setting, diversity is consequently a way of approaching the structure of how we live together, based on the acceptance of a plural vision of the world [10]. We can see then that cultural diversity is perceived here as the integration, rather than the superposition or juxtaposition of cultures and that the information society in which it is expressed is above all a society of shared knowledge. (Word Matters: Multicultural *perspectives on information societies,* 2006, C & F Éditions, *quoted in* Cultural Diversity-Alain Kiyindou). The fight to safeguard endangered cultures is thus a civic duty. How can indigenous cultures and knowledge be integrated without generalizing or particularizing them and how can they be validated with exogenous criteria? The Declaration of Principles of the World Summit on the Information Society, adopted in Geneva in December 2003, stresses the fact that :

> *"- - - applications should be user-friendly, accessible to all, affordable, adapted to local needs in languages and cultures, and support sustainable development".*

Biodiversity, Indigenous Knowledge, and Sustainable Development

The environment, which is rich in biological diversity, offers the broadest range of options for people to rely on for the fulfillment of human survival. Loss of biodiversity influences the local area and its economic bases and social fabric. The experiences of the past few decades have shown that as industrialization and economic development take place in the society, the patterns of production, consumption and the needs have changed, and they have inflicted pressure on people to alter their responses to ecosystems. Conservation and sustainable use of biodiversity therefore become imperative and indeed they are fundamental to sustainable development. This aspect is important in the assessment of biological diversity at world level, though the data reveal that Asia is the most threatened continent. One approach to understand biodiversity is to look at it in a hierarchical manner in which biological organisms are organized. The smallest unit starts from the diversity contained in the genetic material of individual organisms and then goes on to encompass the biological communities in which species are organized and then to cover the wider ecosystem in which they exist. Biodiversity is recognized at three levels viz., genetic, species and ecosystem levels. In all these levels of biodiversity, the components are dynamic in space and time. The genetic composition of species changes over time in response to natural and human induced selection process. The ecosystems strongly respond to external dynamics and internal stresses. The importance of and global commitment towards the conservation of biodiversity is no longer questioned. The accelerating rates of loss of floral and faunal species and the projected negative impacts of this loss of germplasm on humankind have been eloquently described by a growing number of prominent biological scientists such as Solbrig, Wilson and Peter, Abelson, Ehrlich, Beattie, Bower, Brockelman, Bunting, Hoyt, and Loesch. Numerous international foundations, development agencies, and international agricultural research centers are also adding the power of their collective concern and resolve to deal with the circumstances leading to the loss of species. Several influential documents have now been published. Although these publications focus on the immediate and long-term negative biological and economic consequences of the loss of biodiversity, several publications have specially highlighted the complementary importance of cultural diversity that is often reflected in the indigenous knowledge of natural resource management including that of plants and animals. The Global Biodiversity Strategy, for example, nicely portrays the need of conserving biodiversity:

> "– *Cultural diversity is closely linked to biodiversity. Humanity's collective knowledge of biodiversity and its use and management rests in cultural diversity; conversely, conserving biodiversity often helps strengthen cultural integrity and values (World Resources Institute et al. 1992: 21)*".

During the past decade progress has been made in understanding the complementarity of cultural diversity and biodiversity. Understanding the indigenous management strategies of farmers and other rural persons that foster diversity in domesticated and wild species can help in the establishment of national programs for in situ conservation of germplasm that complement the ex situ programs already in existence. "To acquire a comprehensive base of knowledge for genetic resource conservation, the genetic establishment must accept a mandate to be concerned not only with germplasm but also the knowledge systems that produce it" (Brush 1989: 22).

Studies that depicted local communities and their knowledge as 'primitive', 'simple' and 'static' are now countered by a rapidly expanding data base generated by both biological and social scientists that describes the complexity and sophistication of many indigenous natural resource management systems. New studies explore indigenous knowledge related to wild and domesticated plants and animals and the soils and water upon which they depend. The scholars involved in this area of research represent the academic fields of anthropology, agriculture, horticulture, botany, zoology, forestry, agroforestry, fisheries, ecology, wildlife management, and hydrology. The fact that so much effort is now being invested in understanding the basis for indigenous natural resource management indicates that the negative attitudes commonly held about indigenous knowledge during the colonial era have begun to change.

Indic Ethics, Environment Protection, and Mother Earth

Long before ecology became the refrain of the global call out at Stockholm and Rio, the ancient Indic heritage had already provided a spacious spiritual home for the environmental ethos. Laxmi Mall Singhvi (President of the World Congress on Human Rights, Indian High Commissioner to the Court of St James (London) analytically outlines the cultural foundation for environmentally friendly values laid down over many centuries in India. He rightly says the Indic approach to the environment is even today a part of the living legacy of India. That legacy often seems to be embattled and imperiled all around, and yet it is endowed with an uncanny and time-tested resilience. In that resilience, there is hope and promise for India and the rest of the world. The Jain, Vedic and Buddhist traditions established the principles of ecological harmony centuries ago - not because the world was perceived as heading for an imminent environmental disaster or destruction, nor because of any immediate utilitarian exigency, but through its quest for spiritual and physical symbiosis, synthesized in a system of ethical awareness and moral responsibility.

The ancient sacred literature of the Vedas enshrines a holistic and poetic cosmic vision. The Vedic seers regarded the Earth as 'sacred space' for the consecrated endeavours and aspirations of humankind and for the practice of restraint and responsibility. All four major Vedas 'the Rig, Sama, Yajur and Atharva Vedas' recognise the importance of maintenance of the seasons' cycles that are likely to get altered due to the climate change owing to inappropriate human actions. It is remarkable that the people in Vedic times regarded Nature and the environment in a holistic manner and revered each of its constituents and entities by carefully preserving them. The ancient Vedas have several references to environmental protection, ecological balance, weather cycles, rainfall phenomena, hydrologic cycle, and related subjects that directly indicate the high level of awareness of the seers and people of that time. There are many hymns seeking the blessings of the five basic gross elements or the pancha mahabhoota of Nature: akashor firmament, vayu or air, agni, tejas or fire, apah or water, and prithvi or earth. People were careful to refrain from activities that could cause harm to Nature's bounties. It was understood that the well-being of Mother Earth depended on the preservation and sustenance of the environment. The seers of Rig Veda speak on behalf of earth for its principle of replenishment "You give me and I give you". They look at every entity of Nature with the eyes of a friend and sympathiser: "Mitrasyaaham chakshushaa sarvaani bhootaani sameekshe" (Vedic perspective on environment, K. N. Sharma, *The Times of India*, 4 June 2009).

The Vedic Hymn to the Earth, the Prithvi Sukta in Atharva Veda, is unquestionably the oldest and the most evocative environmental invocation. In it, the Vedic seer solemnly declares the enduring filial allegiance of humankind to Mother Earth: 'Mata Bhumih Putroham Prithivyah: Earth is my mother, I am her son.' A soul-stirring prayer is sung in one of the hymns for the preservation and conservation of hills, snow-clad mountains, and all brown, black and red earth, unhurt, unsmitten, unwounded, unbroken and well defended by Indra. The Hymn says, in prayerful thanksgiving and homage:

Earth in which lie the sea, the river and other waters,
in which food and cornfields have come to be,
in which lives all that breathes and that moves,
May she confer on us the finest of her yield.
Earth, in which the waters, common to all,
moving on all sides, flow unfailingly, day and night,
may she pour on us milk in many streams,
and endow us with luster.
May those born of thee, O Earth,
be for our welfare, free from sickness and waste.
Wakeful through a long life, we shall become
bearers of tribute to thee.
Earth, my mother, set me securely with bliss
in full accord with heaven,
O wise one,
uphold me in grace and splendour.

The concept of unity of life is not limited to the human species. It covers all forms of life, which may be classified into: *jarayuja* (viviparous), *andaja* (oviparous), *udbhija* (germinating), and *svedaja* (generated by heat and moisture).

The ecological philosophy of Jainism, flowing from its spiritual quest, has always been central to its ethics, aesthetics, art, literature, economics and statecraft. It is virtually synonymous with the principle of Ahimsa (Non-violence), which runs through the Jain tradition like a golden thread. The term Ahimsa is stated in the negative (a = non, himsa = violence), but it is rooted in a host of positive aims and actions, which have great relevance to contemporary environmental concerns. It is a principle of compassion and responsibility, which should be practised not only towards human beings, but also towards all animals and nature. The Jain scriptures tell us: 'The Arhats (Venerable ones) of the past, present and future discourse, counsel, proclaim, propound and prescribe thus in unison: Do not injure, abuse or press, enslave, insult, torment, torture and kill any creature or any living being.' Compassion and non-violence are the basis of the ancient Jainism. Lord Mahavira proclaimed a profound ecological truth: 'One who neglects or disregards the existence of earth, air, fire, water and vegetation disregards his own existence which is entwined with them.' In The Buddhist Declaration on Nature, The Venerable Lungrig Namgyal Rinpoche, Abbot of Gyuto Tantrik University, quotes Lord Buddha Himself: 'Because the cause was there, the consequences followed; because the cause is there, effects will follow.' He concludes that these few words show that happiness and suffering do not simply come about by chance. A human undertaking motivated by a healthy positive attitude constitutes one of the most important causes of happiness; it is, in the final analysis, rooted in genuine unselfish compassion and loving kindness, seeking to bring about light and happiness for all sentient beings. The Hindus believed that humans, gods and nature were integral parts of one 'organic whole'. Ancient Hindu writers, later on, personified each of the divine force as a Devata or deity worthy of reverence and worship.To Hindus, the concept of environment protection is not a modern phenomenon; they regard that divine forces sustained all living creatures and organic things on this earth. The essential Hindu moral code is to live in harmony with creations including earth, rivers, forests, sun, air, and mountains. This belief spawned many rituals that are still followed by traditional Hindus in India. For example, before the foundation of a building is dug, a priest is invited to perform the Bhoomi Pooja in order to worship and appease mother earth and seek forgiveness for violating her. Even Charvaka, the atheist philosopher of ancient India, who totally rejected Vedas, the Hindu scriptures, considered the principles of Vayu (air) Bhumi (earth), Jala (water), Agni (fire) as important factors in regulating the lives of humans, animals and plants. This Hindu worldview of ancient Vedic times became formalized into the Samkhya system of philosophy that promoted ecology-care in Hindu attitude.

Challenges of Indigenous Knowledge and Cultural and Bio- Diversity: A Plea to International Agencies

There is greater need to discuss the links between nature and culture, and particularly to acknowledge the sacred natural sites and cultural landscapes as of vital importance for safeguarding cultural and biological diversity for present and future generations. Fact remains that the indigenous people regard many sacred natural sites as having great significance for the spiritual well being of indigenous peoples and local communities; hence the need to promote and safeguard cultural and biological diversity, particularly in the face of the homogenizing forces of globalization. There is concern expressed for the sacred natural sites, cultural landscapes and traditional agricultural systems which call for the development and adoption of ethical principles to sustain biological diversity and freshwater resources for present and future generations; for conservation of cultural and biological diversity which hold the key to ensuring resilience in both social and ecological systems. Ultimately there is need to acknowledge the important role of indigenous peoples and local communities as custodians of sacred natural sites and as holders of traditional knowledge, which is fundamental for the preservation of biological and cultural diversity. There is greater urgency today to admire indigenous peoples' rights to their lands and knowledge; and acknowledging the important role of spiritual traditions in the conservation of sacred natural sites and cultural landscapes.

Anthropology's enduring interest in people's knowledge systems has recently attracted the attention of development policymakers and practitioners. 'Indigenous knowledge' has emerged with the focus on popular participation and planning-from-below. It has opened up opportunities for anthropology to engage practically in rural/ folk/ tribal-indigenous locality. But certain questions need universal answers. What is the 'indigenous knowledge' as used in contemporary development discourse? What place does indigenous knowledge have in a globalizing world? As regards the 'Indigenous knowledge' and intellectual property rights, who has the right to own and control knowledge flows? Is knowledge everywhere owned, or is this a western cultural construct? Is there a need to frame research into knowledge traditions in wider legal contexts? How can indigenous knowledge research inform social development without appearing to engage in social engineering? How to facilitate interdisciplinary research between natural and social scientists, and new forms of collaboration in anthropological research? These are indeed the issues surrounding which several panels/sessions are organised in 16th IUAES World Congress. There is need to discuss specifically the discourse of the tangible and intangible heritage vis-a-vis concepts such as value, sustainability and authenticity? What are the implications for heritage research, management and museums? Is it constructive to reorient and reappraise the materiality of heritage? While some of the knowledge elements perform very specific functions of solving health, conservation or production problems, others shape the broader worldview. With passage of time, some of these knowledge, innovation and practices survive in their functional forms and some as part of belief systems, in fact, even as superstitions. Fact remains, however, that in most case, institutional norms, ethical values and cultural codes do evolve along with traditional knowledge. The knowledge systems evolved by people are in stress on account of influences from the modern world, some at their terms and many at the terms at which outsiders determine.

Here we strongly urge to the following world bodies to be alert and be supportive in effective implementation of the programmes. There is need to take serious note of the various international bodies, instruments, programmes, and strategies, such as the International Bill of Human Rights (1966); the 1971 Ramsar Convention on Wetlands of International Importance; The 1972 UNESCO World Heritage Convention; International Labour Organization Convention 169 on Indigenous and Tribal Peoples, 1989; The 1992 United Nations Conference on Environment and Development; The Convention on Biological Diversity (1992); The Seville Strategy for the World Network of Biosphere Reserves of the UNESCO Man and the Biosphere Programme (1996); The mandate of the United Nations Permanent Forum on Indigenous Issues (UNPFII) (2000); The 2001 UNESCO Universal Declaration on Cultural Diversity; The 2003 UNESCO Intangible Heritage Convention; The IUCN International System of Protected Area Categories and the outcomes of the IUCN Vth World Parks Congress 2003; The FAO initiative on "Globally Important Ingenious Agricultural Heritage Systems"; and The UNU initiative on People, Land Management and Ecosystem Conservation.

Today there is greater urgency to be vigilant on part of national authorities, protected area and site managers, indigenous peoples and local communities, the international systems, governments and non-governmental organizations, to consider and implement, where appropriate UNESCO/IUCN Guidelines for the Conservation and Management of Sacred Natural Sites; CBD Akwé:Kon Voluntary Guidelines for the Conduct of Cultural and the Yamato Declaration on Integrated Approaches for Safeguarding Tangible and Intangible Cultural Heritage in order to save Sacred Sites, Lands and Waters traditionally occupied or used by Indigenous and Local Communities.

The chosen themes of Cultural Diversity, Indigenous Knowledge, and Biodiversity Conservation are too focused to be adequately and justifiably analyzed by the specialists in one discipline. Hence, we approached the colleagues in allied disciplines. Thus we have contributions from environmentalists, geographers, biologists, and anthropologists/sociologists compiled in one place. Our scholars have dealt with the issues of the Cultural Diversity, Indigenous Knowledge, and Biodiversity Conservation variously from the standpoints of their disciplinary orientations. However, to a great extent they all portray a definite anthropological perspective in the sense that they are all concerned essentially with the people, their knowledge systems, their traditions/ beliefs, their conservation techniques and their responses to development programmes, all over the world. All papers focus on lone or more of the issues of the Cultural Diversity, Indigenous Knowledge, and Biodiversity Conservation and in doing so they are not confined to Asia/ South Asia alone.

In the very first trend setting article, Dr. M. Sreenathan warns how the increasing threat to Language Diversity has become a global concern as the contemporary political settings, in diverse nation-states universally promote the implementation of 'dominant language' and generally prevent directly or indirectly the inter- generational transmission of smaller languages. The institutional agenda of most States, their respective language policies, literacy –education approaches, the languages of media and such institutionalizations are in favour of ' forced-unifying' of cultures rather than helping in maintaining linguistic/cultural diversity. In fact, the reduction in such linguistic/cultural diversity has irrecoverable impairment on human survival. Being an ethno-linguist the author focuses on the linguistic situation and hence some evidences relating to Indian Language Diversity and its declining trends in order to emphasize the need of interventional language policy for the maintenance of linguistic-diversity is spelled out. The paper illustrates at first, the relation of indigenous knowledge, language diversity and biodiversity, secondly the elucidation of the language diversity of India and then it depicts the declining trend of language, which in sequence demands the interventional language policy. Dr. M.Sreenathan, the author, establishes the explicit symbiotic linkage between environmental issues and the survival of languages. He says, the metaphor of preservation of languages too appeared from within the biological sciences. It is argued that the extinction of languages is part of the larger setting of the near-total collapse of the worldwide ecosystem, and that the struggle to preserve environmental resources, such as the rainforests and unique ethno-botanical knowledge dependant on them, cannot be separated from the struggle to maintain cultural and linguistic diversity. The biological diversity is thus analogous and symbiotically matched with the given cultural and linguistic diversity. Around the world, there is a high level of co-occurrence of flora, fauna, and languages, and humid tropical climates, forested areas, and mountainous regions are especially favourable to biological and linguistic diversification. Environment has been the concern of all sciences – be they social or natural. But in social sciences it did not have the central significance.

In the context of developing the basis within the natural and social sciences for the rational use and conservation of resources of the biosphere, emphasis was led to pursue the environmental approach in social scientific scrutiny. Professor Yogesh Atal being the UNESCO Regional Adviser for Social and Human Sciences in Asia and the Pacific was part of the initiatives undertaken to deal with the situation, mainly through the Man and Biosphere [MAB] Programme, and other programmes. In his crucial article Prof Atal deals with UNESCO's intergovernmental Programme on Man and Biosphere [MAB] in the context of the Social Science Efforts. He says that MAB was never intended to be a preserve for the natural scientists alone. It was conceived as a programme of research aimed towards "developing the basis within the natural and social sciences for the rational use and conservation of resources of the biosphere, and for the improvement of the global relationship between man and the environment". Professor Atal continues to share his rich experiences by focusing on yet other themes of this special volume, that is, the Indigenous Knowledge. He says there is a dramatically growing national and international interest in incorporating indigenous knowledge systems, including traditional ecological knowledge, into truly participatory approaches to development. He says that a local knowledge may be relevant and useful not only at its place of origin but might have wider applications. One major worry of the many enthusiasts of indigenous knowledge systems is the commercialization and museumization of tradition. This is a fact to be reckoned with. The challenge is manifold: how to preserve and record for the posterity the originality of the modes of production of artifacts and pieces of art of the indigenous people? How to ensure a quality life of the indigenous people? How to ensure that the local artists do not get pauperized and marginalized, and their skills are stolen and used through mass medium of duplication? There are people and agencies that express worry about profound loss of indigenous peoples and their knowledge about the natural world constructed by generations from their intimate ties to their locale. They allege that their practices and beliefs are marginalized and neglected because these are regarded as inferior forms of knowing compared to the Western scientific tradition, presented as universally applicable. Western scholars pigeonholed indigenous knowledge in the scaffolding of their knowledge systems. That procrustean method of accommodation of alien knowledge led to several misrepresentations and quite often wrong interpretations and assumptions. It can safely be said that the non-indigenous people made construction of knowledge about, and for, the indigenous people, during colonial period. The "outsiders" took on the role of understanding the "other cultures". That is how the discipline of Anthropology came to be defined. It is this definition that also facilitated studies of communities other than the tribal that belonged to indigenous civilizations. India, thus, offered a good site for research to those anthropologists who extended their scope beyond the tribes to cover indigenous civilizations. However, in such non-tribal societies, nay the civilizations, the insider scholarship contested the social constructions by the outsiders. Of course, such contestations were part of a nationalistic sentiment that grew with the freedom movement. Now a similar reaction is in evidence in case of other tribal communities, which have among themselves a good number of literates and highly educated people, including those trained in anthropology. These insiders question outsider reconstructions of knowledge of their respective societies. Moreover, much of what was written about them in the late nineteenth century, and the first half of the twentieth century has already become dated.

Professor P. R. G. Mathur discusses the issues of Indigenous Knowledge, Forest Ecosystem and Native Medicines amongst the tribes of Kerala, in a critical manner. The main focus is however on one community, the Kurumba, a scheduled 'primitive tribe' of Kerala. The focus of analysis is on the cultural heritage and biodiversity conservation linked traditional knowledge. The paper also discusses briefly the conceptual issues surrounding the themes of Culture, Ecology and Cultural Ecology. The paper also describes the knowledge of the Kani tribe in the field of medicinal plants. The Kani or the Kanikkar tribespeople are now internationally known community for their knowledge in traditional medicine, with the efforts of Tropical Botanical Gardens Research Institute, Trivandrum. A medicinal plant, called Arogya Paccha, used by the Kanikkar for the treatment of diabetes, is now known to larger world. The Coimbatore Ayurveda Pharmacy, TBGRI and the Kani (Kanikkar) tribe have entered into an agreement for sharing the benefits under the Bio-diversity Act. The Coimbatore Ayurveda Pharmacy agreed to pay 10 lakhs Rupees to the researchers of TBGRI, of which 5 Lakhs was paid to the Kanikkar. Tribespeople are traditionally attached to the forest and they consider themselves to be nature's endowment. Their art and culture are replete with references to the forest. There are many rites and rituals, which are devoted to the forest and where forest produce is used by one way or other. Many of the leaves, climbers needed in magical-religious rites are procured from the forest. Many trees in forests are considered to be abode of deities and are worshipped as sacred. Existing forest in India is also the resource base for pharmacopoeia. The tribal people are conversant with the knowledge of use of such medicinal plants occurring in these forest areas. There is a symbiotic relationship between the tribal social organization and forest economy in the specific historical context of India. The overwhelming majority of the tribal people have been living there for centuries and they have evolved a mode of life which, on the one hand is woven around forest ecology and forest resource and on the other, ensures that the forest is protected against degradation by man.

Next paper again deals with the issue of IKS. Sakshi Bhandari, Man Singh Rana and S. S. Samant, from G.B. Pant Institute of Himalayan Environment and Development, Himachal Pradesh, India discuss the issue of Indigenous Knowledge of the Medicinal Plants in Kullu Valley of Northwestern Himalaya, in a critical case study. They argue that indigenous and traditional knowledge are the pillars of any society. Indigenous knowledge of the medicinal plants is crucial for the continued existence of the human beings. The treasury of the diverse medicinal plants available in the vast Himalayan regions has been recorded in ancient Indian scripts as far back as 1000 BC. The Himalaya abounds with unique medicinal plants with potential to be used in the modern medical therapy. Credit goes to the native people for conserving and preserving the old knowledge of the medicinal plants to a great extent. The Kullu valley being situated in the lap of the North Western Himalaya possesses varied topographic and climatic conditions with a wide range of elevation. Because of this varied topography and climatic conditions, the diversity of the medicinal plants in the valley is also very high. The present work explicitly documents the indigenous knowledge of the people of Kullu valley, with the elucidation of 114 species of plants belonging to 82 genera and 47 families. Apiaceae was the most dominant family (06 genera, 10 species) of medicinal plants, followed by Lamiaceae, Ranunculaceae, Asteraceae and Polygonaceae. Of the aboveground plant parts used, leaf was used in majority of cases (40 species), followed by fruit. Of the belowground plant parts used, root (45 species) was used in maximum cases. The results of this study are further discussed in the context of developmental activities and changing socio-economic conditions. With the realization that fast depleting phytodiversity has invaluable therapeutic properties, the current research is undertaken.

The next paper titled 'Indigenous Knowledge Application for Conservation of Bio-Resource in the Cold Desert of the Northwestern Himalaya' is contributed by Santaram S. Oinam, Jagdish C. Kuniyal ,Yashwant S. Rawat, S.C.R. Vishvakarma and Dinesh C. Pandey.They belong to G. B. Pant Institute of Himalayan Environment and Development at Arunachal Pradesh and Himachal Pradesh and the Department of Geography, Kumaun University, Nainital, India respectively. These scholars have found that the people of the northwestern Indian Himalaya practice a variety of indigenous practices to live in by way of storing as well as using their locally available resources. Some of the techniques under these practices such as storage of potato in the sub-soil underground pit, drying up of meat and its storage in living room, storage of food grains in wooden box, and uses of buckwheat fibers in making shoes, are all atypical. The various traditional uses based on uses of natural resources for sustenance, aim at utilizing plant parts based on assessing overall resource capability. Data are collected by conducting extensive survey in four selected villages to assess the status of the indigenous knowledge systems for bio- resources uses. The information about storage of food grains, vegetables, fruits, fodder, fuel wood, use of indigenous container were gathered by recording the responses of the villagers through structured questionnaire. More than 90% of households were interviewed in all four villages. The first hand data about traditional use of human excreta, total production of night-soil compost (NSC), agriculture area covered by NSC and animal dung for manure were obtained through direct interviewing of the family heads. The information was also gathered from secondary sources.

In a brief but stimulating paper "Tradition as a Modern Strategy: Indigenous Knowledge as Local Response to Globalization in Africa" Dr Geoffrey I Nwaka, Professor of History, Abia State University,Uturu, Nigeria, discusses the relevance of Indigenous Knowledge, and how it relates to Modern Science, and to conventional development practice. Indigenous Knowledge is used to refer to the vast and largely undocumented body of knowledge, wisdom, skills and expertise which a given community has developed over time, and continues to develop as it grapples with the challenges of its environment, with outside ideas, and with constantly changing conditions. Indigenous Knowledge represents the heritage of creative thought and practical everyday life, which is passed on orally or through experience from one generation to the next. Indigenous Knowledge is dynamic, and is not really in conflict or in competition with modern science or modernity. The author reviews the World Bank volume - Indigenous-Knowledge: Local Pathways to Global Development –and urges that indigenous knowledge as a model needs rethinking. This paper ponders the challenges of Africa in coping with globalization in a way that is compatible with local values and priorities; and which strikes the right balance between global and local cultures in national governance and development. This paper thus considers how indigenous knowledge and native practice can be put to good use in support of local governance and development in African countries; how development policies and programmes can be made to reflect local priorities, and build upon and strengthen local knowledge, capacity and organization, especially in such vital areas as agriculture and natural resource management, law review and conflict resolution, education, health care and poverty alleviation. Broadly pursuing the view of Marshall Sahlins when he invokes the peoples "to indigenize the forces of global modernity, and turn them to their own ends", since the real impact of globalization depends largely on the responses developed at the local level, this paper acknowledges the renewed interest in Indigenous Knowledge and institutions which are in line with the current advocacy of the minimalist state and the 'enabling approach' as condition for good governance.

In the next chapter titled 'Indigenous Tribal Art: Strategy for Conservation and Promotion' Dr. Somnath Chakraverty, Project Director, Asiatic Society, Kolkata, deals with the earliest evidences of visual art tradition in India in specific context of the prehistoric rock art. He argues for the reconstruction of tribal history in India by considering the pictorial evidences of rock art as dependable and authentic source. He says some other forms of archaeological data, such as the tools and other artifacts, may help reaching some assumptions. Having traveled several world sites and gaining experiences, it is possible for Dr. Somnath Chakraverty to state that in the global ethnographic records on tribal art it is revealed that their visual art tradition is mostly inspired by the aspirations common to the people and it reflects their attitude, need and sentiment towards both internal and external world as also beyond it, i.e. the supernatural domain. In India, most tribes have preserved their similar belief and art traditions. In some selected tribal groups, however, we witness the advanced practice of traditional form of art, wherein tribal artists express aesthetics and creativity instinctively. This aspect needs scientific study. Commercialization of the tribal art and crafts is a current phenomenon and mostly induced by outsiders. Dr. Somnath proposes a strategy and action plan for conservation and promotion of tribal art.

In the next paper titled 'Women's NutriBusiness Cooperatives in Kenya: An Integrated Strategy for Sustaining Rural Livelihoods', Audrey N. Maretzki, PhD, has discussed how rural poverty and human development issues were addressed through implementation of the nutribusiness concept in two rural Kenyan communities. NutriBusiness Project began in 2 Kenyan sites. These locations, though agronomically similar, are culturally different. In both areas, however, women are subsistence farmers, and many belong to one or more village women's self-help groups. Women's groups are organized at the village level and have successfully created small-scale entrepreneurial opportunities for many rural Kenyans. Involvement in these income-generating groups protects the money women earn through collective activities from appropriation by other family members. With funding provided by the Center for Higher Education of the United States Agency for International Development, The Pennsylvania State University and Tuskegee University collaborated with the University of Nairobi in establishing women's NutriBusiness Cooperatives. This initiative enabled approximately 2500 rural Kenyan women farmers to add value to their crops by processing and locally marketing nutritious, convenient, culturally-appropriate weaning food mixes. Implementation of the NutriBusiness model is described and challenges of cultural engagement are highlighted. Nutribusiness involves "activities that address nutritional needs by providing quality foods and food products at affordable prices through small-scale private sector approaches. The nutribusiness concept also incorporates environmentally regenerative Production, storage and distribution techniques that avoid pollution and inappropriate or excessive use of energy and other natural resources."

In nexty paper Professor Georg Pfeffer of Freie Universität, Berlin, discusses the predicament faced by the Tribes of Highland Orissa in the context of the modern development programmes launched in the area. In doing so he refers to relevant points of the book- Tribesmen (1968) authored Marshal Sahlins. He says that when dealing with hill peoples in South and Southeast Asia we seem to sense a good number of structural commonalities, but perhaps we need to clarify these issues.

The issues of the conservation of nature and genetic resources, participatory sustainable resource utilization with a concern for ecosystem, traditional dependence of people on forest resources, the human adaptations and treating the ecosystem as sacred landscape, with sacred species, and calling Khangchendzonga as the guardian deity in Khangchendzonga Biosphere Reserve area is discussed by Dr. Umesh Kumar. The Khangchendzonga Biosphere Reserve is one of the fourteen biosphere reserves in India. Located in Sikkim in the eastern Himalayan Region and named after the world's third highest mountain peak, Mt. Khangchendzonga, it covers an area of 2619.92 square kilometers. Author observed that there is a hierarchy in terms of sequential evolution of the concept of sacredness involving multiple elements -sacred species, stones, land sites at the bottom and the Guardian deity Khangchendzonga on the top. It is observed that this belief plays a vital role in the conservation of nature and finds expression in rites and rituals of the local communities. Nevertheless, in recent times mounting population and increased Himalayan visitation have resulted in the degradation of the ecosystem. The causative factors are dependence of human population on forest for fuel, fodder, timber and non-timber forest produce. An attitude survey done by applying contingent valuation method shows that people are concerned about the conservation of the forest resources. The result has shown the willingness of the people to accept the conservation concerns and also to pay for it. However, it is related with the socio-economic driven concern of the people. It is, therefore, sine-qua-non that socio-economic concerns of the people need to be properly addressed. The experiences gained from the study suggest that making provision of alternative livelihood openings and involving the stakeholders in the conservation efforts can accomplish the aim of conservation of the forest resources.

In the appraisal titled 'Tribes without Forest: A critique of forest and environmental conservation issues', author Dr. J. J. Roy Burman of Centre for Dalit & Tribal Studies, Tata Institute of Social Sciences, Mumbai,observes that the tribes in most parts of India continue to have a symbiotic relationship with the forests. In more recent years however there are instances when the tribespeople are moving out from traditional habitat and there are many who now aspire to earn money and be part of market economy. Author says that many activists and academics are trying to focus the issues of the forest at national level and re-establish the land rights of the tribes. Likewise, many tribes are today demanding their territorial rights (which they lost in the colonial era) over the natural resources and some are even seeking the right to self-determination. Author suggests some remedial actions for compliance.

Professor Ladislaus M. Semali of Pennsylvania State University, USA has raised important issues of Postcolonialism, Survival Strategy and Indigenous Language-

Education Politics in Africa in his essay. This essay exposes the fault lines and contradictions inherent in knowledge production debates and illustrates the challenges of subjugation that oppressive situation presents, particularly the continued absence, erasure, and subordination of local people's knowledge, history, and experience from academic texts, discourses and materials, social and political practices found in curricula and texts in Northern societies. Author suggests conceptualizing African adult basic education broadly to encompass the reality of Africa. Instead of promoting adult basic education-ABE -exclusively as adult learning based on formal schooling pedagogy, jobs, employment, and workplace productivity, author proposes about ABE as a way of knowing, thinking and doing that enables indigenous innovation to build the capacities of farmers, farmers' groups, women's groups, youth and communities to identify their needs, their community assets, the collective capacity for innovation and for creating new alternatives for resource-poor farmers, especially women. This paper documents examples from East Africa to illustrate the dilemmas and contradictions that face communities in this region and their governments in the efforts to overcome poverty and implement the UN Millennium Development goals.

In the last paper - 'Diversity, Pluralism and Convergence: South Asia and India in Perspective' - Dr. N. K. Das deals with issues of "Cultural-Diversity" Pluralism and Convergence which are deeply interconnected in today's world. Author says cultural diversity includes several representations and perceptions, such as race, ethnicity, language, tradition, culture, morality and religion. In order to quantify or estimate cultural diversity we need to count the number of cultures being practiced and the variety of languages spoken regionally or globally. However, in any attempt at measuring the diversity of cultures, the essence and frontier of culture has to be identified. At present, people's values, customs, beliefs and traditional knowledge systems that collectively shape the 'culture' are increasingly recognized as vital sources for grassroots development. In political settlement and management of the issues related to small populations/ tribes/ minorities too "Cultural-Diversity" today plays vital role. Former anthropological theories of culture defined culture as coherent, integrated, ordered, and stable. Today, however, the issues of cultural differences, identity and 'ethnicity', which have emerged as a political factors, are witnessed globally. Globalisation and localization are simultaneously operating today. Today we live in a new geo-religious reality. One of the decisive facts of these days from a global perspective has been the tremendous migration of peoples from one nation to another, both as immigrants and as refugees. People in every part of the world today confront and they frequently endure the plurality of religious traditions and cultures. Indeed, increasing competitions for scarce resources and increasing movements of peoples and their increasing culture contacts have made the terms ethnicity and syncretism as leading concepts. At one level ethnicity also represents common and shared culture. These concepts have generally outdated the concepts of acculturation and assimilation. Indeed, instead of any real 'clash of civilizations', the world is heading for convergence. In this milieu it is all the more fundamental to discuss the theme of community in Indian perspective, mainly in the framework of pluralism in the wider perspective of state. This paper has dealt with the three interconnected conceptions of Cultural-Diversity, Cultural Pluralism and Cultural Convergence, with reference to above-mentioned wider theoretical prelude, particularly in the south Asian/ Indian contexts.

International academic contacts are bound to lead to a series of productive dialogues amongst the colleagues. This should eencourage and foster new approaches of research. We sincerely hope the IUAES World Congress, China, 2009, will spark a dialogue between Chinese anthropologists and non-Chinese anthropologists. On our part, we are extremely pleased to release this volume during the IUAES World Congress.

We are pleased to release this book in commemoration of the 16th World Congress of the International Union of Anthropological and Ethnological Sciences (IUAES) 2009, Kunming, Yunnan, China- 27-31 July 2009. The Editor is thankful to many scholars and individuals who have provided the assistance and ideas for developing the themes and views in this book. If there is any lapse in acknowledgement we would like to be informed so that the corrective measure may be initiated. Editor is especially thankful to many scholars whose brief narratives are reproduced here to pursue the argument for the sake of progression of anthropology. The Editor is very thankful to the Serials Publishers, New Delhi, for bringing out this special volume in a very short time.

LANGUAGE DIVERSITY, INDIGENOUS KNOWLEDGE AND BIODIVERSITY CONSERVATION: The Symbiosis

M. Sreenathan*

Indigenous Knowledge, Cultural-Linguistic Diversity and Biodiversity are intimately united through their mutually supportive roles. Recent studies have provided far-reaching analysis of critical interrelationships between them. This paper seeks to establish the critical and symbiotic relationship amongst the Indigenous Knowledge, Linguistic Diversity and Biodiversity in Indian context by highlighting their mutually supportive roles. In doing so, however, the emphasis is focused on the linguistic situation and hence some evidences relating to Indian Language Diversity and its declining trends are provided in order to emphasize the need of interventional language policy for the maintenance of Linguistic-Diversity. The paper illustrates at first, the relation of indigenous knowledge, language diversity and biodiversity, secondly the elucidation of the language diversity of India and then it depicts the declining trend of language, which in sequence demands the interventional language policy.

Indigenous Knowledge, Cultural-Linguistic Diversity and Biodiversity are intimately united through their mutually supportive roles. Recent studies have provided far-reaching analysis of critical interrelationships between them (Fill and Mühlhäusler, 2001, Maffi, *et al.* 1999, Nabhan 2001, Nations 2001, Oviedo and Maffi 2000, Smith 2001). The ever increasing threat to language diversity is a global concern (Grenoble and Whaley 1996, 1998, Krauss 1992), as the contemporary political settings, in diverse nation-states commonly promote the implementation of dominant language and generally block directly or indirectly the inter- generational transmission of smaller languages. The institutional agenda of most States, their respective language policies, literacy–education approaches, the languages of media and such institutions are in favour of unifying cultures rather than helping in maintaining linguistic/cultural diversity. In fact, the reduction in diversity has irrecoverable impairment on human survival.

* Dravidian University, Kuppam, 517 425, Andhra Pradesh, India

Scholars have established the explicit symbiotic linkage between environmental issues and the survival of languages. In "On the Origin of Species" and "the Descent of Man", Darwin observed parallel between language and species. This metaphor continued to reappear in linguistic discourses particularly in sphere of the ecology of languages. Language death is often compared to species extinction. It is not difficult to ascertain languages, which are predisposed to extinct. The metaphor of preservation of languages too appeared from within the biological sciences. Daniel Nettle and Suzanne Romaine (2000) establish an explicit link between environmental issues and the survival of languages. They argue that the extinction of languages is part of the larger setting of the near-total collapse of the worldwide ecosystem, and in their view the struggle to preserve environmental resources, such as the rainforests and unique ethno-botanical knowledge dependant on them, cannot be separated from the struggle to maintain cultural and linguistic diversity. The biological diversity is thus analogous and symbiotically matched with the given cultural and linguistic diversity. Around the world, there is a high level of co-occurrence of flora, fauna, and languages, and humid tropical climates, forested areas, and mountainous regions are especially favourable to biological and linguistic diversification (The World's Biocultural Diversity: People, Languages and Ecosystems, The Map produced by UNESCO, Terralingua, and World Wildlife Fund for Nature, Heywoosd. 1995).

This paper seeks to establish the critical and symbiotic relationship amongst the Indigenous Knowledge, Linguistic Diversity and Biodiversity in Indian context by highlighting their mutually supportive roles. In doing so, however, the emphasis is focused on the linguistic situation and hence some evidences relating to Indian Language Diversity and its declining trends in order to emphasize the need of interventional language policy for the maintenance of linguistic-diversity is spelled out. The paper illustrates at first, the relation of indigenous knowledge, language diversity and biodiversity, secondly the elucidation of the language diversity of India and thirdly, and then it depicts the declining trend of language, which in sequence demands the interventional language policy.

Languages are an integral component of a nation's rich Intangible Cultural Heritage (ICH). These ICH resources are recognized as seminal to the people's cultural and historical identity. Its magnitude is majestically pronounced, in the following Declaration:

> *"Cultural Diversity is as necessary for Humankind as Biodiversity is for Nature"*
>
> **-UNESCO 2002, Article 1**

Linguistic diversity is indeed essential for ecological stability. Languages reflect their environment (Maffi, 1996, 2001, Milshler, 2001, Mühlhäusler, 2003). The interrelations of ecology and language are well recognized as every language encodes subtle knowledge about environment, medicine, flora and fauna, agriculture and the like. Consequently they persist as being the logo of cultural uniqueness, worldview and repository of history and beliefs they keep shape the identity of the people and region. A language death implies a loss of culture with rich oral tradition, which in turn reduces the survival options for humanity in general.

The forest dwellers, tribes and other rural populations have witnessed increased changes in the settlement ecology as also shifts in traditional occupations. People of India study (K. S. Singh 1994) revealed that the ecological degradation has curtailed the traditional occupations of the tribal communities. The displacement of groups due to forest act, developmental activities and other reasons catalysed alienation among smaller groups. The change in livelihood, displacements etc have seriously affected the language loyalty of these communities as they failed to maintain the traditional way. In India, linguistic and cultural identities are closely interlocked though ethnic and linguistic identity and heritage may not be parallel to each other in several instances. India's Indigenous People define themselves in large part according to the language they speak. Languages of the indigenous tribespeople do not die even in case of drastic social economic change.

India is well recognized as a unique country for its rich Language Diversity. The issue of Mother Tongue is always a grave concern as its very meaning changes in Census Reports. The Indian Census has a record of presenting a fairly systematic account of Mother Tongues since 1881.The language ordinarily spoken in the parental home of a person is considered as mother tongue since the period of 1881 census. According to 1961 Census, there were 1652 mother tongues including 103 foreign tongues. In 1991, the language data were gathered on the basis of parent tongue, specifying the language ordinarily spoken in household of the parents, whether it be the place of habitation or not. Language ordinarily used at household was the determinant of mother tongue in 1901 census. Other than the parent tongue, people were asked to provide information on language in use, outside household, say mostly regional tongue. Home language was included in 1911, 1921, censuses while in 1931, 1941 and in 1951 it was the language first spoken from the cradle.

However, since the time of the 1961 census, the language spoken in childhood based on tongue of the person's mother or the tongue mainly spoken at the household has been considered. In 1971, 1981.1991 and 2001 it was the language spoken in childhood by a person in the household became the criterion. From respondent's declaration census enumeration of mother tongue goes in thousands, which the agency publishes often. For instance out of 3000 mother tongue returns, 1652 were retained in 1961 census. Since 1971, the conditionality of the association of the 10,000 speakers with a tongue to be enumerated in census has come as big blow, for the minor language speakers. Consequentially, 2001 census reported returns of 6661 Mother Tongues. After processing entire 2001 Census lists a total of 122 languages and 234 mother tongues of which, 22 are scheduled languages, were acknowledged. The huge variation exist between raw mother tongue returns and the final Census outcome is mainly due to technical reasons such as multiplication of names of languages and 10000 speaker's criterion. Had the tongues with less than 10000 speakers taken into consideration, the overall tally would have been very high.

As regards Indian surveys of languages and dialects and material on language diversity of India the contributions like "Linguistic Survey of India" and "People of India" cannot be ignored. The Linguistic survey of India had identified 179 languages and 544 dialects. The People of India project identified 325 languages used in households. *Ethnologue* lists 428 languages including 13 extinct languages.

Phylogenetically all the languages are grouped under four major Language Families like Austro Asiatic, Dravidian, Indo Aryan and Tibeto-Burman as well as Andamanese family of languages, which is projected to be in two smaller families (Onge Jarawa and Great Andamanese). Thus we get altogether six language families reported from India. However, the fact remains that in the Indian surveys of languages and dialects and material on language diversity of India disparity exists in terms of number due to varied selection of variables in each survey. Even then what we get is enormous language diversity. The organizations like Census of India, Anthropological survey of India and Linguists at large have proposed different number of tribal tongues. All these propositions undoubtedly accept the fact that the tribal communities have huge number of distinct languages, which comes out to be about 80% of the languages in India. Also it is also a fact that the tribes of India exclusively speak both Austro Asiatic and Tibeto Burman languages. Moreover, in case of Dravidian it is around 75%. But no language family in India remains exclusively "tribal" as People of India project data have revealed (K. S. Singh and Manoharan. 1997).

The diminishing trend witnessed in the field of language diversity is outcome of unfortunate political stratagem in India. The political practice and in fact the executive decisions in India went in favour of slow 'assimilation of smaller languages'; though it was not intended directly as the constitutional provisions for recognition of minority languages and towards multilingual India was well ensured through Articles 120, 345, 346, 347, 350, 1956 seventh Amendment on cultural and educational rights and 350B of the constitution. The foundation of the Eighth Schedule (originally contained 14 languages but now it is of 22 languages) was also meant towards this end. However, the recognition of languages within the Eighth Schedule came to be denounced on various counts. It was alleged that language selection for scheduling is based on selective convenience rather considering any linguistic rights/ language status. It was also debated that the overall impact of the above policy remains favouring assimilation of linguistic identities, derecognising linguistic identities and promoting language erosion. For instance, status fixation of some languages in eighth schedule made others deprived and created linguistic minorities (Chaklader, 1981) which weakened the language loyalties and allowed for ignoring smaller languages especially tribal languages.

Subsequent upon the disturbances over the medium of instruction, and taking in to consideration the plural- linguistic and cultural surface of India, the much laudable Three Language Formula for imparting education was designed and launched. Three language education policy reduced language choice in language education which had enormous impact on minority languages (Abbi. 2004, Bhatt and Mahboob 2002, Rajeswari, 2002). In the absence of education material in own language and in view of the slightest choice for language provided through education policy, the tribes and other minorities were forced to settle on 'regional tongue' for betterment. As a result of such unfavourable social ecology, majority of tribal languages are subsumed by dominant regional languages (Biligiri 1969, Karunakaran 1983, Khubchandani 1983, Abbi (1995), Istaque, 1999, Rajeswari, 2002).

Language endangerment is caused variously through social, economic and administrative measures and while the results are by and large felt adversely, indeed there are some success stories. As regards above mentioned governmental policies introduced in India there are scholarly works highlighting both the positive and negative aspects. Language impairments are also related to people's migrations, and also the urbanisation factor. Endangerment is also caused by displacement from traditional habitat due to various reasons, extinction of population due to diseases or natural disasters and the politics of 'settlement' of 'immigrants/

'refugees' in county's pristine eco-linguistic tribal settings. These are some of the reasons, among others, by which mother tongues become endangered, resulting in declining speaker's strength (Great Andamanese, for instance).

In the sphere of the language endangerment the issue of the language shift becomes relevant too. Language shift is a culturally, socially and economically related process (Hoijer, 1948, Fishman 1976, Milroy and Milroy 1985). Language shift is explained mainly in terms of industrialization, urbanization, political reorganisation, and administrative favour as also policy of standard language promotion in administration, education and mass media. The changes in the arrangement of the economy may lead the speakers of small languages to become bilingual. Bilinguals may subsequently abandon their ancestral tongue (Annamalai 2000). Scholars have pointed to such predicaments in their long time surveys and assessments, particularly in relation to tribal languages (Raza and Ahamaead 1990).

There is no doubt that the tribal language shifts demonstrate the gravity of language sink among the tribes of India. While discussing the trend of vanishing linguistic diversity in general, Abbi (2004) states " – associating with the dominant regional language is considered as a step towards merging with the mainstream. This implies a direct correlation between the process of submerging identities and the reduction of linguistic diversity. Abbi (2004) further observes, "The inevitable fears of the tribes about being pushed back – desires to rise up to the elite and superior languages and amalgamate with the mainstream – factors discouraging the lower rung language speakers to exercise their linguistic rights". The fact remains that the very elite-oriented ideology of development and language management inherently promotes the process of assimilation rather than maintenance of smaller linguistic identities. Any genuine effort of the communities in focusing their language rights cantered on conservation and preservation of the cultural identity is ignored as sectarian and divisive.

The general trend noticed in the rate of endangerment faced by the languages in India is that the languages surviving with mono ethnic base are more in danger than multiethnic based languages (Sreenathan 2009). UNESCO (2003) follows Nine-Point based Language vitality and endangerment assessment. The vitality index ranges from vulnerable to extinct. The criteria followed are, Absolute number of speakers, proportion of speakers within the total population, intergenerational language transmission, community member's attitudes towards their own language, shifts in domains of language use, Governmental and institutional language attitudes and policies including official status and use, Type and quality of documentation, Response to new domains and media, and availability of materials for language education and literacy. Based on the above criteria, UNESCO has listed 196 languages under threat in India as vulnerable (84), definitely endangered (62), severely endangered (6), critically endangered (35) and extinct (9). (*http://www.unesco.org/culture/ich/index.php?pg=00206*). The languages included within above list covers languages belonging to all language families of India keeping Tibeto-Burman at the top in the list of languages.

India is divided into numerous eco-cultural zones, where ethnic communities pursue their traditional economic activity and maintain their cultural-linguistic identity. The diverse languages of India are variously located in these eco-zones of the country. Within these zones several smaller languages survive till date. The richness of indigenous knowledge of these zones is primarily stored in these smaller languages, which by and large remain uninterrupted, but are increasingly threatened lately. The fact is that the greater parts of the indigenous knowledge remain in phonocentric and body-centric mode than scripto centric. Gradually, however, as in case of the language, the local indigenous knowledge is also facing extinction. These losses to knowledge resources are caused mainly by the shift in livelihood, displacement of tribes, and eventual death of the language. These factors severely affect the knowledge transmission.

The problem of language endangerment is serious in India, particularly among the smaller groups. This situation necessitates exhaustive surveys of language speakers in order to make clear assessment of the statuses of languages and to suggest measure for language revitalization. Questions of survival of indigenous knowledge and smaller languages are fundamentally and decisively related. This is because they are complimentary to each other. The intergenerational transmission of language is a must for the preservation of indigenous knowledge, which in turn is a prerequisite for the Biodiversity Conservation.

As a Policy Intervention, it may not be prudent to preserving the language alone by allowing continuing ecological abuse. A holistic ecological-cultural-linguistic initiative is destined keeping in view the basic fact that language death directly erases indigenous knowledge and traditionally preserved knowledge of Biodiversity Conservation. These engross the concern for the preservation of the prevailing cultural milieu, as far as possible. Such an effort will infuse the sense of belonging among forest dwellers/ tribes in true sense and they will come forward to protect the environment, as they value their symbiotic relation with the forest

environment traditionally. Indeed the Biodiversity Conservation cannot be achieved without the supportive community participation.

References

Abbi A. (1995), "Small Languages and Small Language Communities". *International Journal of the Sociology of Language,* 116: 175–85.

Abbi, A. (2004), *Vanishing Diversities and Submerging Identities: An Indian case,* Forum: Bracelona.

Ali, Reza, (2003), "Understanding Urbanization," in S. A. Zaidi, Ed:, *Continuity and Change: Socio Political and Institutional Dynamics in Pakistan.* Karachi: City Press.

Annamalai (2000), *Managing Multilingualism in Indian Language and Development.* New Delhi: Sage Publications.

Bhatt, R. M. and Mahboob, A. (2002), In: B. Kachru and S. N. Sridhar, Eds, *The Minority Languages and their Status: Languages in South Asia.* London: Cambridge University Press.

Biligiri, H. S. (1969), "Problems of Tribal Languages in India". In N. Ray Ed. *Language and Society in India,* 245–50. Shimla: Institute of Advanced Study.

Carlson, T. J. (2001), Language, Ethno-botanical Knowledge and Tropical Public Health. In L. Maffi Ed. *On Bio-cultural Diversity: Linking Language, Knowledge and the Environment:* 489-502. The Smithsonian Institute Press.

Census of India, *Census of India Reports of 1951, 1961, 1971, 1981, 1991, 2001.* New Delhi: Office of the Registrar General of India.

Chakladar, S. (1981), *Linguistic Minority as a Cohesive Force in Indian Federal Process.* New Delhi: Associate Publishing House.

Daniel Nettle and Suzanne Romaine (2002), *Vanishing Voices-The Extinction of the World's Languages* USA: Oxford University Press.

Fill A. and Mühlhäusler, P. Eds (2001), *The Ecolinguistic Reader: Language, Ecology and Environment.* Continuum.

Fishman, Joshua A. (1976), *Bilingual Education: An International Sociological Perspective.* Rowley, MA: Newbury House. xiii, 208 pages.

Grenoble, L. A. & Whaley, L. J. (1996), Endangered Languages: Current Issues and Future Prospects. *International Journal of the Sociology of Language* 118: 209-223.

Grenoble, L. A. & Whaley, L. J. Eds (1998), *Endangered Languages: Current Issues and Future Prospects.* Cambridge University Press.

Haugen, E. (1971), The Ecology of Language. *The Linguistic Reporter. Supplement* 25, 19- 26. Reprinted in Haugen 1972: 324-329.

Heywoosd, V. H. (ed.) (1995), *Global Biodiversity Assessment.* Cambridge & New York: Cambridge University Press & UNEP (United Nations Environmental Program).

Hoijer, Harry (1948), Linguistic and Cultural Change. *Language*, 24 (4), 335-345.

Ishtaq (1999), *Language Shift among the Scheduled Tribes in India: A Geographical Study*, New Delhi. Motilal Banarsidass.

Karunakaran, K. (1983), *Sociolinguistic Patterns of Language Use*. Chidambarm: Velan Press. (All India Tamil Linguistic Association Publication 20).

Khubchandani, L. (1983), *Plural Languages, Plural Cultures: Communication, Identity, and Sociological Change in Contemporary India*. Honolulu, East West Center: University of Hawaii Press.

Krauss, M. (1992), *The World's Languages in Crisis*. Language 68: 1, 4-10.

Maffi, L. (ed.) (2001), *Language, Knowledge and the Environment: The Interdependence of Cultural and Biological Diversity*. Smithsonian Institute.

Maffi, L. (1996), Language, Knowledge and the Environment: Threats to the World's Biocultural Diversity. *Terralingua Newsletter* 2, December 1996.

Maffi, L. Skuntnabb-kangas, T. & Andrianarivo, J. (1999), Linguistic Diversity. In D. A. Posey Ed. *Cultural and Spiritual Values of Biodiversity. A Complementary Contribution to the Global Biodiversity Assessment*: Intermediate Technology Publications, for and on behalf of the/United Nations Environmental Programme.

Milshler, B. D. (2001), Biodiversity and the Loss of Lineages. In L. Maffi Ed. *On Biocultural Diversity. Linking Language, Knowledge and the Environment*: 71-81. The Smithsonian Institute Press.

Mühlhäusler, P. (2003), *Language of Environment - Environment of Language. A Course in Ecolinguistics* Battlebridge.

Nabhan, G. P. (2001), Cultural Perceptions of Ecological Interactions: An "Endangered People's" Contribution to the Conservation of Biological and Linguistic Diversity In L. Maffi Ed. *On Biocultural Diversity. Linking Language, Knowledge and the Environment*: 145-156. The Smithsonian Institute Press.

Nations, J. D. (2001), Indigenous Peoples and Conservation. In L. Maffi Ed. *On Biocultural Diversity, Linking Language, Knowledge and the Environment*: 462-471. The Smithsonian Institute Press.

Nigam, R. C. Language *Handbook of Mother tongues in Census*, Census Centenary Monograph No. 10, 1972.

Oviedo, G. & Maffi, L. (2000), *Indigenous and Traditional Peoples of the World and Ecoregion Conservation: An Integrated Approach to Conserving the World's Biological and Cultural Diversity*. WWF International & Terralingua.

Pandharipande, Rajeshwari V. (2002), Minority Matters: Issues in Minority Languages in India, *International Journal on Multicultural Societies*, Vol. 4, No. 2 *http://www.unesco.org/most/vl4n2pandhari.pdf*

Pandharipande, R. (1992), "Language Shift in India: Issues and Implications". In: W. Fase, K. Jaspaet and S. Kroon, Eds. *Maintenance and Loss of Minority Languages*. Amsterdam: John Benjamins Publishing Company.

Nettle, D.; Romaine, S. (2000), *Vanishing Voices: The Extinction of the World's Languages*. Oxford: Oxford University Press.

Nettle, D. (1999), *Linguistic Diversity*. Oxford: Oxford University Press.

Pandit, Prabodh B. (1976), *Languages in Plural Society*. Delhi: Manohar.

Patnayak. D. P. (1981), *Multilingualism and Mother Tongue Education*. Delhi, Oxford University Press.

Razz, M. and Ahmed, A. (1990), *An Atlas of Tribal India*. New Delhi; Concept Publications.

Schermerhorn, R. A. (1978), *Ethnic Plurality in India*. Tucson, Arizona: University of Arizona.

Singh, K. S., (1994), *The Scheduled Tribes, People of India,* Vol. III. Anthropological Survey of India and Oxford University Press.

Singh, K. S. and Manoharan, S. (1997), *Language and Scripts, People of India,* Vol. IX. Anthropological Survey of India and Oxford University Press.

Smith, E. A. (2001), On the Coevolution of Cultural, Linguistic, and Biological Diversity. In L. Maffi (Ed.). *On Biocultural Diversity. Linking Language, Knowledge and the Environment*: 95-117-The Smithsonian Institute Press.

Sreenathan. M. (2009), Language Plurality and Functional Heterogeneity among People of India. In *Identity, Cultural Pluralism and State-South Asia in Perspective*. Eds. N. K. Das and V. R. Rao New Delhi: Macmillan and ASI.

Sreenathan, (2008), Dravidian Tribes and Languages, Dravidian University, Kuppam.

Srivastava, R. N. (1977), Indian Bilingualism-Myth and Reality in Gopal P. Sharma and Kumar Suresh. Ed. *Indian bilingualism,* Agra: Central Institute of Hindi.

UNESCO (2003), *Language Vitality and Endangerment*. UNESCO *Intangible Cultural Heritage Unit's Ad Hoc Expert Group on Endangered Languages*. Approved 31 March 2003 by the Participants of the International Expert Meeting on UNESCO Programme Safeguarding of Endangered Languages, UNESCO, Paris-Fontenoy, 10-12 March 2003.

SOCIAL SCIENCE INPUT TO MAN AND BIOSPHERE [MAB] PROGRAMME

Yogesh Atal*

Population explosion, fast depletion of national resources, energy crisis and the pollution of the environments had become the matter of global concern. It is in such a milieu that UNESCO's intergovernmental programme MAB was launched. Author says that inclusion of social sciences in MAB was to bring 'Man' into prime focus, for what if the environment survived and the Man and his product 'culture' disappeared. He says that it is worthwhile to discuss the contemporary issues of biodiversity conservation and cultural diversity from the perspectives of the early efforts such as MAB.

The decade of the 1960s was the decade when the world began to suffer from the "future shocks"—a phrase popularised by Alvin Toffler. Population explosion, fast depletion of natural resources, energy crisis, and pollution of the environs, including damage to the ozone layer, had become matters of universal concern. It is in this context that slogans discouraging exploitation of scarce energy resources were raised. Simultaneously, need for appropriate technology, use of local resources and return to old and traditional ways of living, innovation of biogas and the like were advocated. For all the damages done to the environment it was Man, with a capital M, who was held responsible. Man was declared guilty of exploiting the nature. "Save the environment" became the key concern. Since environment is a broader term that includes both natural and man-made environments, environmentalists proposed the term Biosphere for the natural environment.

It is in such a milieu that UNESCO's intergovernmental Programme on Man and Biosphere [MAB] was officially launched in 1970. It was oriented towards actual management problems arising from the interactions between human activities and natural systems. The official

* Professor Yogesh Atal, Pent House, B-502, Residency Towers B, ARDEE City, Sector 52, Gurgaon-122003

document on MAB clarified the orientation of the Programme in the following manner:

> *Although Man's interactions with his environment have continually been undergoing change, it is the increasing scale and rate of change in many situations, which is threatening to exceed the present adaptive, and carrying capacity of the various natural and socio-cultural systems that collectively constitute the biosphere. MAB Programme is conceived for the analysis of change in Man's interactions with various ecosystems, or what are called physiographic units. Change in these interactions has not only time and space dimensions but also social and scale dimensions. Changes occurring in the human populations, in the pattern of division of labour, in science and technology, and in the structure of attitudes and goals of societies, have affected the entire gamut of man-environment relationships.*

It is obvious from the above that the concern for the environment put Man in the dock. The National MAB Committees set up by the Member-States had high representation of scholars from physical and biological sciences. Of the fourteen programme areas that were delineated for MAB most research projects were again in the field of biological sciences.

Soon after joining UNESCO as its Regional Adviser for Social and Human Sciences in Asia and the Pacific towards the end of 1974, one of the tasks of this author was to collect filled questionnaires sent to the various MAB Committees, which included social scientists, in the Asian region. Incidentally, this Programme is located in the Science Sector of UNESCO, and there was then very little communication between MAB programme officers and the Division within the Sector of Social Sciences dealing with environment-related issues. My visit to the various countries in the region to enquire about the questionnaire yielded the expected result. Since there was no social science involvement in MAB the committees had nothing to report. I took upon myself the task of encouraging social science input to MAB.

Trained in anthropology, and as a votary of interdisciplinary research, I found MAB to be an ideal starting point for my work in the Asian region. It was also a rare instance where funds for social science programme were contributed by another sector. I rediscovered the fact that most MAB Committees focussed on the Biosphere and neglected the *social* dimension. I was confronted with questions such as these: What contributions can social sciences make to MAB? Are there any social scientists who have researched on Biosphere? Are techniques available in social sciences for the investigation of this terrain? Can social scientists participate in a joint research team with natural scientists? And, to cap it all, are social sciences really scientific?

MAB was never intended to be a preserve for the natural scientists alone. It was conceived as a programme of research aimed towards "developing the basis within the natural and social sciences for the rational use and conservation of resources of the biosphere, and for the improvement of the global relationship between man and the environment". Inclusion of social sciences in MAB was to bring Man into prime focus, for what if the environment is saved and the Man—and his product, *Culture*—disappeared?

The reason why social sciences did not partake in MAB was partly related to the dominance of the natural sciences in the national committees on MAB, and partly to the indifference of the social scientists themselves. To be sure, environment has been the concern of all sciences - be they social or natural. But in social sciences it did not have the central significance.

Man's environment can be divided into natural and cultural. Adding time dimension, we may talk of the past, present, and future of these environments. Confronted with the responsibility of promoting MAB in social sciences, I evolved a paradigm that I would like to present here. The disciplines dealing with the different aspects of the totality of environment are easy to identify. For example, the past of the natural environment is investigated by geology and palaeontology, and the past of the cultural

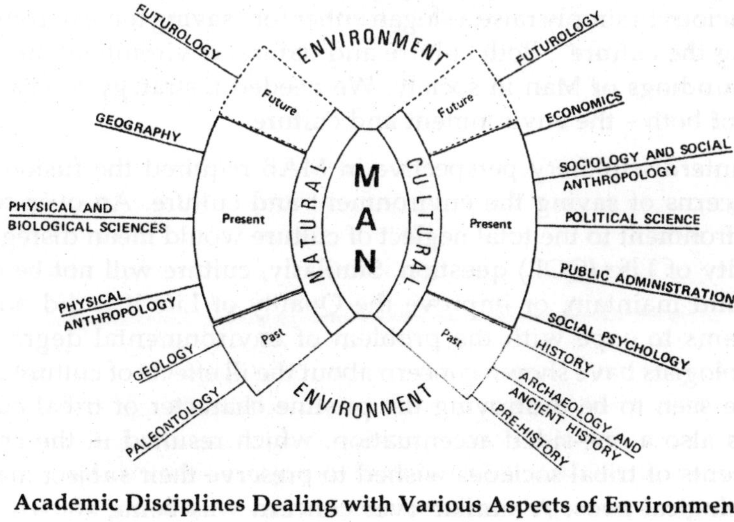

Academic Disciplines Dealing with Various Aspects of Environment

environment is handled by prehistory, archaeology and ancient history. Similarly, the present of the natural environment is the focus of physical anthropology, physical and biological sciences, and geography; whereas the present of the cultural environment is studied by history, social psychology, public administration, political science, economics, and sociology / social anthropology. But when it comes to the future, it is the newly emerging discipline of futurology - combining concerns both of the physical and biological sciences and social sciences - which is at the forefront. See the following diagram:

It is clear from the above diagram that the subject of environment has been studied from the perspective of individual disciplines. In Anthropology, for example, we have been defining culture as a product of interactions between Man and Nature, Man and Supernatural, and Man and Man - constituting the triumvirate of economy, religion, and social structure and polity. Ethnographies have devoted considerable attention to habitat. Primitive economies have been heavily dependent on the natural surroundings, and therefore man-nature relationships were seen primarily from an economic angle. Anthropologists were the first to question the deterministic role of the environment in relation to culture by offering examples of different cultures in a similar environment, and similar cultures in different environments. Their position was in contrast with those of the geographers.

What we needed in MAB was a truly trans-disciplinary perspective, culling out the important contributions made by different sciences and integrating them into a new paradigm. In such a perspective it would have been fallacious to simply raise a slogan either for "saving the environment", or "saving the culture". Both culture and natural environment are part of the surroundings of Man in society. We needed a strategy to ensure the survival of both - the environment and culture.

The interdisciplinary perspective in MAB required the fusion of the twin concerns of saving the environment and culture. An over-concern with environment to the total neglect of culture would mean disregarding the Quality of Life (QOL) question. Similarly, culture will not be able to survive and maintain, or improve the Quality of Life if it did not have mechanisms to cope with the problem of environmental degradation. Anthropologists have shown concern about the ill effects of culture contact that were seen to be destroying the pristine character of tribal cultures. That was also a one-sided accentuation, which resulted in the criticism that students of tribal societies wished to preserve their subject matter as anthropological zoos. A similar over concern was being shown by the environmentalists to save the environment and preserve the ecological diversity. This one-sided accentuation was later toned down when the term "sustainable" development was coined and adopted at the Rio Conference - the Earth Summit - in 1992.

When the slogan for the protection of environment was raised and given a universal colour, it was basically the problem of the developed societies who, through the development of new technologies and expensive life styles, had already begun damaging the environment. But the crisis of the North was generalised as the crisis for the whole world and environment was given priority attention. In the enthusiasm for the new concern it was almost forgotten that a basic distinction existed between the developed and the developing societies insofar as environment was concerned. The developed societies had the environmental crisis that was the outcome of the very process of development. Since the developing societies were far behind the race - with little urbanization and limited industrialization - they had not damaged their environment to that extent. Seen this way, the problem for the developed societies was to arrest the process of environmental decay, and to ensure de-pollution and rational use of the energy resources, along with a search for alternatives. In contrast, the problem for the developing countries was to have a second look at the development blueprints and to take prophylactic actions to prevent occurrence of the kind of crisis that the North was experiencing. The development model, adopted by most of the developing societies, was essentially the western, capitalistic model, which was intended to initiate a process of homogenization - a process that would gradually erase cultural diversity and create look-alike societies. The 1970s, thus, confronted a situation where ecologists were making a case for maintaining ecological diversity, and the developmentalists were undermining cultural diversity. All failures in development, for example, were attributed to tradition and to local culture. A dichotomy between tradition and modernity provided the base for the analysis of social and cultural change. Modernists were ready with their obituary to tradition.

In such a climate of opinion, quite naturally Man was declared the key culprit, and all focus of studies in the developing societies relative to MAB was seen in the context of adversative relationship between Man and his environment. While the city and the industrial townships did attract some attention, studies focussing on rural and tribal areas found one theme of great concern, namely *Shifting Cultivation*. In the several national meetings that we in UNESCO convened in Asia to develop a list of research topics Shifting Cultivation was suggested as an important topic because this was seen as a practice that was damaging the forest cover and needed to be halted. When the 10th International Congress of Anthropological and Ethnological Sciences was convened in India in 1978, UNESCO sponsored a post Congress symposium on this topic that was held in Bhubaneshwar (19-24 December 1978) with a view to developing a perspective on this age-old practice that engaged several tribal populations in large number of Asian societies.

The practitioners of Shifting Cultivation have always been viewed from the perspective of the outsider who treated them either as a different and a closed system, or viewed them as a satellite system having deleterious effects on their society and the surroundings. The first perspective led to the unintended consequence of "leave them alone" philosophy, and the second to the missionary zeal reflected in "change-them-fully" agenda. Both these perspectives are outsider perspectives and are biased against the people who lead the life in such an economy. The outsider treats the shifting cultivator as primitive and backward, and feels alarmed about the destruction of the natural environment of the neighbouring upland. The only option that the outsider has proposed was to move towards settled agriculture. The problem was never seen from an "emic" perspective.

The English terms such as "shifting cultivation" or "slash- and-burn cultivation" had disparaging connotations, and indicated only some cultivation techniques and not the social system. It gave the impression that populations keep on shifting, and also that there are no other forms of economic activity in such societies. These are false notions and therefore anthropologists suggested to use the term "Swidden"[1] , which is derived from the Old English swithen (meaning to singe, burn the top). Swidden refers to a diversity of agricultural systems in which fields are cleared and prepared using axe, adze, or sword, and fire, and are cultivated for a short period and then fallowed for a period to allow fresh vegetation. Thus Swidden is characterized by a cycle of clearing, burning vegetation, planting cultigens, weeding, harvesting, and fallowing[2].

Practiced for millennia, in the tropical ecosystems with high rainfall and poor soils, Swidden was perhaps the best suited but it had constantly been condemned. The congregation of the anthropologists at Bhubaneshwar had a close look at the problem and raised very pertinent questions:

1. Is Swidden a practice peculiar to the primitive tribes? In Sri Lanka, it is practised by Sinhala speaking people; in Korea, it is practised in the northernmost mountainous part by those people who escape to the mountains for political, economic, or religious reasons.

2. Is Swidden to be viewed only as an economic activity, or need it to be studied in specific historical and socio-political contexts? Is it not the case that the tribal has been made a refugee in his own habitat?
3. Is Swidden really uneconomical? Does it destroy the environment, or is it the simple fire phobia of the non-tribal that regards this form of cultivation as bad?
4. Can there be a positive policy towards Swidden cultivation? Rather than condemning it as bad - without proper assessment of the extent of damage caused by it to the biosphere - would it not be advisable to improve the methodology of shifting cultivation so that yield is increased and any damage to the environment is minimised?

In the interaction that I was able to initiate between the natural and social scientists, in the framework of MAB, it was accepted that any situation of man-environment relationship is basically exploitative in the sense that, in order to survive, Man has to exploit the resources of his surrounding environs, be they plants or the animals. Therefore, saving the environment at the cost of Man and his culture is an untenable proposition. The injection of the concept of "sustainability" tried to bring balance in our approach vis-à-vis the biosphere.

The concept of 'sustainability' is still differently defined; the basic idea is that we have to have a development that can be sustained. This is how Agenda 21 of the Earth Summit held in Rio de Janeiro, Brazil, in 1992 (3-14 June) interpreted this concept. The road from Rio to Copenhagen, where the World Summit for Social Development was held in 1995, further refined the concept by adding that the development has to be humanly sustainable. While Rio Summit talked of maintaining ecological diversity - by ensuring that the endangered species of plants and animals must be prevented - the Copenhagen Summit brought back *culture* to the central stage and suggested that the common problems that the world confronts do not have common solutions. We have to look for culture-specific solutions.

I mention this to emphasise the point that the worry about the environment should be seen in a proper perspective. Such a perspective ought to de-emphasise one-sided concern for environment, and the solutions for the impending crises ought to be sought in the context of cultures. Culture should be a variable of all our development planning. The untested recipe of replacing all tradition with the so-called modernity - understood as practices of the North - has not always worked. The review of development results towards the end of the last century indicated that economic development bereft of concerns for the social and cultural spheres is hazardous. This acknowledgment prepared the ground for a plurality of models for development and progress while highlighting the crises that the entire humanity faces. Certainly, environmental crisis is one that is of universal concern but it needs different corrective actions in different social and cultural settings. Strategies and solutions that may work in a given society may not always be the appropriate ones in another setting.

The admission of this social reality secured a place of prominence for the social sciences in development dialogue, but only in the last decade of the last century. Until then, it was economics that ruled and the role of culture remained unrecognised. For the first time in the history of the United Nations an open invitation was issued to the social sciences. It was accepted that economic development has to subserve the cause of social development. Poverty, unemployment, and socially disruptive tendencies need a holistic social science approach and not mere economic development.

This is certainly a matter of celebration for us, the social scientists; but we should not oversell our bill of goods. It would be wrong to use this opportunity to reintroduce the cultural bias to the total neglect of the biosphere. We have to assure the survival of both nature and culture, and this is possible only through maintaining diversity in both the fields.

Diversity does not mean insularity. In a world on the path to globalization, one cannot prescribe a halt to interactions. We have to learn to live together in a symbiotic relationship. What the 'primitive' tribes did in the past vis-à-vis their biosphere has now to be remodelled where different cultures in a common biosphere evolve a symbiosis to ensure sustainability both of the environment and of the culture.

This is not an easy affair. If we have seen in the past decades the end of the cold war, and the collapse of communism, we have also witnessed rise of ethnicity and ethnic and communal violence. If we have marvelled at ourselves for making tremendous advances in science and technology, we have also suffered from unintended negative consequences of such development on our environment and on our populations. Therefore, while emphasising the importance of culture in our calculations for development we must not minimise the gravity of environmental crisis. As Gro Harlem Brundtland – Chairperson of the World Commission on Environment and Development said, "Our Common Future" requires us to move from one earth to one world. This one world of many cultures and many voices faces severe environmental problems that were created with the rise of human civilization. During the period of 900 days of the work of the World Commission on Environment and Development – from October 1984 through April 1987 – following major disasters occurred all caused by human mismanagement:

- The drought-triggered environment-development crisis in Africa peaked, putting 35 million people at risk, killing perhaps a million.
- A leak from a pesticide factory in Bhopal killed more than 2000 people and blinded and injured over 200,000 more.
- Liquid tanks exploded in Mexico City, killing 1,000 and leaving thousands more homeless.
- The Chernobyl nuclear reactor explosion sent nuclear fallout across Europe increasing the risk of future human cancers.
- Agricultural chemicals, solvents, and mercury flowed into the Rhine River during a warehouse fire in Switzerland, killing millions of fish and threatening drinking water in the Federal Republic of Germany and the Netherlands.
- An estimated 60 million people died of diarrhoeal diseases related to unsafe drinking water and malnutrition; most of the victims were children.[3]

All the examples cited by Brundtland convey the disastrous consequences of industrialization and urbanization. The fear is that if such development advances to cover the hitherto untouched rural and tribal areas they would equally be entering the danger zone. The blurb of the book, Our Common Future, serves notice that the time has come for a marriage of economy and ecology, so that governments and their people can take responsibility not just for environmental damage, but for the policies that cause the damage. Some of these policies threaten the survival of the entire humanity.

As we entered the twenty-first century, we witness the growth of two trends encouraged by our review of past development efforts: namely, the environmental movement and the campaign for the protection of the indigenous populations. Both these movements have activated many NGOs and social activists. On surface, these movements appear reasonable; but discerning eyes also detect political subtexts in them. Studies of these movements in social scientific terms, without subscribing to any particular bias, would indeed be a welcome move.

Similarly, it is the concern with cultures of the indigenous peoples expressed in the development reviews that prompted the United Nations to declare an International Decade for the Indigenous People in 1995. Upon its conclusion, a second decade has also been dedicated to it which began in 2005 and would conclude in 2014. This gives us - anthropologists - a new stimulus to return to our original interest, that of the study of the tribal societies. But while doing so, we must accept the point that today's tribes are not the same as those described in the ethnographies of the nineteenth century and the early twentieth century. Present day tribes would defy the traditional definition of the tribes as primitive, exotic, backward, and isolated groups. A great deal of change has occurred in them. Although there are pockets of underdevelopment in tribal areas, the people treat their educated and urbanised compatriots as positive reference groups. In such a situation, the attitude of charity or mercy by the "outsiders" would not be very welcome. Of course, the indigenous people have begun asserting their cultural identity, and reviving their lost tradition, but would hesitate to re-enter their primitive past. A judicious mix of the tradition and modernity is needed and is happening as a result of their interactions with the wider society.

We must admit that in many of the tribal societies the "insider" scholarship is now contesting 'outsider' reconstructions of knowledge of their respective societies. At the same time, there is a real danger to the tribal cultures in the sense that they might disappear as forces of modernization and globalization become more potent. There are people and agencies that express worry about profound loss of indigenous peoples and their knowledge about the natural world constructed by generations from their intimate ties to their locale. They allege that their practices and beliefs are marginalized and neglected because these are regarded as inferior forms of knowing compared to the Western scientific tradition, presented as universally applicable.

There is growing interest in incorporating indigenous knowledge systems, including traditional ecological knowledge, into truly participatory approaches to development. Moreover, it is also being emphasised that such knowledge may be relevant and useful not only at its place of origin but might have wider applications. It would, however, be wrong to over-argue the case of indigenous knowledge. The new fund of knowledge that the humanity has accumulated in different cultural settings over the millennia is part of the world heritage and not a monopoly of any single society. To deny entry to such fruitful knowledge and live in a cloistered world is an unacceptable prescription. It would be a disservice to insulate these communities and deprive them of the available stock of knowledge. If new medicines have been discovered to prevent debilitating diseases hitherto unattended these must be made available. Glorification of past, or of prevalent practices, should not lead to ethnocentrism. We need both indigenization of the outside knowledge and universalization of parochial wisdom that is advantageous to the wider humanity.

One major worry of the many enthusiasts of indigenous knowledge systems is the commercialisation and museumization of tradition. This is a fact to be reckoned. The challenge is manifold: how to preserve and record for the posterity the originality of the modes of production of artefacts and pieces of art of the indigenous people? How to ensure a quality life of the indigenous people? How to ensure that the local artists do not get pauperised and marginalized, and their skills are not stolen and used through mass medium of duplication?

As students of culture, we know that no culture is static. Changes in them occur both from within and without. It involves a process of attrition and accretion. Through non-use, or reduced use, cultural traits move towards the periphery of the culture and may even undergo hibernation. Similarly, new traits may enter either through invention or discovery or as innovations from abroad. Their acceptance is thoroughly screened by the cultural monitors. Thus, one should not repent over the disappearance of traits in any living culture, nor should one lament over arrival of new traits. Let cultures exercise their resilience.

It would be wrong to approach the question as an outsider considering either the desirability of preserving the culture, or of changing it wholesale. We must also not think that it is only the underdeveloped that are responsible for damaging the environment alleging that they are thoroughly ignorant. The wisdom contained in folk culture ought to be recognised and spread beyond the confines of the culture of its origin; similarly, doors must be opened for entry of good and useful wisdom produced in other cultural contexts. Concern in MAB was oriented towards the future. As anthropologists we are also now invited to move from the paradigm of the "primitive and the past" that prompted many to propagate a policy of preservation - interpreted as anti-change - to a policy of envisioning the future that would develop a protocol for conserving the desirable and discarding the damageable, on the one hand, and innovating and importing the traits and technology considered necessary for fashioning the future, on the other.

Anthropology in the 21st Century faces new challenges. To meet them, its interdisciplinary orientation will have to be preserved. Breaking the discipline in water-tight compartments of specialties - as is the current trend - is taking away the strength that has characterized it. Let us remind ourselves that Anthropology has been defined by our predecessors as the Study of Man - at all levels of cultural development; we are obliged to honour that commitment.

Notes

1. In the three UNESCO volumes that I edited this term has been used. It was first used by K.G. Izikowitz in 1951 in his book *Hill Peasants in French Indochina*; Ethnografiska Museet. Eilert Ekwall has given the rationale for the use of this term in his article "Slash-and-Burn Cultivation", in *Man*, 55 (144), pp.135-136. 1955.
2. See Harold Conklin, *Hanuno's Agriculture*. FAO, Rome 1957.
3. *Our Common Future*, Oxford University Press, New York. 1987. p. 3.

This is a revised version of the Inaugural speech titled "MAB in UNESCO and MAN in MAB" delivered by the author at the National Conference on Man in Biosphere, organised by the Anthropological Survey of India at the Central Regional Centre, Nagpur (26-28 February 2007). Views expressed are of the author.

ON STUDYING INDIGENOUS KNOWLEDGE

Yogesh Atal*

In this paper author discusses the early concerns of the anthropologists in studying tribal societies having what was called indigenous civilizations. He says India offered a good site of research for anthropologists. With his experience in UNESCO, when he was an adviser, author elucidates how the demands to attend to the needs of the indigenous peoples arose. He states that the tasks remained incomplete after the observance of the decade of 1995-2004 as the International Decade of World's Indigenous Peoples, hence a second decade (2005-2014) has been declared as the decade of the indigenous peoples. Thus in discussing the issues of the indigenous knowledge today we remain part of a contemporary international agenda.

Some time towards the conclusion of the last century, when the world community was taking stock of the achievements of various development decades since the setting up of the United Nations, there arose a demand to attend to the needs of the indigenous populations. As a consequence, the United Nations decided to observe the decade of 1995-2004 as the *International Decade of the World's Indigenous Peoples*. Since the agenda of the Decade required more time, a second Decade has been declared in continuation of the earlier Decade. The Second Decade that began in 2005 would conclude in the year 2014. Any discussion of indigenous people or indigenous knowledge till 2014 accordingly should be regarded as part of this international agenda.

The overpowering processes of colonization that followed the industrial revolution influenced all the non-Western societies, including the tribal communities. It is during that process that the science of Anthropology grew. Missionaries and political administrators were the first to reach the tribal communities who lived in comparative isolation, and led a life that was quite distinct from the colonisers. These societies were characterised as queer, exotic, and primitive, and their strange ways of life became the

* Professor Yogesh Atal, Pent House, B-502, Residency Towers B, ARDEE City, Sector 52, Gurgaon-122003

subject matter of many descriptive accounts published for the Western audience. Later, it was realised that a deeper understanding of their cultures and behaviour was necessary for an efficient administration of the area. Thus, anthropology entered the training curricula of the administrators chosen to rule these colonies. Concern with the past of the mankind also led to evolutionary theories that put these societies at lower levels of development and the western societies at the top of the pyramid. Implicit in this kind of exercise was the belief that there is a single course of evolution and that the practices of the primitives will have to be replaced by those evolved by the Western societies. That was the prescription to make the primitives civilized. Opposed to this approach were many anthropologists and social workers who felt concerned about the ill-effects of cultural contacts with the outside world that were destroying their distinctive cultural traits and subjecting them to the exploitation by outsiders. Their plea for the preservation of tribal cultures was eloquent and forceful. But, others, who alleged that anthropologists were treating Tribes, as "Anthropological Zoos", thereby obstructing their progress, misunderstood it.

It can safely be said that construction of knowledge about, and for, the indigenous people was made, during that period by the non-indigenous people. The "outsiders" took on the role of understanding the "other cultures". That is how the discipline of Anthropology came to be defined. It is this definition that also facilitated studies of communities other than the tribal that belonged to indigenous civilizations. India, thus, offered a good site for research to those anthropologists who extended their scope beyond the tribes to cover indigenous civilizations. However, in such non-tribal societies, nay the civilizations, the insider scholarship contested the social constructions by the outsiders. Of course, such contestations were part of a nationalistic sentiment that grew with the freedom movement. Now a similar reaction is in evidence in case of other tribal communities which have among themselves a good number of literates and highly educated people, including those trained in anthropology. These insiders question outsider reconstructions of knowledge of their respective societies. Moreover, much of what was written about them in the late nineteenth century, and the first half of the twentieth century, has already become dated.

Written in the idiom of the "eternal present", as if the societies were non-changing, the ethnographies do not correspond to the actually existing realities of today. The Gonds of Bastar today are very different from those described by Verrier Elwin. The image of the tribe has changed. No doubt, there exist tribal habitats, there are large pockets of the illiterates amongst them, and those living in remote areas continue with several age-old practices, including wearing the traditional attire and jewellery. But there are others who have attained national stature. Take for instance, the case of Mr P.A. Sangma who established high standards of performance as Speaker of the Lok Sabha. This tribal from the North-East is a national figure who, according to some, had the potential of becoming the Prime Minister of India! His command over Hindi and English, his professionalism, his stature as a national leader are indeed worthy of praise and serve as an example for others. Back in his tribal habitat he may still wear the traditional attire, but in Delhi he merges with modernity. Without loss of tribal identity, people like Sangma are changing the profile of their primordial cultures. And now, his daughter – in her twenties – has become a Minister at the Centre; she took her oath of office, to the surprise of many, in Hindi.

In the midst of all this, there is a genuine concern shown by many that the tribal cultures might disappear as forces of modernization and globalization become more potent. There are people and agencies that express worry about profound loss of indigenous peoples and their knowledge about the natural world constructed by generations from their intimate ties to their locale. They allege that their practices and beliefs are marginalized and neglected because these are regarded as inferior forms of knowing compared to the Western scientific tradition, presented as universally applicable. Foreign scholars pigeonholed indigenous knowledge in the scaffolding of their knowledge systems. That procrustean method of accommodation of alien knowledge led to several misrepresentations and quite often wrong interpretations and assumptions.

Our past development efforts, in which we laid emphasis on exogenous change, have taught us that introductions of innovations without regard for the recipient culture has, in many cases, led to costly failures, including erosion of biological diversity. Advocates of Human Rights have gone to the extent of attributing violation of human rights in those cases where the participation of local communities has not been secured in development projects. Neglect of traditional knowledge, according to many, amounts to ignoring available and relevant information. They allege that foreign experts only indulge in transplanting their institutions and practices rather than finding local solutions to local problems. It is the review of past practices that have suggested that we must think globally but act locally. This prescription does not suggest *insulation* from the outside; it only broadens our vision and strengthens our foothold in our roots. Mahatma Gandhi also stressed to keep all the windows open to let the wind in from all sides, but not to be swept away.

It is the over attachment to the so-called "modern" that has caused deficits in our development profiles. Of course, it was an easy route for the analysts to blame all our developmental failures to our "insensitive" cultures and traditions. We wrongly believed that the modernity is to be built on the ashes of the tradition. Time has come to realize that while different societies might have common problems to combat, there are no common solutions. Since a common problem may be the result of one or more of the factors, its solution has to be situation specific, and not a generic prescription.

We had mistakenly written premature obituaries to our culture and tradition. For the first time, the World Summit for Social Development, organised under the auspices of the United Nations System in the year 1995, declared that we have to give culture a place of centrality. Like biodiversity, we need to preserve cultural diversity. The world of tomorrow will be a world not of a common homogenized culture, but a world of rich cultural diversities.

There is a dramatically growing national and international interest in incorporating indigenous knowledge systems, including traditional ecological knowledge, into truly participatory approaches to development. Moreover, it is also being emphasised that such knowledge may be relevant and useful not only at its place of origin but might have wider applications. We are familiar with the debate about the patent for *Haldi* –turmeric – that we have been using not only to colour our curries but also for medicinal purposes. I received a message from a fellow anthropologist telling me that the cure for the deadly Dengue fever exists in the traditional system – the juice of two green papaya tree leaves can perform this miracle. There is also a claim for an herbal "viagra", and of several other aphrodisiac herbs – such as Ginseng of Korea – that belong to the non-allopathic pharmacopoeia. Already in India we are now witnessing a trend towards increasing use of Ayurvedic medicines, available in modern packages at the chemists' shops. Swami Ramdev's yoga movement is gaining worldwide following.

One major worry of the many enthusiasts of indigenous knowledge systems is the commercialisation and museumization of tradition. This is a fact to be reckoned with. The challenge is manifold: how to preserve and record for the posterity the originality of the modes of production of artefacts and pieces of art of the indigenous people? How to ensure a quality life of the indigenous people? How to ensure that the local artists do not get pauperised and marginalized, and their skills are stolen and used through mass medium of duplication?

Some efforts are being done in this direction. I gather that the Central government has involved the National Institute of Fashion Technology in developing a Geographical Indication Project to study traditional handicrafts in the Bastar region and have them patented. This will be done first for the bell metal artefacts known as *Ghadhwa Kala*.

Here we may discuss the fear surrounding the disappearance of tradition. As students of culture, we know that no culture is static. Changes in them occur both from within and without. It involves a process of attrition and accretion. Through non-use, or reduced use, cultural traits move towards the periphery of the culture and may even undergo hibernation. Similarly, new traits may enter either through invention or discovery, or as innovations from abroad. Their acceptance is thoroughly screened by the cultural monitors. Thus, one should not repent over the disappearance of traits in any living culture, nor one should worry over arrival of new traits. Let cultures exercise their resilience. We must also admit that as we cannot prevent death of an individual, despite all medical intervention, we may also not be in a position to prevent all attritions in a given culture.

Take language for example. While there are around six to seven thousand languages spoken all around the world, there are only eight that are spoken in several cultures. More interesting is the point that 96 per cent of the currently live languages are spoken by only four per cent of the world's population, and 80 per cent of these languages are confined to single countries. In Africa, more than 200 languages have fewer than 500 speakers each and may soon die out. The death of these languages is inevitable, and soon the total number of world languages may be reduced to half the present number. For the linguists, this should be a serious challenge. But the recipe of their revival seems impractical. What the linguists might do, as a service to posterity, is to record these languages and ensure their archival documentation. Even with the reduction in the number of languages, cultural diversity has not been eroded; and this is a fact to be rejoiced.

One thing that is definitely needed is for the scholarship to return to the tribal habitats. The old enthusiasm of studying the tribal groups is waning out despite the growing number of departments of anthropology in the universities and colleges. It is a matter of great worry that such departments are overwhelmed by physical anthropologists. My Alma mater, Saugar University, that had one of the finest departments of Anthropology led by late Professor S.C. Dube does not have, for years, even a permanent lecturer in social anthropology. The situation of Raipur University, which once belonged to the state of Madhya Pradesh, is no better. In this regard, I would like to pay my tribute to a person who gave up his economics training and flourishing family business to devote all his life to collect items of folk art from all over India. His private collection finds no match anywhere in the country. I salute Shri Niranjan Mahawar, who now resides in Raipur, for his dedication and devotion and hope that his efforts get due recognition. Let me hope that others would follow his noble example.

The time has come when the fruitless debate on tradition versus modernity needs to be closed. Historians of knowledge generally fall into two categories: the adumbrationists who attribute every thing to the past, to the tradition and do not acknowledge any novelty of innovation; and the palimpsests that refuse to acknowledge the shoulders of the past on which the novelty is mounted. Let us accept that we cannot recreate our past and live in it; and also that the present and the future require the foundations of the past. It is the amalgam of the old and new that defines our present and would fashion our future.

In fact, this was the policy towards the tribes that was formulated during the Nehru era. Enunciating his *Panchsheel* for the tribal policy, Pandit Nehru said:

> *I am alarmed when I see...how anxious people are to shape others according to their own image or likeness, and to impose on them their particular way of living...I am not sure which is the better way of living, the tribal or our own. In some respects, I am quite certain their's is the better. Therefore it is presumptuous on our part to approach them with an air of superiority, to tell them how to behave or what to do and what not to do. There is no point in trying to make of them a second-rate copy of ourselves.*

However, Nehru made it clear that he was not in favour of an isolationist policy. Thus, in the Foreword to the book, *A Philosophy for NEFA*, authored by Verrier Elwin, he remarked:

> *We cannot allow matters to drift in the tribal areas, or just not take interest in them. In the world of today that is not possible or desirable. At the time we should avoid over-administering these areas and, in particular, sending too many outsiders into tribal territory. ...We should rather work through, and not in rivalry to, their own social and cultural institutions.*

This is an excellent summary message, and continues to be relevant even today. There is definitely an urgent need to take a balanced view of the emerging reality and make proposals for the administration and the academics that are realistic and do-able, avoiding over-accentuation of a partial point of view.

Note

1. As a former official of the United Nations System, and as one who had the responsibility of promoting Social and Human Sciences in the vast Asia-Pacific region, Professor Atal has often discussed the issues involving indigenous knowledge systems including traditional ecological knowledge of the tribes and other people. *Editor*

This is the revised version of the Keynote Address delivered by Professor Yogesh Atal, Ph.D., D.Sc. (Hons), Formerly UNESCO's Principal Director for Social Sciences, at the National Seminar - Indigenous Knowledge: Implications for Development, Organized jointly by Barkatullah University and Indira Gandhi Rashtriya Manav Sangrahalaya, IGRMS, Bhopal- November 21-23, 2006.

INDIGENOUS KNOWLEDGE, FOREST ECOSYSTEM AND NATIVE MEDICINE:
Vision of Biodiversity Conservation among the Tribes of Kerala

P. R. G. Mathur*

This paper aims to describe and analyse the Indigenous Knowledge of Forest Ecosystem and Native Medicines among the Kurumba, a 'primitive tribe' of Kerala. The focus of analysis is on the cultural heritage and biodiversity conservation linked traditional knowledge. The paper also discusses briefly the conceptual issues surrounding the themes of Culture, Ecology and Cultural Ecology. The paper also describes the knowledge of the Kani tribe in the field of medicinal plants. The Kani or the Kanikkar tribespeople are now internationally known community for their knowledge in traditional medicine, with the efforts of Tropical Botanical Gardens Research Institute, Trivandrum. A medicinal plant, called Arogya Paccha, used by the Kanikkar for the treatment of diabetes, is now known to larger world. The Coimbatore Ayurveda Pharmacy, TBGRI and the Kani (Kanikkar) tribe have entered into an agreement for sharing the benefits under the Bio-diversity Act. The Coimbatore Ayurveda Pharmacy agreed to pay 10 lakhs Rupees to the researchers of TBGRI, of which 5 Lakhs was paid to the Kanikkar. Tribespeople are traditionally attached to the forest and they consider themselves to be nature's endowment. Their art and culture are replete with references to the forest. There are many rites and rituals, which are devoted to the forest and where forest produce is used by one way or other. Many of the leaves, climbers needed in magical-religious rites are procured from the forest. Many trees in forests are considered to be abode of deities and are worshipped as sacred. Existing forest in India is also the resource base for pharmacopoeia. The tribal people are conversant with the knowledge of use of such medicinal plants occurring in these forest areas. There is a symbiotic relationship between the tribal social organization and forest economy in the specific historical context of India. The overwhelming majority of the tribal people have been living there for centuries and they have evolved a mode of life which, on the one hand is woven around forest ecology and forest resource and on the other, ensures that the forest is protected against degradation by man.

* Chairman, International Commission on Urgent Anthropological Research, South Indian Regional Centre, Ananthakrishna International Centre for Anthropological Studies (AICAS), Agraharam (PO), Palakkad 678571, Kerala, India, *E-mail: drprgmathur@yahoo.co.in*

Conceptualizing the Culture, Ecology and Cultural Ecology

Culture theory is a branch of anthropology, semiotics, and other related social science disciplines such as political economy, in particular, but also sociology and communication (to name a few). Culture is a learned behaviour (Malinowski 1944, Tyler 1871) and itself satisfies the basic needs of a community in a given environment. An environment offers many resources, which are taken as part of the culture. For Tyler (1871: 1), a culture is "that complex whole which includes knowledge, art, beliefs, morals, law, customs and any other capabilities and habits acquired by man as a member of society". Malinowski (1931: 621) treated 'social heritage' as culture and such a social heritage was taken as the key concept of Cultural Anthropology. He observes: "Culture comprises inherited artifacts, goods, technical processes, ideas, habits and values". He has also said "culture is the integral whole consisting of implements and consumers 'goods, of constitutional charters for the various social groupings, of human ideas and crafts, beliefs and customs". (Malinowski 1949). Herskovits emphasizes the technological aspect of culture while defining culture as the 'man made part of the environment'. According to Kroeber (1948), culture is a superogranic and super individual in that, although, carried, participated in and produced by organic individuals, it is acquired; and it is acquired by learning'. And it is these, which guide the behaviour of man. For Claude Levi-Strauss (1968) culture derives from dialectic between idea and activity. He stresses culture as mere surface representation of underlying principles of human mind. He also assumes that the universals of human culture never exist as manifest fact, but remain at the level of structure alone.

UNESCO Observed

> *Cultures are not cast in stone: they have a past, a present and a future. Nor do they reflect a consensus, either within or between societies, but are manifestations of power. However, cultures are characterized not only by their diversity but also by their likenesses (UNESCO 1995:37).*

Ecology is concerned with active mutual relationship between living organisms and the given environmental situation. The environment and ecology have a tremendous impact on human society. In ecological study the element of adaptation formed the key concept. Since the organism and environment do not remain constant, the process of adaptation is taken as dynamic. Julian H. Steward said that culture change takes place to facilitate adaptation. Nash (1967: 249) describes that "ecology is just that: a setting, a framework, a ground for the weaving of a figure determined by other ecological factors. Ecology is sub-social or exogenous factor in relation to the social system". It is the notion of "adaptive interaction", which forms the basis of Cultural ecology. Julian Steward (1955: 82) defined cultural ecology as the interrelationships between living organism and their environment. Thus Cultural ecology is concerned with the interrelationships between cultural system and the environments within which they exist. Further, Ember (1977: 46) observes: "just as the structural functionalist may not be able to show that a particular custom is 'functional' so the ecologist may not be able to show that a particular custom is 'adaptive'. For the ecologist cannot subtract or replace a cultural trait in order to see if it really affects the society's chances of survival". Now a new ethnographic approach, known as ethno science, attempts to derive these rules from the logical analysis of ethnographic data. The ethno scientist seeks to understand the natives' world from their point of vies.

The ecology of an area influences and gets influenced by the technology and the material products of people. In this connection Beals and Hoijer (1971) observed

> *"Technology is the sum total of the techniques possessed by members of a society; that is, the totality of their ways of behaving in respect to collecting raw materials from the environment and processing these to make tools, containers, food, clothing, shelters, means of transportation, and many other materials goods. What is usually called material culture, on the other hand, refers to the sum total of the artefacts (manufactured goods and devices of all sorts) resulting from technology. Whereas most other animals simply utilize the natural environment as such for food and shelter, changing it relatively little in the process, man alters or transforms his environment. He makes tools of wood, stone, shell, bone and metal to increase his efficiency in using the environment. - - -In a strict sense, material culture is a result or product of it" (Beals and Hoijer, 1965: 298).*

Knowledge about ecology or study of interrelationship of organisms and their environment helps us to have an important insight into the type of food, technology of food procurement, consumption, and etcetera of the people. At the same time the consumption of a particular type of food does not totally depend on the climate or physical environment. Nevertheless, methods of food procurement are by and large in accordance with the local resources.

According to Steward (1955: 40-41), "The method of cultural ecology involved the analysis of: (1) The interrelationship between environment and exploitative or productive technology, (2) The interrelationship between 'behaviour' patterns and exploitative technology, and (3) The extent to which those behaviour patterns affect other sectors of culture".

The major focus in cultural ecology according to Steward is the international analyst of environmental -cultural relationships. Steward (1955: 82) put forward the notion of "adaptive interaction" which forms the basis of cultural ecology. Thus the ecological anthropologists are concerned with man-environmental relationships from the point of view of observer. Anderson (1973: 197) has observed, "More generally, the hypothesis of the adaptation of human populations to specific environmental conditions by means of socio-cultural institutions or behaviour has been widely employed and has produced interesting interpretations. The concept of cultural materialism may be described as a general theory of socio-cultural change. Marvin Harris has developed this theory after analyzing a number of adaptation studies especially on some 'primitive' societies in Africa. Marvin Harris (1969) observes that "Cultural determinism involves the concerted action of three classes of phenomena: technology, economy and natural environment". Indeed there is a definite relationship between plants, animals including human beings and the environment in which they live. Land, air, water, plants and animals of all kinds are the very important elements of ecological equilibrium. Man is the chief animal who is generally responsible for the destruction of environment. A number of modern scholars now admit that primitive communities have shown a better understanding of the essentials of "conservation" than the modern complex societies.

The Biosphere Reserves: Sites of Traditional Ecological Knowledge (TEK)

Human populations are often widely dispersed within Biosphere Reserves (BRs). As elsewhere in the developing world traditional peoples living in forested area have always been integral parts of eco-system, in the midst of nature and the natural resources. Living within the natural environments, traditional communities have derived many of their livelihood requirements from the rich biodiversity around them. Eco-systems such as forests not only meet a number of livelihood needs of the indigenous communities through products such as timber non-timber forest products (NTFPs) but also sustain traditional agriculture practices. All these forest linked activities of the indigenous peoples mediated through a rich Traditional Ecological Knowledge (TEK). TEK has economical, ecological and social culture dimensions. Traditional ecological knowledge (TEK) and its worth for biosphere reserves management has been considered by the UNESCO. It is emphasized that the communities living in these reserves have a rich cultural heritage and possess diversity conservation linked traditional knowledge. According to UNESCO there is a worldwide network of Biosphere reserves, which now comprises 411 sites in 94 countries, covering the bulk of climate zones, eco-systems and socio-economic conditions. Silent Valley is part of the Nilgiri Biosphere Reserves and the Kurumba territories are situated around the Silent Valley.

Tribespeople, Forest and issue of "Primitive Tribal Groups"

Tribal people have been sentimentally attached to the forest and they consider themselves to be nature's gift. Their art and culture are replete with references to the forest. There are many rites and rituals, which are devoted to the forest and where forest produce is used by one way or other. Many of the leaves, climbers needed in magical-religious rites are procured from the forest. Many trees in reserve forests are considered to be abode of deities and are worshipped as sacred. The fact that they perform some sort of reverence before actually cutting a tree is an indication of their sense of attachment and respect. Existing forest in India is also the resource base for pharmacopoeia. The tribal people are conversant with the knowledge of use of such medicinal plants occurring in these forest areas.

There is a symbiotic relationship between the tribal social organization and forest economy in the specific historical context of India. The overwhelming majority of the tribal people have been living there for centuries and they have evolved a way of life which, on the one hand is woven around forest ecology and forest resource and on the other, ensures that the forest is protected against degradation by man and nature. The tribal people in India cannot exist without forest. In fact, the very existence of these people depends on forest to such an extent that they cannot be visualized in the absence of forest. Tribes and forests are ecologically and culturally inseparable. They have co-existed since time immemorial. If they can sustain, and reinforce their forest-relationship in future will depend on their individual placement in the context of proposed new legislations and other policy of the state which might intervene.

The issue of defining the 'tribe' or the 'primitive tribe' in India is replete with controversy and debate. The term 'indigenous people' is also problematical in Indian context. There are broad criteria set for selection of the community as a tribe or 'primitive tribe'. The criteria and norms considered for identification of a tribe as primitive tribal group are the pre- agricultural level of technology; extremely low level literacy (below 2%), near stagnant or diminishing population and practice of simple technology. According to John W. Cole and Eric W. Wolf (1974) the "primitive societies can be treated as systems whose steady state is maintained through negative feedback, whereas complex societies are involved with surrounding nations are systems dominated by positive feedback'. There are 75 primitive tribal groups in India, of whom five tribes live in Kerala. The primitive tribal groups identified in Kerala are Kurumba of Attappady (1267), Kadar of Parambikulam, and Nelliyampathy forest (1521), Koragar of Kasargod (1300), Kattunaickan of Wayanad (11001), and Cholanaickan of Nilamboor (360).

Biosphere Ecosystems, Scheduled Tribes and their Main occupations:

1. Kasaragod: This zone comprises of two districts of Kasaragod and Cannanore. The major tribe living in this zone is the Koraga, an artisan community.

2. Wayanad: The average elevation of the Wayanad plateau above sea level is 3000 ft. The numerically dominant Schedule tribes inhabiting the region are the Paniyans, Kurichians, Kattunaickans, Adiyans, Mulla Kurumans, Urali Kurumans. As per the SC/ST Amendment Act of 2002 Thachanadan Moopan, Karimpalan, Kadar (Wayanad Kadar of Wayanad), Tenukurumban and Jenu Kurumban have been included in the ST list of 2002. Consequent upon the large-scale influx of plainsmen especially the Christians from the former Travancore state, the tribal population of Wayanad has been reduced to a minority. Nonetheless the zone has about 40% of the tribal population of the state. The Mullakurumans and Kurichians are agriculturists. The Kattunaickans are food gatherers and hunters, while the Tenukurumban, Jenukurumban subsist on food gathering and hunting. The Vettukuruman or Urali Kuruman subsisted on hand made pottery. They had become wage labourers due to the introduction of industry-manufactured aluminum, plastic pots and vessels in this zone.

3. Nilambur: Nilambur is well known for its evergreen forests. The Nilambur forest division is situated in Malapuram district. Major Scheduled tribes living in this area are Cholanaickan, Aranadan, Allar, Paniyan and Kurumans. The Cholanaickan, one of the primitive tribes of Kerala, inhabit the natural caves of the reserved forest of Karulai range and the Chugathara range of the vested forest in the Nilambur valley. The Cholanaickans are 'cavemen of Kerala' and they subsist on food gathering and collecting of minor forest produce, to a great extent. The other tribal community of this zone included in the SC/ST list of 2002 is Malapanikkar. The upper valley of Nilambur gets 4000mm during the southwest of monsoon lasting from June to August.

4. Attappady: Attappady is one of the prominent forest regions of Kerala. This valley is situated in the Mannarghat Taluk of Palghat District. Most parts of the valley have an elevation ranging from 2000 ft. to 3000 ft.

The three tribal communities living in this valley are the Irula, Muduga, and the Kurumba. In the SC/ST Amendment Act 2002 Muthuvan and Mudugar and Muduvan are treated as synonymous communities although they are linguistically, racially and culturally different tribes. According to the census of 2001, the literacy rate of Irula is 49.05%, Kurumba (48.59%) and Mudugar (41.52%).

5. Parambikulam: The zone is located in the Chittur taluk of the Palghat District. The most important tribe, which inhabits the region, is the Kadars of Cochin (Ehrenfels 1952). In the Census of 1971 they were numbered 1120. As per the 2001 the population of Kadar was 2745. As per the SC/ST Amendment Order 2002 the Wayanad Kadar (have been bracketed along with the Kadar of Cochin, although racially, culturally and linguistically they are different communities. Mahamalasar are also found in this zone. Above all Malayan and Eravallen are distributed in Muthalamada Panchayat and Perumatty Panchayat.

6. Idukki: Idukki comprises the mountainous taluks of Pirmade, Udumbanchola, Devicolam and Thodupuzha. It has an area of 5068 sq. kms. About half of the area in the zone comes under Government Reserve Forests. But it is to be mentioning here that hundreds of acres of forestland have been encroached upon by the settlers and they are fighting for getting the Pattayam. This has resulted in degradation of evergreen reserve forest and tribes of this area have become the victims of deforestation. The main Schedule Tribes living in this area are Urali, Muduvan, hill Pulayans, Mala Ulladans and Mala Arayans.

7. Trivandrum: The well-known Schedule Tribe inhabiting this zone is the Kanikkar of Travancore. The Kanikkar were largely food gatherers and shifting cultivators in the past. However, through the efforts of Tropical Botanical Gardens Research Institute, Trivandrum, the Kani or the Kanikkar tribespeople are internationally known community for their knowledge in traditional medicine. A medicinal plant, called Arogya Paccha, used by the Kanikkar for the treatment of diabetes, is now known to larger world. The Coimbatore Ayurveda Pharmacy, TBGRI and the Kani (Kanikkar) tribe have entered into an agreement for sharing the benefits under the Bio-diversity Act. The Coimbatore Ayurveda Pharmacy agreed to pay Rupees 10 Lakhs to the researchers of TBGRI, of which 5 Lakhs was paid to the Kanikkar tribespeople.

Ecological and Demographic Structure of Western Ghats

As per Census of India, 1991, India's tribal population was about 68 million (8 per cent of total population). It increased to 84 million (8.2%) in 2001. As per the census of 2001, the total tribal population of Kerala state was 3.64 lakhs. The tribal population elsewhere has been growing at a higher rate, but the tribal population of the peninsular south has been growing at the lowest rate. And, the rate apparently declined from about 2.2 per cent during 1971-81 to 1.53 per cent during 1981-91. The Western Ghats has a length of 1600 km. (1, 39,000 sq.km.) and stretches over 134 Taluks lying in the States of Maharashtra, Karnataka, Kerala, Tamil Nadu and Goa. The Western Ghat region is a treasure house of rare medicine plants and animals. According to the 1971 Census the total population of the Western Ghat region was 275 lakhs, which increased to 490 lakhs in 2001. About 59% of the population in the Western Ghat region is distributed in Maharashtra and Kerala which together account for nearly half of the area. The pressure of increasing population on land and vegetation and undesirable cultivation practices has resulted in ecological and environmental degradation and the problem of deforestation. The eco-system of the region had to face harsh conditions like submersion of large areas under river value projects and increasing felling of natural forest for raising commercial plantation and also the encroachment of forestland by outsiders.

The Kurumba Settlement Pattern and their Ecology

Attappady is a high level valley (elevation range from 400 metres to 1700 metres +MSL) in the Western Ghat range, south of the towering Kora Kundha range of mountains of the Nilgiris district, Tamil Nadu. The Bhawani River drains the area. The ridge of the Western Ghats constitutes the rain shadow. Attappady is an extensive east sloping gently undulating plateau, sandwiched in between the Nilgiris to its north and the Palghat Hills to its southeast and west. Once it was heavily forested but at present is practically barren. The valley is in three distinct sub regions: the south western with denuded forests and human settlements, the north eastern with scattered deciduous forest and townships and the northern-western, with heavy rainfall, is in the mountainous wet evergreen reserve forest. These roughly coincide with the settlements of the Irula, the Muduga and the Kurumba tribes respectively. There are traditional social ties between Muduga and Kurumba tribes and intermarriage takes place between them. The Kurumba are identified as a 'primitive tribe' subsisting on shifting cultivation and collection of minor forest produce. The Irula have adapted to plough cultivation; the Muduga have been largely alienated from their land holdings and hence subsist on farm labour.

The Kurumba hamlets are located in the northwest part of the Valley. The Silent Valley Reserve Forest is their western boundary. The hamlets are distributed far and wide and the area is ridden with precipitous slopes and deep gorges. The annual rainfall in the Kurumba land ranges between 2500mm to 4000mm. Gusty winds with heavy rains lash the area for days together from June to August. The forests around their hamlets are rich in flora and fauna. Out of the total 16 Kurumba hamlets, 10 are in reserve forest and the rest in the Vested Forest ('Vested forests' are those which used to be in private possession until they were taken over by Government in 1971). The Kurumba have contacts with forest officers, forest labourers, petty traders and other non-tribals. They speak a dialect, which is an admixture of Malayalam, Kannada and Tamil. The Kurumba were leading a nomadic life in the forest practising shifting cultivation on a wide tract of land. The Kurumbas of Attappady traditionally dwell in linear structures, which are divided into compartments for each conjugal family to live with privacy. There are two or three such structures to accommodate all the families in a hamlet. During the agricultural season, they erect small huts; in these huts they transfer their belongings from their permanent hamlets. The season of cultivation starts with the onset of monsoon and lasts for five to six months, viz., from September to February. They abandon these temporary huts after gathering their harvest and return to their hamlets. They draw water from nearby streams and springs.

Shifting Cultivation, Food Gathering /Hunting and Fishing Economy of the Kurumba

The number of households in a hamlet varies from 5 to 32 with an average of 15. The land is owned communally, but each family does cultivation individually on separate plots. The Kurumba cultivate at a time nearly one fifth of the total land in the hamlets, the remaining area being left unused. A particular plot is used for two to three years and then they shift to another. Finally they may return to the first plot after twelve to fifteen years by which time it would have regained its lost fertility. The Kurumba cultivate sizeable quantities of cereals, legumes and vegetables and follow a mixed crop pattern, which include ragi (Elleusine coracora), avarai (Dolicnos lablad), Sami (Pinicum spa) and tuvarai (Cajanus Cajan). They also grow vegetables, plantains (Musa paradisica), Mango, tamarind and pappaya around their hamlets. During the lean months, they collect roots, tubers, fruits, nuts and mushrooms, etc. They also hunt animals with traps and country made guns. Using pellet bows they catch birds. Fishing is done with hook and line, wattle traps and stupefying techniques. The food gathering and hunting contribute substantially to their sustenance. The Kurumba also collect minor forest produce such as soap nuts, dammar resin, wild cardamom, gooseberry, oil seeds, honey, bees wax etc. The peak collection periods are from October to December and March to June. The produce is sold to the Kurumban Girijan service Co-operative Society Ltd. They raise poultry and rear goats, and cattle for milk products. They sometimes keep cattle for sale after fattening. However, beef eating is taboo for them.

During the pre-agricultural time man used to roam about in a definite territory in quest for food. This nomadic life pattern may still be observed in the case of surviving, gathering and hunting community like the Kurumba of Attappady. The other noteworthy food gathering-hunting tribe depending on a primitive way of life are the Cholanaickan of Nilambur. The tribal societies living by food gathering and hunting did not posses containers or utensils. Hence, storing the surplus, if any, for the rainy season posed a lot of problem. The tools and implements at the disposal of the Kurumba were so crude that the output in terms of quantity of food procured was generally too meagre in proportion to the input involved i.e., time and labour. Gradually Kurumba developed better technology, tools and implements and developed the existing one. Thus the crude hand axes and choppers gave away to blade and flake tools. But the digging stick always remained. Then the Kurumba evolved throwing weapons or missiles like throwing club, bow and arrow, javelin and spears, and harpoons for fishing, noose and traps for hunting or so on.

The Kurumbas being a food gathering community use throwing weapons/missiles for hunting. Besides, these they also use nooses, nets, traps and pets like dogs for hunting expedition. The Kurumbas use nets of various types, nooses and traps. Such nooses and traps can be divided into the following categories: 1. Such nooses are laid on the ground and the target animals are forced to tread over them and thus they get trapped. 2. The popular technique of catching birds is to spread some adhesive material over a wooden sheet or any other thing and broadcast food grains around it. Tempted by the food grains birds come down and rest their feet over the adhesive and are thus trapped.

The Kurumba make baskets of various shapes and form square, cylindrical, triangular, open or with a lid, tightly knitted or loosely plaited from bamboo strips and reeds. These baskets are used for storing paddy, ragi and chama. The Kurumba manufacture a variety of musical instruments. Among them are the dhavilu, a small drum made of wood and ox skin, and porai, a large drum having an earthen frame work, both having top and bottom made of oxen hide. The drums and other musical instruments are used during marriage and death and funeral ceremonies.

Fishing has been an important aspect of the Kurumba economy. The practice of fishing through elaborate technique may be traced back to the upper Palaeolithic times. Among the Kurumba different techniques of fishing have been in vogue depending upon the local ecology. The prevalent fishing techniques are fishing by hand, fishing by poisoning, fishing by hooks and rods, fishing by stopping the flow of water over a patch of land, fishing by weapon, fishing by nets and fishing by noose and traps. The Kurumba live in small groups and maintain consanguineous ties, kinship playing the most important part in their social structure. Although they lead a nomadic life but their range of mobility is confined to their territory. With the advancement of cultural contact the land hungry non-tribal started pushing the Kurumba into more and more interior and relatively inaccessible areas with scant resources. Wherever, state-sponsored developmental programmes were implemented their impact left the Kurumba either to take the new economy and technology or simply become the victims of depopulation.

Conservation of Fire, Fire-making Techniques and Food Practices

The Kurumba learnt many a thing from the nature and fire is one of them. Though it cannot be said with certainty as to when and where exactly Kurumba started using fire but it can be stated without the fear of contradiction that right from the beginning fire has occupied a very important place in the Kurumba's life. Conservation of fire was the first step toward gaining control over it. Once the tribesmen became convinced of the multifarious uses of fire, they learnt how to make fire through the process of friction. Initially fire was not meant for comfort and luxury but as a means of survival for the Kurumba. Later on fire became a part of religious rituals among them and the fire was and is still used as a sacred object for worship and invoking blessing; Gods or Goddesses of fire have been a part of Kurumba ecology and culture, folklore and mythologies.

Different tribes use varying techniques for cooking food depending upon their beliefs, available material and local environmental condition. The staple food of the Kurumba is ragi. They keep a reserve of ragi stored for use over prolonged time whereas rice is to be purchased from the market and is not economical. Ragi puttu is the major item of their food. In preparing it the Ragi powder is added to the boiling water and it is stirred constantly until it gets thoroughly pasty. This paste is eaten by swallowing peace by peace. The Kurumba supplement their diet with chama, edible roots, fruits and tubers of various creepers. They also relish pork and chicken, domestic and wild fowl and meat of deer, jungle sheep and goat, etc. They used to roast the meat in fire instead of cooking. Jack fruits and mangoes are consumed in plenty during their seasons. The Kurumba take their meal twice daily in the morning, and in the evening. Some-time their abject poverty compels them to forgo their morning meal and be content with an evening meal. Their morning meal consists of either boiled rice or boiled vegetables or ragi paste. They also take chama as a subsidiary food. The supper is taken between 6 and 8 p.m. and this consists of ragi paste or boiled chama. The cooking medium is either ground nut or coconut oil. Turmeric and chillies are used as condiments. Often married couples eat from a single plate. It is not unusual for young girls and the mother to eat from the same plate and boys to join their father in eating food together. Biri and Ganja is the most popular item of smoke. Liquor is not infrequently consumed by the Kurumba. Children invariably suffer the pangs of stomach during the whole day, in anxious expectation of the return of their parents in the evening. Eggs are a luxury. Beef is taboo for the Kurumba. Some of the families in Anavayi and Thadikundu possess a few fowls. They do not sell eggs unless pressed by exigencies. The Kurumba drink tea and coffee when they visit Mukkali, 20 km, from their Anavayi settlement.

The Attappady population increased in the 20th century and some forest streams began to be polluted by population pressure. The Kurumba managed to avoid contamination by switching from drinking stream water and fresh milk to tea, coffee and sometime alcohol, all of which would be free from bacterial organism. The new balance within the given ecology that this change brought about was certainly one factor in the remarkable increase in the tribal population ever since the advent of British in Malabar. At the same time, at this stage, drinking habits in their habitat were undergoing an equally radical transformation.

The Kurumba Tattooing, Dress Pattern and Ornaments

The practice of tattooing has been prevalent among the Kurumba. Different motives are attributed behind the practice of tattooing like the enhancement of beauty and sexual attraction, health, sign of identification, warding off evil spirits etc. Perhaps, except the pupils of the eyes, tattooing may be done on almost anywhere in the body but the most favoured parts are forehead, nose, arms and chest. Among the Kurumba tattooing is done by their own specialists and occasionally by professionals against payment at fairs and festivals. Initially tattooing was done by sharpened bones of birds, fishes and other animals, but now one comes across mechanised devices for this purpose. Some of the marks found among Kurumba are floral designs, snakes, flowers, fishes, combs and sometimes simply names. The pictures of lions, swords and various gods and goddesses are also not rare as tattoo marks.

The Kurumba men wear a loin cloth round their waist to cover the lower part of the body. The Kurumba women usually wear a long piece of cloth called Chela, round their waist, permitting a portion of it to drape their torso unto the armpit covering their breasts fully. Saffron, deep blued and deep green and red are some of their favourite colours. Ornaments are one of the most popular and oldest ways of personal adornment among the Kurumba. Now we have in our possession evidence to prove that the practice of wearing ornaments or jewellery go back definitely to middle Palaeolithic and upper Palaeolithic times. In the earliest stage some vital parts of animals and birds were used along with seashells, bones and horns for making ornaments. The Kurumba for personal decoration also used leaves and flowers. The motives behind ornamentation are their use as a prophylactic against the evil spirits, improvement of personal appearance and attraction of opposite sex through this enhancement of sexual appeal. The Kurumbas say that the fear of ferocious animals and warding off evil spirits is the prime motive behind ornamentation. Living in the midst of nature, the Kurumba used to preserve the nails and teeth of the lions and tigers, hoofs of swift animals and feathers of beautiful birds. Later he made them into ornaments and started wearing them. In this connection Mathur (1977) observes "a chain of beads with chequered colours is the most popular among the Kurumba women. These ornaments are bought from vendors of neighbouring markets. One of the most valuable ornaments is a chain made of coins. Old eight anna coins and four anna coins are seen riveted to a chain after making eyes for them. Some of the elderly women plug their ears with rolls of Palmyra leaf coloured red. Necklaces made of glass beads are also worn by young women. This corporal decoration is well loved by old men as well. They wear rings and ear ornaments. It is not unusual to meet an old Kurumba man with long hair which is oiled and combed."

Mooppan: Traditional Chief, Soil-expert-cum-priest and Custodian of Customary laws

The most eminent political leader of sort in this tribe is the Mooppan, the paramount chief of the Ooru (hamlet) a man whose powers are now greatly diminished but who in earlier times was responsible for mediating between the community and the outside world. The Ooru Mooppan is the headman of the hamlet and he has continued to mediate between the Kurumba and other tribal communities like Irula and Muduka of Attappady and also with forest officials on those issues that concerns the entire tribal community. He is assisted by a three member council of elders namely, Mannukkaran, Kuruthalai and Bhandari. He is responsible for mediating among the individuals on the basis of traditional laws and customs. In other words he is responsible for maintaining the customary law of the community and inflicting punishment on those who violate the code.

The Mannukkaran is another important member of the tribal council. He is responsible for agricultural practices of the Ooru. Mannukkaran should have adequate knowledge of the fertility of the soil and seeds to be sown for shifting cultivation. It is he who performs certain rites and ceremonies in honour of Karadaivam or village deity for bumper crops at the time of sowing and first harvest. Kuruthalai and Bhandari assist the Mooppan in his functions. Thus, Mannukkaran, the soil-expert-cum-priest in every Ooru is responsible for mediating between man and God. His ability to gain the attention of the village and win their support in crucial times depends upon the fertility of the soil and the cattle and also the well-being of the whole community.

Indigenous Medicine, Peoples' Definition and Classification of Illness and their Cure: Method of Transfer of Knowledge

The complex connection between a tribal therapeutic system and the ecology and culture within which it operates are realms of medical anthropology. As a medical ethnographer we are concerned with the traditional peoples' definition and classification of their medicines and their cures. Central to this process is the profession of the therapist because it is that specialist who makes the relevant diagnostic decision. We have tried to explore how therapists and such related specialists as midwives and exorcists try to affect the health and development of each person and how a patient would seek or even avoid therapeutic assistance in accordance with a culturally specific fabric of ecological knowledge, choices in values that traditional peoples nurture.

Traditional therapist, midwife and exorcist play crucial but diverse role in indigenous healing system. The midwife is concerned with the yet unborn. The therapist deals with the problems of the living beings (women and animals), whereas the exorcist mediates between the tribal community and the ghosts of the dead. Each is thus relied upon for mediation in a well-defined sphere. This kind of mediation that involves the individual Kurumba in wider set up of the medicine-men and local forest differs from the comparable mediation in the Western medical world. We normally pay our physician for his professional services when we consult him, but

Kurumba does not pay him directly for any mediation and indeed it is by no means always the suffering individuals who make the decision to call in a mediator. A token fee, travel expenses or a small gift would constitute the material reward that most therapists would expect. The prestige that comes from serving their community-members is in fact a more important consideration for all mediators and most of the therapists and midwives (who are women in the Kurumba society). The therapists try their best but their fellow tribesmen do not expect miracles from them. It is worth noting that the Kurumba credit only their male exorcists with some miracle heeling powers. Most of the Kurumba hamlets do not have their therapists but we met two, the late Mudhamoopan of Anavoyi and the Valliamma of Veerannur, who used to live in Palapetta and Chindaky respectively. Generally when a therapist, particularly a midwife, goes to treat somebody she notices which girl is regularly present and over a series of cases in that particular Ooru, she slowly teaches her craft of gynecology so that she can carry on the skill. This is in fact what Valliamma, a famous tribal medicine woman, experienced as she herself learnt the skill from her uncle Mudhamooppan aged 105 and also from her husband's father.

A therapist among the Kurumbas often teaches the secrets of craft to daughters and sons and sometimes to the son's wife. No coercion is adopted; it is a self-selecting process for someone to become a therapist. The older ones want the younger generation to learn from them, with proper motivation. All the younger therapists take charge of their Ooru (hamlet), thus the old ones need to work less but, will handle the most serious cases and may be consulted by the young therapists or midwives. Even so, there are some who do not divulge professional secrets until they are about to die. These treatments include medicines for cancer and plants that can cure a girl's infertility and snake bite.

A therapist has his or her own stipulation for selecting and training member of young generation and tries to enforce his or her own standard of practice. Furthermore, the numbers of her or his patients dwindle when a therapist gets old. The younger therapists are encouraged as learning and handling treatment important also because the old hands may not be strong enough to deliver a child as many of the Kurumba women are turning to modern medicine. Thus, women therapists generally deal with gynecology and obstetrics whereas men deal with skin diseases, defective limps, deafness snake bites, jaundice, dysentery etc. while women specialize on all illnesses affecting women and children. Otherwise, therapists of either sex do treat patients of either sex in so far as modesty will allow. The manner of treatment varies somewhat, however in that male therapists often use spells (Mantra) in their curing techniques whereas female therapists rely more on herbal medicine.

There is no school or other formal institution for training Kurumba therapists. When a Kurumba suffers from illness he first goes to a therapist in his own or a neighbouring hamlet (Ooru). If that therapist cannot diagnose a cure the patient goes to seek the advice of a more distant therapist who is reputed for his abilities with an appropriate treatment only. If the tribal medicine men fail to cure the patient, the latter will go to an allopathic doctor who generally lives at Agali, the Block headquarters. If the treatment recommended by modern medicine man is too costly a poor tribal may be obliged to continue his treatment at the hands of a Kurumba therapist. There is also some variation in respect of payments. It is usual to give a small fee to all therapists, males or female, for any kind of treatment. Kurumba specialists like Valliamma or his son Ravindranath expect a fee from rupees 250 to 300 towards the cost of medicine for 3 weeks.

We have briefly discussed above how the individuals for the job of the midwives from the new generation are chosen for training. A midwife generally gives some tips to Kurumba women and some training too whenever a delivery occurs in the village and she is invited. A midwife not only assists in the delivery of babies but she is also asked to minister the different health needs of parturient woman and the new born. She is trusted and consulted as she becomes skilled as a healer of diseases as well. Sometimes she supervises birth among the domestic animals. Often there is more than one midwife in a hamlet. Other tribal women are asked to attend a delivery if they have helped one before. A midwife is a polluted through each birth for 3 days. As per norms, she washes also the clothes in that place. And if it is mother's first delivery she throws her clothes away. Thus we see a wide sphere of treatment, healing and training in vogue among the Kurumbas of Attappady.

Exorcists and Shamans

Both the exorcists and shamans operate in the Kurumba tribe. The exorcist seeks to expel an evil spirit from a person or place, and the shaman acts as a medium between the visible world and the invisible spirit world and who practices magic or sorcery for purposes of healing, divination, and control over natural events. The Kurumba exorcists are always male. The tribesmen wear talismans to ward off fever and evil influences. The most feared Manthravadies (exorcists) in Attappady area belong to the Kurumba community. One of them, Mudhamooppan, aged 105, used to be called in on all occasions of sorcery and magic to propitiate or scare the demon of disease. It has also been observed that the Kurumba officiate as exorcists to the other tribal communities of Attappady, namely, Irula and Muduka and also non-tribal people. They offer much supernatural protection to victims of sorcery of other malicious Manthravadies. Mudhamooppan has the unique distinction of combining the arts of a medicine- man, exorcist and shaman. His daughter Chelli is also a well-known shaman. She invokes both malevolent and benevolent spirits for causing and curing illness. She can convert friends into enemies, it is believed. Comparatively speaking several experts operate in society, but the enjoy different statuses. Thus the midwives and exorcists are the specialists but they differ in status. The midwife deals with 'birth' and pollution of blood and is always a female; the exorcists/shamans, who deal with the danger that spirits bring, are invariably males. The exorcist/shaman ranks higher in status and the midwife is lower in esteem.

Indigenous Classification of Local Medicine

Since there are no clear-cut differences in the classification of the indigenous medicine, an attempt has been made to differentiate and cluster together some of these indigenous medicines for the purpose of identification. I have identified three major types of indigenous medicine among the tribes of Attappady - Herbal medicine, Ritual medicine and Mystical medicine. The first category of Kurumba Indigenous medicine is the Herbal medicine. This group of medicine is made from leaves, bark of trees, plants, juices and other parts of plants. They are mainly used for curing biological diseases, such as arthritis, asthma, diarrhea, eye-disease, pneumonia, cholera, malaria and other general diseases. The second type of medicine is Ritual medicine. This ritual medicine involves sacrifices, eating of some specific kind of food and giving various prescribed gifts. They are performed to heal social, psychological and psychosomatic diseases. The third type of disease is mystical disease. The mystical disease includes curses, incantations, and some other diseases. The indigenous medicines among the Kurumbas and Irula are thus recognized first as protective medicine, second as Therapeutic medicine, and third as Success medicine. We will discuss this typology below.

Protective Medicines and Faith Healers

It is relevant to discuss the concept of protection in indigenous culture of the Kurumbas. In Kurumba Indigenous culture there exist a number of items which mean evil in various manners. There is also existence of evil eyes, enemies, sorcerers, wizards and evil spirits and ill-wishers. There is the enemy. The actions and pursuits of these enemies is a major source of fear and anxiety. The Kurumba believe that all evil and pain have causes and are attributed to the above mentioned ill-wishers. Among the Kurumba of Attappady, there is a believe that every person has at least one known or unknown enemy called Sathru. The activities of Sathru can bring painful consequences. It may be abnormal behaviour, sudden loss of children and property, chronic illness and even death. Thus the Kurumba believe that incidents like infant mortality, bareness in women, impotence in men, accident of any kind, dullness in school children and all other bad things are attributed to enemies of different kinds. Constant fear and insecurity may also be caused by caused by hostile environment other than malignant forces.

Another major way of obtaining protection against enemies in tribal society in Attappady is the use of charms and amulets and charms are generally obtained from medicine men who are healers and diviners. They are used for diverse purposes but mainly as protective devices to prevent the enemies, witches and wizards, and evil spirits from entering a house and attacking a person. It is also used to nullify all the attempts of enemies or sorcerers. They are prepared with different ingredients according to the purpose of the charm or amulets. Charms are tied with animal skin. Others are wrapped and tied with some black and white threads. Some also require the recitation of some potent words and prayers to go along with the charms for their effectiveness. Those words must be recited exactly according to the prescription of the medicine-man otherwise it may not be efficacious. Charms are used by the Kurumbas during hunting, to get protected from wild animals attack, snake bites and against wicked supernatural beings.

The worldview and religious beliefs of the tribesmen are closely associated with the notions and causes of illness. This tribe believes in supreme spirits take the Kakkilinga, also known as Karadeivam. Sometimes, he is identified with "Malleeswaran" a needle shaped peak towering about 200 meters, Malleeswaran is a "Sanskritised" form of Lord Shiva of the Hindu pantheon. The spirits of ancestors are worshipped, relics being often carried in wicker baskets, normally kept in the Mannukkaran's house. Female deities like Mari, Kali, Velugan Patta, Benjaminthayi etc. are believed to cause illness when displeased. Annual offerings are made to these deities. Dances and feasts accompany their propitiation. Malevolent spirits are always on the look out for creating mischief including illness. An individual alone on a forest path is vulnerable to the mischief. Such an attack is termed Kannithattal. Sometimes, malevolent spirit may attack a person in the form of wind, when it is called Kattuthattal especially in the case of children's diseases. There are some gifted individuals among the Kurumba who have command over these mischievous spirits and can order them to leave the victims alone. If such faith- healers are commissioned to treat the victim the individual recovers his health. The faith- healers are regularly commissioned to treat the victims in this tribe and neighboring tribes. The Kurumba conduct numerous rituals and religious practices for preventing mysterious diseases believed to be caused by the spirits of the ancestors. They conduct Pachachavu, post-mortuary rites in honour of their ancestors. This involves a kind of vigorous dance in which the headman is accompanied by men and women to the rhythm of drums and pipes. There is another ritual called "Seeru" in which they collect the right collar-bones of those who died 10 to 15 years ago and these are kept in a small chariot. These bones are worshipped for seven days. As many as 25 goats are sacrificed, in honour of their ancestors. They also collect the spleen of these goats, and give them as an offering to appease the dead. These bones are later preserved under a memorial stone. Today, the Kurumba have responded to the various development programmes initiated by the State Government. They have adapted to many technological innovations. Traditional and modern systems of knowledge go hand in hand in the present day Kurumba cultural set-up.

Indigenous Medicine among the Kurumba of Attappady, Kerala

Therapeutic Medicine

Head Ache

KURUMBA MEDICINE

Crush a piece of fresh stem of leaves of thalasithari (Clematis gouriana), squeeze the juice and pour into the nose;

Mash the leaves of Mukkuthikodi (Bidens pilosa) and smear over the forehead;

Mash the leaves of the Tamarind tree (Tamarindus indicus) and apply over the forehead for an hour;

Grind the root of the above, smear over the body and take bath in the evening;

Mash the leaves of thottavadi (Mimosa pudica) and turmeric (Curcuma Longa) and smear over the forehead;

Grind garlic and sputum on the threshold of the house, and smear over the body.

Worship Velugan Patta (Ancestor spirit) and benjamintaayi (Goddess) and smear coconut oil over the forehead.

Fever and Head Ache

KURUMBA MEDICINE
Mash the root and leaves of Kurumthotti (Sida retus) and apply over forehead before bath;
Grind the leaves and roots of Karuuppu cedi (cannabis sativa) and smear all over the body;
Worship Velugan Paatta (Ancestor spirit) and Benjámintaayi (goddess) and drink turmeric water;
Grind the leaves of Veppai maram (Azadirachta indica) and smear all over the body, especially for children.

Dysentery

KURUMBA MEDICINE
Prepare a curry of Kuppa keera and karim keera (Portulaca oleracea) and venkayam (Alium sativum) and eat;
Eat the sap of vazhaa pindi (Musa paradisiacea) and matalanaranga (Punica granatum) and the tender leaves of panai (Borassus flabelliformis).

Cholera

KURUMBA MEDICINE
Grind finely the bark of teak (Tectona grandis) and Veetti (Dalbergia latifolia) and Kodivetti mix in milk and drink in small doses.

Vomiting

KURUMBA MEDICINE
Grind the bark of nelli (Emblica officinalis) and drink, this may be taken to alleviate cough also;
Chew the root of Ulakudi (Trumfetta pilosa) and swallow the juice.

Stomach Ache

KURUMBA MEDICINE
Mash the bark of muringai (Moringa olefera) and drink the juice twice a day;
Grind the northbound root of Ulakudi cedi (Triumfetta pilosa) and drink the juice;
Dilute salt in water and drink

Chest Pain

KURUMBA MEDICINE

Grind the roots of Kothamalli cedi (Coriander sativum), Mullakkeera cedi Kuppa keera cedi (Portulaca oleracea) and drink the juice.

Oedema

KURUMBA MEDICINE

Squeeze the leaves of niirpidissi (Ammania baccifera)and smear all over the body and take bath after half an hour;

Grind the roots of kothamallicedi (Coriander sativum), Mullakkeeraccedi and Kuppa keera cedi (Portulaca oleracea) and drink the juice;

Grind the root of Mullu venga (Pterocarpus marsupium), liver of cock and the leaves of Muringa (Moringa olefera) and drink the juice.

Jaundice

KURUMBA MEDICINE

Grind the fine parts of kiizharnelli (Phyllanthus neruri) and add to it black goat's milk and drink;

Grind the tuber of puumparuthi (Gossypium arboreum) add to the urine of white sheep and drink;

Mash the bark of vaka (Albizzia lebleck), Karimaram (Terminalia alata) and ezhilampala (Alstonia scholaris) and drink the juice.

Piles

KURUMBA MEDICINE

Grind Chukannulli (Allium cepa) and Portulaca sp. and apply over the piles;

Tie the meat of tortoise in the bark of Gardenia latifolia and push into the rectum;

Grind the leaves and roots of Mimosa pudica and Kuzhiana (ant-lion) and drink the juice;

Mash the head of the tortoise and push into the rectum with the thumb of the left hand - the tortoise head is generally dried and kept preserved;

Take the bark of pulasi maram (Butea frondosa) and grind with coconut (Cocos nucifera) shell and apply over the piles.

Epilepsy

KURUMBA MEDICINE

Eat the meat of crow after frying it in coconut oil;
Grind the scrapings of bamboo (Bambusa arundinacea) and Manjikalan cedi (Hibiscus vitifolis) and the bark of ciingantholi (Capparisdivaricata) mix in water and drink;
Wear amulet and black thread after incartation of spells;
Grind the leaves of Kulamavu (Gullenia excelesa) and the earth collected from the four corners of the house, mix in human urine and water, keep in a bamboo measure, smear all over the body and propitiate Velugan patta and Benjamintaayi.

Snake bite

KURUMBA MEDICINE

Recite the spells in honour of Siva, Kali and Garuda and fan the patient with leaves of Eruku (Calotropis gigantea);
Mash the root of Kaattu Kolinji (Tephrosia purpurea), Pooveru (Rauvolfia serpintina) with salt and coriander seeds mix in water and give to drink;
Mash the root of Rauvolfia serpentiana and apply over the bitten part;
Mash the root of Vellarakkan cedi (Calotropis gigantea) with Tephrosia pumpurea and Rauvolfia serpentiana and give the juice to drink;
Grind the root of Ponnarali (Cascabela thevetea) and give the juice to drink;
If bitten by a Python, grind the roots of Palakapayyani (Oroxylum indicum) and give the juice to drink;
Mash the root of Dalbergia latifolia, bark of Kanjiram (Strychnos nux vomica) and apply over the bitten part;
Grind the root of Chandragiri (Pterocarpus santalinus), mix with water and give to drink, also apply over the bitten part;
Grind the root of Vanchi cedi (Vaccinium neigherrenses), mix in water and give to drink, apply over the bitten part.

Family planning

KURUMBA MEDICINE

Mash the leaves of tamarind (Tamarindindicus) and smear over the body of the woman, bathe her in flowing water before intercourse for causing her to conceive;
Grind the tubers of missakkei (Clemantis gauriana); husband should cause the wife to drink the portion for three days for aiding conception;
Mash the roots of patti keerai and mullakkeerai (Portulaca spp.) mix in milk, the wife should drink it and apply it all over the body of the husband for preventing pregnancy.

Fertility treatment

KURUMBA MEDICINE

Mash leaves of tamarind (Tamarindindicus) and smear over the body of the woman, bathe in flowing water before intercourse for causing her to conceive

Drink the ground tubers of missakkei (Clemantis gauriana)

Burns

KURUMBA MEDICINE

Powder the charcoal of coconut shell (Cocos nucifera) to a fine paste, mix with coconut oil and smear;

Fry the leaves of Cajanus cajan into powder, mix with coconut oil and smear;

Fry the leaves of Emblica officinalis powder, mix with coconut oil and smear.

Eye pain

KURUMBA MEDICINE

Mash the leaves of Ponnavira (Cassia senna) and Savola Ulli (Allium cepa) dilute with water, eye drop;

Mash the dry ginger (Zingiber officinale) and pour the juice in the eyes;

Mash the roots of Sankuchichedi (Abrus precatorius) filter through cloth and use as eye drop.

Abscess

KURUMBA MEDICINE

Grind the tuber of maavalinga (Decalepis hamiltonii) and apply;

Grind the leaves of Murukku (Erythrina indica) and smear.

Wound

KURUMBA MEDICINE

Mash the leaves of appasappa (Eupatorium odaratissima) and cowri cedi and apply the juice over the wound, bandage;

Grind the leaves of ellakkara (Singesbeckia orientalis) and smear;

Mash the leaves of Kathivettu (Pachygone ovata) and smear;

Grind the bark of Karimaram (Terminalia alata) and apply.

The stifling rain forests with such rich bio-diversity had given birth to a vast number of uses and applications of the flora and fauna of the eco system of which these tribal communities are a part. It is not surprising that, over the centuries, the autochthonous Kurumba have achieved sustainable equations with their rich forest based environment. The important element in these equations has been the recognition of the curative power of the plant species which are meticulously used in the treatment of specific individual diseases. However, we should not hastily jump into the conclusion that the Kurumba materia medica is only the reflection of a dead tradition. The curative/ protective/ healing practices of these tribespeople described above are part of the booming continuous cultural tradition.

Concluding Observations

> *"The interplay of ecology, sociology, economics, anthropology and culture is to be tied together to design meaningful biodiversity management strategies in an ecologically and socially heterogeneous environment"* –
>
> **UNESCO (1995)**

> *Over the centuries, every culture, every society has built up a body of technical and practical expertise, which is still being enriched. Some of this derives from an attempted general and comprehensive interpretation of the world, while some meets the need to organize knowledge and know-how somewhat along the lines of the various Western Scientific disciplines. The fairly widespread dissemination of such knowledge and the existence of reserved pools of know-how in both traditional modern societies result in cultural divisions, which are very often social divisions as well.*
>
> **UNESCO (1995: 108)**

In this paper our concern has been with the Indigenous Knowledge of the tribespeople living in the forest ecosystem and depending on their indigenous mmedicine and local medicine men and women specialists. We also described in brief the tribal peoples' own vision of biodiversity conservation. Tribal health and medicine are pragmatically integrated with all aspects of their life and culture. Nature and "super-nature' are both involved. In the tribal concept of health the actions of each individual have repercussions on the well being of the community as a whole and therefore they are everyone's concern. Benevolent and malevolent deities react to each and every human action, which in turn affect the people's health. Thus, worship is as important as medication. The tribal medicine or ethno-medicine has become a treasure hunting ground for other medical systems and multinational drug firms. It is seen that the professionals of Ayurvedic and allopathic systems approach the tribal healers and ask about the ingredients of their curing recipes. The tribe's traditional knowledge is usurped and the intellectual property of the tribes alienated. The tribe's right over their knowledge on the medicinal herbs and that of other realms should be safeguarded. The variety of crafts, techniques, products and knowledge of flora and fauna of the tribal communities has been acclaimed as unique by many experts. The tropical rain forests with much varied and rich bio-diversity had given birth to a vast number of uses and applications of the flora and fauna of the eco system of which the tribal communities are a part. However, gradually outsiders exploit this traditional knowledge for commercial purposes, whereas the tribal communities suffer from want.

In this respect the case of the 'Kani' tribe of Kerala is unique. According to UNESCO, "The case of 'Kani' tribe, where the cultivation and the value addition to ethno-biologically important medicinal plant species could improve the quality of life of these people is an interesting example. The extraction of the active principle from medicinal plant species like 'Trichopus Zeylanicus' and three other medicinal plants as ingredients used in a formulation 'Jeevani' which has revealed to remove fatigue and energize the body, due to the presence of certain glycolipids and non-steroidal compounds with profound adaptogenic and immune-enhancing properties is remarkable.

In view of the success of the ethno medicine associated with the Kani Tribe as also the exposure of this ethno medicine with outside world, certain points described below become notable for wider consideration:

(1) Encouraging and Enabling the local people doing traditional cultivation of the medicinal plant species,

(2) Empowerment of the community for equal sharing of the economic benefits arising from the value added pharmaceutical products sold in the market.

(3) Promoting traditional medicine, which may still have remained isolated, which need to be stimulated in a major way.

(4) The database of the tribal medical /healing system rests on oral traditions of a few surviving practitioners. An exceptional and rare human asset is likely to be lost, if conscious efforts are not made at once to preserve this tradition.

The ethno-medicine is exposed to threats from "modern" scientific systems, including Ayurvedic and allopathic systems, which enjoy governmental/ market support. Traditional healing Techniques of the tribal communities contain locally suitable and effective drugs in the plant species, some of which are in endangered category. The Bio-diversity Act of 2003 (Government of India) is intended to: provide for the determination, preservation, protection and improvement of tribal traditional knowledge system related to medicine, agricultural practices, knowledge on wild flora and fauna used for food shelter etc. Thus, the government cannot allow the priceless heritage to be sold in cheap deals. Benefit sharing cannot be reduced to financial compensation for giving conglomerate to access to and monopoly rights over collectively held biological resources and knowledge. In the protection of traditional knowledge, innovations and practices of tribal communities, there is no need of speculative contracts with royalties.

Violation of the above Act including investigation survey, research analysis, documentation, reproduction or marketing of any tribal intellectual property should be punished with a fine of three Lakh or rigorous imprisonment for a period of not less than three years. The benefits secured on the basis of usurpation of any components of tribal medicine should be recovered from the usurpers and in its place and this may he handed over to the original custodian of the knowledge system without paying any compensation.

Traditional Medicine is the sum total of all the knowledge and practices whether explicable or not, used in diagnosis, prevention and elimination of physical, mental or social imbalance and relying exclusively on practical experiences and observation handed down from generation to generation. The tribes particularly the Kurumba and Irula of Attappady depend on collection of minor forest produce and medicinal plants. However, in recent years they have been hit hard by the liberalization and globalization in Kerala. Some developing countries and some western countries have adapted the traditional medicine in curative aspects of health. Although the Kurumba use four kinds of rare herbs for the treatment of cancer, they do not want to divulge. There is a traditional medical centre run by a healer exclusively for the treatment of cancer.The worst sufferers of the environmental degradation are the tribal communities like the Kurumba. Except for the Silent Valley, the forests in Attappady have witnessed violent human interference after Independence. With the opening of the area for the extraction of bamboos by the Gwalior Rayons, many of the indigenous species endemic to the area have been permanently lost. It is not now possible to ascertain whether they had in the past attributed Kurumba pharmacopoeia; point is that they should have been substituted by several other species.

In recent years there is a Growing interest in the Traditional Medicine among the Social scientists, Modern Medicine Practitioners, Health Planers and Administrators Consequently the WHO and UNICEF and developing countries like India, China, Egypt etc. have recommended the inclusion of Traditional Medicine and its Practitioners in primary health care on the grounds that the Practitioners of Traditional Medicine will be fitted in to the cultural heritage of the people. As a matter of fact the Government of India has included the Traditional Medicine care in the existing health care system programmes. It is therefore recommended that there should be an integration of modern and indigenous medicine in a meaningful manner and the rights of the tribes and their benefits should not be ignored.

According to UNESCO 1995 (Page No. 112) that " In the medical field (pharmacopoeia and medicine proper) there have been increasing numbers of experiments with the adoption of traditional technologies, in particular in pharmacology, or with the combining of traditional and modern expertise, for example pairing witch-doctors or healers with psychiatrists in some African countries, notably Senegal."

"Thus, although traditional folk medicine may appear fragile as compared with its scientific Western equivalent, often imported and imposed without discernment, many projects are aimed at recording tradition and reconciling it with modernity. In Central Africa, for instance, cells of traditional healers have been incorporated into modern medical teams in order to protect patients from the harmful effects of mixing traditional and modern prescriptions. Traditional practitioners in several regions have been trained in environmental health, preventive care, and nutrition and child care. Once trained, they join modern health-care teams. Similar steps have been taken to improve the training given to village birth attendants."

Donal Worster in his article (1993) published in the book *Global Ecology* has rightly observed,

> *"We must make our first priority in dealing with the earth the careful and strict preservation of the billion-year-old heritage achieved by the evolution of plant and animal life. We must preserve all the species, sub-species, varieties, communities, and ecosystems that we possibly can. We must not, through our actions, cause any more species to become extinct. To be sure, we cannot stop every death or extinction, since the death of living things is part of the inevitable workings of nature. But we can avoid adding to that fateful outcome. We can stop reversing the processes of evolution, as we are doing today. We can work to preserve as much genetic variety as possible. We can save endangered habitats*

and restore those needed to support that evolutionary heritage. We can and must do all this primarily because the living heritage of evolution has an intrinsic value that we have not created but only inherited and enjoyed. That heritage demands our respect, our sympathy, and our love"-

Donal Worster (1993)

Acknowledgement

Author is extremely grateful to Dr. N.K.Das, Visiting Fellow, ASI and Editor, JSA, for editing this paper thoroughly and for providing some important comments and observations included in this paper.

References

Anderson, James N., (1973), "Ecological Anthropology and Anthropological Ecology". In 'Handbook of Social and Cultural Anthropology' John, J. Honigmann. Chicago: Rand Mc Nally and Company.

Beals, R.L. and Hoijer, (1953/1965 edition) an Introduction to Anthropology. New York: The Macmillan and Company.

Beattie, John, (1964), Other Cultures. Routledge and Kegan Paul.

Benedict, Ruth, (1934), Patterns of Culture. London: George Routledge and Sons. Also see 1935 and 1946 editions.

Bottomore, Tom, (1975), Marxist Sociology. London: The Macmillan Press Ltd.

Bottomore, T. B., (1956), Marx's Social Theory. London: Walts.

Brown, A. R. Radcliff, (1952), Structure and Function in Primitive Society. London: Cohen and West Ltd. Also 1959, 1965 edition.

Chaudhuri Buddhadeb, (1986), Tribal Health: Socio-Cultural Dimensions, Inter-India Publications.

Ember, Carol: C and Ember, Melvin, (1977), Cultural Anthropology. New Jersey: Prentice Hall Inc.

Feinberg Richard, (1979), "Schneider's Symbolic culture Theory: An Appraisal". In Current Anthropology, September.

Gluckman, Max., (1949), an Analysis of the Sociological Theories of Bronislaw Malinowski. Oxford University Press.

Gluckman, Max., (1954), Rituals of Rebellion in South-East Africa. Manchester. Manchester Uni. Press.

Gluckman, Max., (1955), Custom and Conflict in Africa. Oxford Basil Blackwell. Also 1956 and 1970 edition.

Harris, Marvin, (1966), The Cultural Ecology of India's Sacred Cattle, Current Anthropology. 7.

Harris, Marvin (1968), the Rise of Anthropological Theory. New York, Thomas Y. Crowell Co. Also, 1969 edition.

Herskovits, M. J., (1947), Man and His Works. Illinois.

Herskovits, M. J., (1951), Cultural Anthropology. Oxford and IBM Publishing Company. New Delhi. Also, 1955 and 1974 editions.

Honigmann, John J., (1973), Handbook of Social and Cultural Anthropology. Chicago: Rand Mc Nally and Company.

Kluckhohn. C. and W. H. Kelley, (1945), the Concept of Culture. The Science of Man in the World Crisis. (Ed. R. Linton), New York.

Kroeber, A. L., (1948), Anthropology. New York. Harcourt, Brace and World INC. Also, 1923 and 1967 editions.

Kroeber, A. L. and Parsons Talcott, (1958), "The Concept of Culture and of Social System". *American Sociological Review*. Vol. 23.

Malinowski, B., (1931), Culture. *Encyclopaedia of the Social Sciences*, Vol. 4. New York.

Malinowski, B., (1944), A Scientific Theory of Culture and Other Essays. Carolina: The University of North Carolina Press.

Malinowski, B., (1958), The Dynamics of Culture Change. New York: Yale University Press. Also 1945 edition.

Mathur, PRG. (1977), Tribal Situation in Kerala, Published by Kerala Historical Society Trivandrum, Printed at St.Joseph Press, Trivandrum.

Mathur, PRG., (1978), The Mappila Fisherfolk of Kerala, A Study in inter-relationship between Habitat, Technology, Economy, Society and Culture, Kerala Historical Society, Kerala University, Trivandrum.

Mathur, PRG. (1978), Kurumbas of Attappady in Primitive Tribes, 1st step Sharma, B.D. and Sinha, S.C. (Ed) Published by the Ministry of Home Affairs, New-Delhi (1978).

Mathur, PRG., (1979), The Khasi of Meghalaya (Study in Tribalism and Religion), Cosmo Publishers, Ansari Road, New Delhi.

Mathur, PRG, (1980), The Cholanaickans – Cavemen of Kerala in Occasional Papers on Tribal Development, In Xth International Congress of Anthropological and Ethnological Sciences and Tribal Development,1978 Ministry of Home Affairs, Government of India(1980) B.D.Sharma (ed).

Mathur, PRG, (1982), Political Awakening among the Tribes of Wayanad, In Singh K. S. (ed), Tribal Movements in India, Vol. I, Delhi: Manohar (1982).

Mathur, PRG. (1985), Kurichians and Customary Law, Cochin: University Law Review (C.U.L.R) Published by the School of law studies, Cochin University.

Mathur, PRG, (1989), Workshop proceedings Tribal Habitat and Environment, Published by IGRMS, Bhopal.

Mathur, PRG, (1989), Applied Anthropology, Planning and Development Administration – Law and Practice, In L.K.A. Iyer 125 Birth Anniversary, Edited by A.K.Danda and S. B. Chakravarthi, Anthropological survey of India.

Mathur, PRG., (1989), Applied Anthropology, Planning and Development Administration - Law and Practice: Human Science, Anthropological Survey of India, Calcutta

Mathur, PRG., (1989), Solar Lighting in Kerala's Tribal Development. *The International Journal for Rural Development Practitioners*. Vol. 1, No. 4

Mathur, PRG., (1991), Tribal Medicine: A Study in Irular Science and Superstition in Tribal Culture and Thought (ed. B.N. Saraswathy).

Mathur, PRG., (1992), Paper Contributed on Continuity and Change in Tribal Society in Kerala in Continuity and Change in Tribal Society edited by K.S. Singh published by the Indian Institute of Advanced Study.

Mathur, PRG, (1992), "Tribal Medicine" in Dravidian Encyclopedia Vol. III

V.I. Subramoniam (ed), Published by the Dravidian Linguistics Association, Trivandrum, Kerala.

Mathur, PRG., (1994), Traditional Medicine among the Kurumba of Kerala in Bulletin of the International Committee Urgent Anthropological and Ethnological Research, No. 36 1994.

Mathur, PRG., (1994), Social Stratification among the Muslims of Kerala, Bulletin of International Committee on Urgent Anthropological Research, Published under the auspices of UNESCO, Vienna.

Mathur, PRG., (1996), Kadar in Encyclopedia of Dravidian Tribes Vol II, The International School of Dravidian Linguistics.

Mathur, PRG., (1996), Tribal Movements among the Dravidian Tribal Communities, Edited by T. Madavamenon, Vol. I, Page 85-88.

Mathur, PRG., (1996), Marketing of Honey by Dravidian Tribal Communities in Kerala, Edited by T. Madavamenon, Vol. I, Page 163-166.

Mathur, PRG. (1996), Customary Law among Matrilineal Dravidian Tribes, in Encyclopaedia of Dravidian Tribes (Vol. I) T. Madhavamenon (ed), Page 204-208, Published by the Dravidian Linguistics Association, Trivandrum, Kerala.

Mathur, PRG, (1996), The Development Experience and Evolution, in Encyclopaedia of Dravidian Tribes (Vol. I) T. Madhavamenon (ed), Page 305-313, Published by the Dravidian Linguistics Association, Trivandrum, Kerala.

Mathur, PRG, (1996), Criteria for scheduling of Tribes, in Encyclopaedia of Dravidian Tribes (Vol. I)T. Madhavamenon (ed), Page 322-328, Published by the Dravidian Linguistics Association, Trivandrum , Kerala.

Mathur, PRG., (1996), Environmental Degradation and the Endangered Dravidian Tribes, in Encyclopaedia of Dravidian Tribes (Vol. I)T. Madhavamenon (ed), Page 340-345, Published by the Dravidian Linguistics Association, Trivandrum, Kerala.

Mathur, PRG. (1996), Kadar - A Primitive Tribe of Kerala, in Encyclopaedia of Dravidian Tribes (Vol II) T. Madhava Menon (ed), Published by the Dravidian Linguistics Association, Trivandrum, Kerala.

Mathur, PRG, (1998), Tribal Movement in Lakshadweep and Southern India: In Antiquity to Modernity in Tribal India Vol IV, Tribal Movements in India, Edited by K. S. Singh, Page No.318-336.

Mathur, PRG. (1998), Traditional Health Care System and Eco Restoration of Medicinal Plants - A Case Study. The 21st Century: The Century of Anthropology. The International Union of Anthropological and Ethnological Sciences (IUEAS). The 14th International Congress of Anthropological and Ethnological Science.

Mathur, PRG., (2000), Kerala Fisherfolk Ritualistic and Cosmic Elements. Prakrti : The Integral Vision. Vol. I, Edited By B. N. Saraswati.

Mathur, PRG., (2003), Tribal Development and Violation of Human Rights in XV ICAES 2K3 Humankind/Nature Interaction: Past, Present and Future, International Union of Anthropological and Ethnological Sciences (IUAES).

Mathur, PRG. (2003), Melakkarar - The Traditional Musicians of South India. Bulletin of the International Committee on Urgent Anthropological and Ethnological Research. IUAES, Publication under the auspices of the UNESCO, Vienna.

Mathur, PRG. (2003), Crop Diversity and Tribal Development in Kerala, Attappady Co operative farming Society (ATCOFARMS) - A case study . Edited by Justice K. Sukumaran. Vol. VII, No. 30-31. Niyama Samiksha Cochin.

Mathur, PRG., (2003), Cultural Heritage of Cholanaickan and Kurumba Tribes of Kerala, Edited by Justice K. Sukumaran. Vol. VII, No. 30-31 Niyama Samiksha Cochin.

Mathur, PRG. (2003), Tribal Development and Violation of Human Rights, Edited by Justice K. Sukumaran. Vol. VII, No. 30-31. Niyama Samiksha : Cochin.

Mathur, PRG., (2003), Ecology, Environment, Society and Culture (in press).

Mathur, PRG., History, Society and Culture among the Marginal Communities of South India. Mimeographed.

Mathur, PRG. Kshetrasampada of Guruvayur Sri Krishna Temple (Indira Gandhi National Centre for Arts, Ministry of Culture, New Delhi).

Mathur, PRG. Ecology, Technology and Economy: Continuity and Change among the Fisherfolk of Kerala. Indira Gandhi Rashtriya Manav Sangrahalaya, Ministry of Culture, Bhopal.

Paul Hockings, (1980), Sex and Disease in a Mountain Community. New Delhi: Vikas Publishing House Pvt Ltd.

Rappaport, R. A. (1963), Aspects of man's influence upon island ecosystems: Alteration and control. In F.R. Fosberg (ed), Man's Place in the Island Ecosystem, pp. 155–174. Honolulu: Bishop Museum Press.

Steward, Julian H. (1955), *The Theory of Cultural Change: The Methodology of Multilinear Evolution*. University of Illinois Press, Urbana, 1955.

Tyler, E.B. (1871), Primitive Culture: Researchers into the Development of Mythology, Philosophy, Religion, Art and Custom, John Murray, London, Vol. 1.

UNESCO The Culture Dimension of Development towards a Practical Approach (1995) Paris.

Worster Donal (1993), in Global Ecology by — —.

INDIGENOUS KNOWLEDGE OF THE MEDICINAL PLANTS IN KULLU VALLEY OF NORTHWESTERN HIMALAYA: A Case-Study

Sakshi Bhandari*, Man Singh Rana & S. S. Samant

Indigenous and traditional knowledge are the pillars of any society. Indigenous knowledge of the medicinal plants is crucial for the continued existence of the human beings. The treasury of the diverse medicinal plants available in the vast Himalayan regions has been recorded in ancient Indian scripts as far back as 1000 BC. The Himalaya abounds with unique medicinal plants with potential to be used in the modern medical therapy. Credit goes to the native people for conserving and preserving the old knowledge of the medicinal plants to a great extent. The Kullu valley being situated in the lap of the North Western Himalaya possesses varied topographic and climatic conditions with a wide range of elevation. Because of this varied topography and climatic conditions, the diversity of the medicinal plants in the valley is also very high. The present work explicitly documents the indigenous knowledge of the people of Kullu valley, with the elucidation of 114 species of plants belonging to 82 genera and 47 families. Apiaceae was the most dominant family (06 genera, 10 species) of medicinal plants, followed by Lamiaceae, Ranunculaceae, Asteraceae and Polygonaceae. Of the aboveground plant parts used, leaf was used in majority of cases (40 species), followed by fruit. Of the belowground plant parts used, root (45 species) was used in maximum cases. The results of this study are further discussed in the context of developmental activities and changing socio-economic conditions. With the realization that fast depleting phytodiversity has invaluable therapeutic properties, the current research is undertaken.

***Keywords:** Medicinal plants, indigenous knowledge, Kullu valley*

Introduction

The treasury of the diverse medicinal plants available in the vast Himalayan regions has been recorded in ancient Indian scripts as far back as 1000 BC. The Himalaya abounds with unique medicinal plants with potential to be used in the modern medical therapy. In the Indian Himalayan Region (IHR),

* G. B. Pant Institute of Himalayan Environment and Development, Himachal Unit, Mohan-Kullu, 175 126, Himachal Pradesh, India, *E-mail: sakshi_gbpi@rediffmail.com*

there are over 1748 plant species; (1685- angiosperms, 12- gymnosperms and 51- pteridophytes), including 1020 herbs, 335 shrubs and 330 trees of medicinal value (Samant *et al.*, 1998). The documentation of the indigenous knowledge is important as it can slowdown the erosion of the valued traditional know-how. Unfortunately, indigenous knowledge on usage of medicinal plants in various regions of Northwest Himalaya has not been documented. Out of the above mentioned medicinal plants in IHR, 643 species of medicinal plants are identified in Himachal Pradesh alone (Samant *et al.*, 2007).

Kullu district comprises of five major valleys (*viz.* Banjar, Siraj, Parbati, Kullu and Lug valley). Studies on indigenous knowledge of phytodiversity (Dhaliwhal & Sharma, 1999, Rawat & Singh, 2000) and ethnobotany (Dobriyal et al. 1997; Sharma et al., 2004; Thakur, et al. 2007) have been reported from different parts of the Kullu district which is restricted to few representative villages. Kullu valley is explored only for floristic description and vanishing indigenous knowledge related to medicinal plants is not addressed so far. Therefore, the present study was carried out in the Kullu valley of Himachal Pradesh, North Western Himalaya.

The valley starts from Aut (1000m) in south and extends towards north direction along river Beas (the main drainage system of the valley) up to the Rohtang crests (3978m). This valley is about 80 Km long and 3 Km wide (maximum) in the north. The area lies between 31^{0}21'N and 32^{0}59'N and 76^{0}49'E and 78^{0}59'E, comprising a total of 5503 Km^2. The average rainfall is 80cm. Temperature ranges between 52^{0}C to 38.8^{0}C. The valley is undergoing rapid transformation due to its being a well renowned tourist spot and is therefore, more market oriented. Because of this market based economy the traditional knowledge is depleting at an alarming rate as in many parts of Himalaya (Uniyal et al., 2003). Hence the present study of documentation of the traditional knowledge of the people of Kullu valley becomes relevant.

Land and People

Kullu valley originally bore the name of 'Kulantapitha' meaning the end of the inhabitable world - the utmost limit of human settlement. Kullu has the distinction of having the oldest existing democracy in the world in village 'Malana'. The fairs & festivals, customs and traditions, attire & occupation explain the hard- earned life style of the natives of Kullu valley. Kullu Dusherra, Kulluvi cap and Kulluvi apple have gained international fame and are known all over the world. The customs and rituals practiced in the valley represent the simple way of life of the natives, living in close harmony with Mother Nature. The people worship deities, sages, snake gods and other powerful gods and goddesses mentioned in primeval Indian scriptures. There is a rich tradition of folk arts in Kullu valley. The bulk of inhabitants of the valley comprises of Hindus followed by Buddhists and smattering of others belonging to Sikhs, Jains and Christians. Hindus are divided into Rajputs (Kanets, Khasas), Brahmins, Khatris, Kolis and Dumna. The main occupation of these native inhabitants is agriculture along with horticulture and livestock rearing. The extraction of medicinal plants forms major source of the secondary income for these native inhabitants. The natives possess great deal of indigenous knowledge about medicinal plants and pass it orally from one generation to next.

Methodology

Indigenous knowledge of local inhabitants about the use of native plants was collected during the field trips through interviews. The elders and knowledgeable persons were mainly interviewed. Data was collected on local names of plants, parts used and ailments treated. The collections were identified using standard regional floras (Collett, 1902; Dhaliwal & Sharma, 1999; Aswal & Mehrotra, 1994, Singh & Rawat, 2000). The indigenous uses are mostly based on the surveys; however information on indigenous uses has also been updated with the help of secondary information (Jain, 1991). The data thus collected were pooled and analyzed.

Table 1
Medicinal Plants, Local Names, Plant Parts used and Uses in Kullu Valley

Taxa	*Local name*	*LF*	*Part used*	*Uses*
Alliaceae				
Allium humile Kunth.	Fourn	H	Lf	Indigestion, Stomach disorders
A.wallichii Kunth.	-	H	Bb	Indigestion
Anacardiaceae				
Pistacia integerrima Stew.	Kakarsingi	T	Fr	Cough, cold
Apiaceae				
Angelica glauca Edgew.	Chora	H	Rt	Dysentery, stomach complaints, vomiting
Bupleurum falcatum L.	Nimla	H	Rt	Abdominal inflammation, fever, liver complaints
Heracleum candicans Wall. ex DC.	Padiyala	H	Wp	Leucoderma, menstrual problems, piles
Pimpinella acuminata (Edgew.) Cl.	-	H	Wp	Diarrhoea, dysentry

P.diversifolia DC.	-	H	Rt	Cold, cough, digestive disorder
Pleurospermum angelicoides (DC.) Cl.	-	H	Rt	Antihelminthic, gastric, stomachache
P. candollii (DC.) Cl.	-	H	Lf	Bodyache
Selinum candollii DC.	-	H	Rt	Cough, asthma, hysteria
S.tenuifolium Wall.	Matoshal	H	Wp	Insecticidal, nervine, sedative
S.vaginatum Cl.	Matoshal	H	Rt	Nervine sedative
Asparagaceae				
Asparagus filicinus Buch.-Ham.	Shoutjalari	Sh	Fr, Rt	Antihelminthic, rheumatism, bleeding from nose, cough, dysentery, gonorrhoea, headache, menstrual and gastric problems
Asteraceae				
Achillea millefolium L.	-	H	Lf, Rt	Carminative, tonic, stimulant, tooth ache, cough, cold
Ainsliaea aptera DC.	-	H	Rt, Lf	Stomachache, urinary problems, fever
A.latifolia D.Don	-	H	Rt	Colic
Arctium lappa L.	Nakli kunth	H	Rt	Gastric, burns
Jurinella macrocephala (Benth. ex Hk. f.) Aswal & Malhotra	Jugal dhoop	H	Rt	Antiseptic, colic, fever, laxative
Saussurea heteromala (D.Don) Hand.-Mazz.	-	H	Lf, Rt	Leucoderma, fever, wounds, colic
Berberidaceae				
Berberis jaeschkeana Schneid.	Kashambal	Sh	Rt, Fr	Astringent, blood purifier, diuretic, eye disease, jaundice, menorrhoea, skin disease
B.lycium Royle	Kashambal	Sh	Rt, Fr	Jaundice, eye disease
Cannabaceae				
Cannabis sativa L.	Bhang	H	Lf, Sd, Fr, Fl	Antihelminthic, appetite, bowel complaints, bronchitis, cold, cough, cramp, eye disease, gonorrhoea, laxative, narcotic, nervine stimulent, piles, skin disease
Cucurbitaceae				
Melothria heterophylla (Lour.) Cogn.	Balakakri	H	Rt, Lf, Fr	Antifertility, cuts, diabetes, fever, stomachache
Cuscutaceae				
Cuscuta reflexa Roxb.	Amar bel	H	Wp	Bodyache, burns, cuts
Dioscoreaceae				
Dioscorea deltoidea Wall. ex Kunth.	Shingdi-mingli	H	Tu	Dysentery, piles

table 1 contd.

Ericaceae				
Gaultheria trichophylla Royle	-	Sh	Lf, Fr	Cough, cold
Rhododendron arboreum Sm.	Brass	T	Fl, Lf	Headache, fever, wounds, nose bleeding
R.campanulatum D. Don	Shargal	Sh	Rt, Lf, Fl	Boils, cold, cough, headache, rheumatism, skin disease, tonic, fever
R.anthopogon D.Don	-	Sh	Lf	Bronchitis, cold, cough
R.lepidotum Wall.	Shargal	Sh	Lf	Bronchitis, cold, cough
Fabaceae				
Astragalus chlorostachys Lindl.	-	H	Lf	Tonic, febrifuge, tuberculosis
A. himalayanus Klotz.	-	H	Sd	Colic, leprosy
Parochetus communis Buch.-Ham. ex D.Don	-	H	Lf	Stomach diseases, ear ache, cuts, wounds
Fumariaceae				
Corydalis govaniana Wall.	Bhutkeshi	H	Wp	Antipyretic, diuretic, eye disease, gastric pain, liver complaints, muscle pain, skin disease, syphilis, tonic
Gentianaceae				
Swertia angustifolia Ham. ex D.Don	Chirayata	H	Wp	Malaria, fever
S.cordata Wall.ex Cl.	-	H	Wp	Antihelminthic, antipyretic, laxative, stomach disorders
Geraniaceae				
Geranium nepalense Sw.	-	H	Rt	Cuts, jaundice, toothache, ulcer, wounds, stomach complaints
G.wallichianum D.Don ex Sw.	Chowarhi	H	Rt	Astringent, ear and eye diseases, toothache
Hypericaceae				
Hypericum uralum Buch.-Ham.	-	Sh	Sd	Food poisoning, abortifacient
Iridaceae				
Iris kumaonensis Wall. ex D.Don	-	H	Rt, Lf	Pimples, ringworm, fever, urine complaints, sores
Juglandaceae	Akhrot	T	Bk, Lf,	Frost bite, rheumatism, sores of
Juglans regia L.			Fr	toes, toothache
Lamiaceae				
Ajuga bracteosa Benth.	Neel-kanthi	H	Lf	Blood purification, burns, boils, cold, fever
A. parviflora Benth.	Neel-kanthi	H	Lf	Febrifuge

table 1 contd.

Elsholtzia ciliata Hyland.	-	H	Fl	Skin disease, diarrhoea, stomachache
E. fruticosa (D.Don) Rehder	Buthi	Sh	Lf, Fr, Sd	Relieve sciatica
Mentha longifolia L.	Kusma	H	Wp	Antiseptic, carminative, digestive, wounds
Origanum vulgare L.	Ban-tulsi	H	Wp	Bronchitis, colic, diarrhoea, fever, hysteria
Prunella vulgaris L.	-	H	Wp	Lung complaints, cold, fever, gastric complaints, headache, liver complaints
Thymus linearis Benth.	Ban ajwain	Sh	Wp	Antihelminthic, skin disease, stomachache
Liliaceae				
Cardiocrinum giganteum (Wall.) Makino	-	H	Bb, Lf, St	Antiseptic, wounds, bruises
Polygonatum cirrhifolium (Wall.) Royle	Salam misri	H	Tu, St	Fever, blood purifier, cuts, wounds
P. verticillatum (L.) All.	Salam misri	H	Rh	Nervine tonic
P. multiflorum (L.) All.	Salam misri	H	Rh	Urinary problems
Trillidium govanianum (Wall. ex D.Don) Kunth.	-	H	Tu	Dysentery
Malvaceae				
Sida cordata (Burm.f.) Brossum	-	H	Wp	Cuts, pain in back, snake bite
Meliaceae				
Melia azedarach L.	-	T	Fr, Lf	Antihelminthic, antiseptic, blood purification, headache, insecticidal, rheumatism, skin disease, wounds
Moraceae				
Ficus palmata Forsk.	Fagda	T	Fr, Lf	Dysentery, indigestion, laxative
Morinaceae				
Morina longifolia Wall. ex DC.	-	H	Rt	Boils, wounds
Oleaceae				
Jasminum humile L.	Kuda	Sh	Fl, Lf, Rt	Skin disease, blood disease, heart problems
Olea ferruginea Royle	Koahu	T	St, Oil	Rheumatism, Toothache
Orchidaceae				
Dactylorhiza hatagirea (Don) Soo	Panja	H	Rt	Astringent, bone fracture, expectorant, tonic, wounds
Habenaria edgeworthii Hk.f. ex Collett	-	H	Tu	Blood purifier

table 1 contd.

Oxalidaceae				
Oxalis corniculata L.	Malori	H	Wp	Digestive disorders, dysentery, scurvy, skin disease, stomachache
O.latifolia Kunth.	Malori	H	Wp	Cough, cuts, diarrhoea, digestive disorders, dysentery, fever, stomachache
Papaveraceae				
Meconopsis aculeata Royle	Mushkanda	H	Wp	Backache, colic, renal pain, tonic
Parnassiaceae				
Parnassia nubicola Hk. f.	-	H	Tu	Snake bite
Plantaginaceae				
Plantago himalaica Pilger	Shokha ra poucha	H	Wp	Stomach disorders, fever
P.ovata Forsk.	Shokha ra poucha	H	Wp	Gonorrhoea, dysentery, diarrhoea, fever, rheumatism, cough
Poaceae				
Cymbopogon distans (Nees) Wats.	-	H	Sd, Infl	Cough, cold
C. martinii (Roxb.) Wats.	-	H	Lf, Oil	Skin diseases
Cynodon dactylon (L.) Pers.	Joob	H	Wp	Dysentery, hysteria, headache, menstrual problems, piles
Saccharum spontaneum L.	Philoo	H	Lf	Asthma, cholera
Podophyllaceae				
Podophyllum hexandrum Royle	Bankakri	H	Rt, Fr, Sd	Cancer, cough, wounds, diarrhoea, fever, gastric ulcers, hepatic diseases, purgative, skin diseases
Polygonaceae				
Fagopyrum dibotrys (D.Don) Hara	Paphra	H	Rt, Lf, Sd	Vermicide
F.esculentum Moench	Ghangri	H	Rt, Lf, Sd	Lung disorders, rheumatism, typhoid, urine complaints
Polygonum affine D.Don	-	H	Rt, Sd	Cold, diarrhoea
P.amplexicaule D. Don	Dori ghaa	H	Rt, Lf	Cough, dysentery, tonic
Rheum australe D.Don	Chuchi	H	Rt	Abdominal pain, asthma, bronchitis, fever, cuts, dysentery, laxative, eye disease, piles, skin disease, sprain, wounds
R.speciforme Royle	Chuchi	H	Infl, Rt	Abdominal disease, boils, astringent, purgative, wounds
Rumex acetosa L.	Jungli palak	H	Lf, Fr	Stomach diseases

table 1 contd.

R.nepalensis Spreng.	Malora	H	Lf, Rt	Boil, diuretic, purgative, scurvy, swelling of muscles
Primulaceae				
Primula denticulata Sm.	Jaibeez	H	Fl	Diabetes, urinary ailments
Punicaceae				
Punica granatum L.	Daru	Sh	Rt, St, Fr, Lf	Antihelminthic, cholera, dysentery, eye problems, pimples, stomachache
Ranunculaceae				
Aconitum heterophyllum Wall. ex Royle	Patish	H	Rt	Antihelminthic, cough, diarrhoea, digestive complaints, dysentery, fever, gastric problems, vomiting
A.violaceum Jacq. ex Stapf.	Meethi Patish	H	Rt	Gastrointestinal complaints, renal pain, rheumatism, stomachache
Actaea spicata L.	Mamira	H	Lf, Fl	Sedative, sciatica, body inflammation
Anemone obtusiloba D.Don	Mamiri	H	Rt, Sd	Menorrhoea, rheumatism, purgative
Delphinium denudatum Wall. ex Hk. f. & Th.	Laskar	H	Rt	Antihelminthic, respiration problem, toothache, ulcers
D.vestitum Wall. ex Royle	-	H	Wp	Antidote to snake bite, cuts, wounds, fever, diarrhoea
Thalictrum foliolosum DC.	Mamiri	H	Rt	Eye diseases
Rosaceae				
Duchesnea indica (Andres.) Focke	Bummaru	H	Wp	Cuts, eye disease, swelling, ulcer on tongue
Potentilla argyrophylla Wall. ex Lehm.	Dori	H	Wp	Wounds as analgesic
P.atrosaguinea Lodd.	Dori	H	Lf	Wounds as analgesic
Prinsepia utilis Royle	Bhekhal	Sh	Sd, Fr	Burns, cuts, rheumatism, wounds
Rubus biflorus Buch.-Ham. ex Sm.	Anchha	Sh	Fr, Rt	Diarrhoea
R.ellipticus Sm.	Kala Aanchha	Sh	Fr, Rt	Dysentery, malaria, stomachache, worms
R.paniculatus Sm.	Lal Anchha	Sh	Lf, Fr	Diarrhoea, stomachache
Rubiaceae				
Rubia manjith L.	-	H	Rt	Antidote to scorpion bite, snake bite, astringent, chest complaints, lecuoderma, inflammation, jaundice, liver complaints, paralysis, menorrhoea, urine complaints, ulcer, stomachache
Rutaceae				

table 1 contd.

Boenninghausenia albiflora (Hk.f.) Reichb. ex Meissn	Pissumer	H	Rt	Antiseptic, cuts & wounds, vomiting, dysentery
Skimmia laureola Sieb. & Zucc. ex Walp.	Nair	Sh	Lf	Tooth care, mouth wash
Zanthoxylum armatum DC.	Timber	Sh	Fr, Sd, St	Cough, cholera, fever, eczema, itching, piles, tonic, toothache
Saxifragaceae				
Bergenia ciliata (Hew.) Stercb.	Pashan ved	H	Rt, Lf	Asthma, boils, cuts, wounds, burns, fever, liver complaints, piles, kidney stones, urine complaints
B.stracheyi (Hk. f. & Th.) Engl.	Pashan ved	H	Rt, Lf	Diuretic, fever, ophthalmia, tonic, cuts, wounds
Scrophulariaceae				
Picrorhiza kurrooa Royle	Karroo	H	Rt	Abdominal pain, anaemia, cold, dyspepsia, diarrhoea, influenza, jaundice, purgative, dysentery, fever
Valerianaceae				
Valeriana hardwickii Wall.	Nihanu	H	Wp	Mental disorder, insecticide
V.jatamansi Jones	Nihanu	H	Wp	Antidote to poisonous sting of Insects, hysteria, skin diseases
Violaceae				
Viola biflora L.	Vanafsha	H	Lf, Fl, Rt, Sd	Antiseptic, antispasmodic, cold, cough, emetic, fever, laxative, leucoderma, skin disease
V.canescens Wall. ex Roxb.	Banaksa	H	Lf, Fl	Asthma, bronchitis, cold, cough, eye disease
Zingiberaceae				
Hedychium spicatum Sm.	Ban haldi	H	Rh	Asthma, blood purification, bronchitis, nausea
Roscoea purpurea Sm.	-	H	Wp	Tonic, cuts
Gymnosperms				
Taxaceae				
Taxus baccata L. subsp. *wallichiana* (Zucc.) Pilger	Rakhal	T	Bk,	Anti cancerous
Pteridophytes				
Athyriaceae				
Diplazium esculentum (Retz.) Sw.	Lingdi	H	Frd	Constipation
Equisetaceae				
Equisetum arvense L.		H	Wp	Kidney affection, acidity, dyspepsia

Results and Discussion

The Kullu valley being situated in the lap of the North Western Himalaya possesses varied topographic and climatic conditions with a wide range of elevation. Because of this varied topography and climatic conditions, the diversity of the medicinal plants in the valley is also very high. In the present study, a total of 114 species belonging to 47 families and 82 genera were recorded (Table 3). The information on botanical binomial, local name of the plant, plant part used to cure the ailment and the ailment for which it is used has been given in Table 1. In terms of number of plant species, Apiaceae was the dominant family followed by Lamiaceae, Ranunculaceae, Asteraceae and Polygonaceae (Table 2). Different plant parts were used as a medicine by the people of Kullu valley. Of the aboveground plant parts used, leaf was used in majority of cases (40 species), followed by fruit. Of the belowground plant parts used, root (45 species) was used in maximum cases. The whole plant of 25 species was used as medicine (Table 5). The plants were used for curing a variety of diseases from most common cold to even advanced diseases including cancer. For example, bark of *Taxus baccata* subsp. *wallichiana* is used for the treatment of cancer; rhizome of *Hedychium spicatum* is used in asthma, blood purification, bronchitis and nausea; *Podophyllum hexandrum* in cancer, cough, ulcer, hepatic diseases, fever and diarrhoea; fruits and stem of *Zanthoxylum armatum* in cough, cholera, fever, eczema, itching, piles, tonic and toothache and flowers and leaves of *Rhododendron arboreum* used in Headache, fever, wounds and nose bleeding.

Maximum number of plants was used for curing stomach disorders followed by fever, cold & cough and cuts & wounds (Table 4). It was also noted that a single plant species had multiple medicinal values like *Picrorhiza kurrooa, Viola biflora, Bergenia ciliata, Aconitum heterophyllum, Rheum australe etc.* But as in other parts of the Himalaya, the loss of medicinal plant diversity is one of the fast spreading current trends in the valley also. Reduction in medicinal plant diversity is a domino effect of many factors particularly living conditions which stimulates perception or per se the perceptions of people develop according to the available natural resources. With the changing socioeconomic and socio-cultural context, the population of medicinal plants are depleting increasingly. There is a need to understand the real value of this rich medicinal plant diversity for improving the yield and product quality in a sustainable way for the social upliftment of the hilly people in this part of Himalaya. Also there is a huge scope for medicinal plant based enterprises and related avenues in the valley. The present documentation of indigenous knowledge of Kullu valley opens new avenues to scrutinize such a rich natural resource for investigating the potential of herbal medicine for sustainable development.

Table 2
Dominant Families of Medicinal Plants in Kullu Valley

Family	*Genera*	*Species*
Apiaceae	6	10
Lamiaceae	6	8
Ranunculaceae	5	7
Asteraceae	5	6
Polygonaceae	4	8
Rosaceae	4	7

Table 3
Taxonomic Description of the Medicinal Plants in Kullu Valley

	Families	*Genera*	*Species*	*Herbs*	*Shrubs*	*Trees*	*Ferns*
Angiosperms	44	79	111	89	18	4	-
Gymnosperms	1	1	1	-	-	1	-
Pteridophytes	2	2	2	-	-	-	2
Grand Total	47	82	114	89	18	5	2

Table 4
Number of Plants used for Treating Various Diseases

Disease	*Number of Plants Used*
Stomach disorders	31
Fever	25
Cold and cough	22
Cuts and wounds	20
Dysentery	16
Skin diseases	14
Eye problems	10
Female disorders	8
Headache	6

Table 5
A Comparison of the Plant parts used for Medicinal Purposes

Aboveground plant parts used	*Number of Species*	*Belowground plant parts used*	*Number of Species*	*Whole plants used*
Leaf	40	Root	45	25
Fruit	19	Tuber	5	
Seed	15	Rhizome	3	
Flower/ Inflorescence	11	Bulb	2	
Bark/ stem	7			
Frond	1			
Total	93		55	25

Acknowledgements

The authors are thankful to the Director, G.B.Pant Institute of Himalayan Environment & Development, Kosi-Katarmal, Almora for facilities and motivation. Local people of Kullu valley are also acknowledged for their valuable cooperation. Help received from Dr. Manoher Lal, Mr. Aman Sharma and Ms. Shalini Vidyarthi is also highly acknowledged.

References

Aswal, B. S. and Mehrotra, B. N. (1994), *Flora of Lahaul-Spiti*. Bishen Singh Mahendra Pal Singh, Dehradun.

Collett, H. (1902), *Flora Simlensis*. Thacker Spink. & Co. Calcutta and Simla, Reprinted 1971. Bishen Singh Mahendra Pal Singh, Dehradun.

Dhaliwal, D. S. and Sharma, M. (1999), *Flora of Kullu District* (Himachal Pradesh). Bishen Singh Mahendra Pal Singh, Dehra Dun.

Jain, S. K. (1991), *Dictionary of Indian Folk Medicine and Ethnobotany*. Deep Publications. New Delhi.

Samant, S. S., Dhar U. and Palni L. M. S. (1998), *Medicinal Plants of Indian Himalaya: Diversity, Distribution, Potential Values*. Himvikas Publication No. 13, Gyanodaya Prakashan, Nainital.

Samant, S. S., Pant, S., Singh, M., Lal, M. Singh, A., Sharma, A. and Bhandari, S. (2007), Medicinal Plants in Himachal Pradesh, North Western Himalaya, India. *International Journal of Biodiversity Science and Management*, 3: 234–251.

Singh, S. K. and Rawat, G. S. (2000), *Flora of Great Himalayan National Park*, Himachal Pradesh, Bishen Singh, Mahendra Pal Singh, Dehradun.

Uniyal, S. K., Awasthi, A. & Rawat, G. S. (2003), Developmental Processes, Changing Lifestyle and Traditional Wisdom: Analyses from Western Himalaya. *The Environmentalist*, 23: 307-312.

Dobriyal, R. M., Singh, G. S. Rao, K. S. and Saxena, K. G. (1997), Medicinal Plant Resources in Chhakinal Watershed in the Northwestern Himalaya. *Journal of Herbs, Spices and Medicinal plants*, 5(1): 15-27.

Sharma, P. K., Chauhan, N. S. and Lal, B. (2005), Studies on Plant Associated Indigenous Knowledge among the Malanis of Kullu District, Himachal Pradesh. *Indian Journal of Traditional Knowledge*, 4(4): 403-408.

Thakur, S. D., Hanief, S. M. and Chauhan, N. S. (2007), Multipurpose use of Plant Species in the Kullu Valley of Himachal Pradesh (India). *Journal of Non-Timber Forest Product*, 14(2): 139-146.

INDIGENOUS KNOWLEDGE APPLICATION FOR CONSERVATION OF BIO-RESOURCE IN THE COLD DESERT OF THE NORTHWESTERN HIMALAYA

Santaram S. Oinam*, Jagdish C. Kuniyal, Yashwant S. Rawat*** S. C. R. Vishvakarma*** and Dinesh C. Pandey******

Indigenous knowledge systems play a major role in sustainable use and conservation of bioresources in many parts of the world. The Lahaul valley located in northwestern Himalaya is one such geographical entity having rich culture and the customary practice of indigenous knowledge to sustain their life in an otherwise harsh cold climatic condition. The present in-depth study about the indigenous uses of bioresources was carried out in four revenue villages in the Lahaul valley. The people here practice indigenous techniques for the storage, use and management of their local resources. Some of the indigenous practices for storage of cultivated crops (i.e., food grains, vegetables, fruits), fuel, fodder and several other uses of remaining bioresources in nutshell are described in this paper. The paper also touches the traditional uses of human excreta and animal dung for manure and to develop woolen goods in the area. The present study not only establishes the validity of traditional knowledge but also indicates the urgency to keep them in sustainable mode. Indigenous knowledge if not conserved properly will be seriously threatened under pressure of modernization and especially on account of the apathy among new generations.

Keywords: *Indigenous knowledge, bioresources, storage, night-soil compost, Lahaul*

Introduction

The indigenous knowledge of an area is product of the needs of an area to survive judiciously by using the local resources to the best of the ability and with care. Such knowledge is of greater value in the life of the people

* G. B. Pant Institute of Himalayan Environment and Development, N.E. Unit, Vivek Vihar, 791113, Arunachal Pradesh, India

** G. B. Pant Institute of Himalayan Environment and Development, Himachal Unit, Mohal-Kullu, 175 126, Himachal Pradesh, India

*** G. B. Pant Institute of Himalayan Environment and Development, Kosi-Katarmal, Almora- 263 643, Uttaranchal, India

**** Department of Geography, DSB Campus, Kumaun University, Nainital (U.A), India

living in the harsh cold climatic conditions. In such conditions there is greater urgency to cope with the problems of the rational management of bioresources. A rational and fair observance of the conservation of bioresources in unkind conditions is the outcome of the continuous struggle and learning as posed by the challenges in such area and handling the opportunities provided by the nature[1]. The fact is that the existing customary practices and the enduring indigenous knowledge that remain in practice is mainly due to the actuality of the confronting the challenges of such harsh cold climatic conditions of the area. Such traditional knowledge of the indigenous people has continuously been updated from one generation to another with passage of time. Thus the existing knowledge has become perfect over time and is ever readapted to the new situations faced by the local people in their surrounding environment. The new experiences that are witnessed about bioresource use and practice are influenced by the greater needs for the rational management of local natural resources under severe physio-climatic conditions. In the past, the communication distance from one community to another in such difficult geographical area had hindered the exchange of ideas. Gradually the people realized the importance of interacting with neighbors. These interactions led to establishing a solid base for the sustenance of indigenous people. Today, the people of the northwestern Indian Himalaya are proud holder of such rich knowledge in conserving and managing the locally available scarce resources under hard-pressed environmental conditions.

The native people of the northwestern Himalayan region used to collect foodstuff from a variety of sources. In view of the harsh climate the danger of damage to the foodstuff was always felt. Hence they realized the need of the appropriate storing of the available food and the yields collected through cultivated crops and through other bio-resource uses, which are unique. Such requirement for appropriate storing of the available food and the yields led to gradually developing the indigenous methods for preservation in the face of the cold and harsh climatic conditions and in view of the fact that their land was locked for larger part of the year, particularly in the Lahaul valley. These regions physically inaccessible during winters are characteristics for undulating relief features, remoteness and sluggish development activities. Population pressure, and only the limited scopes for development of new markets and transportation facility have collectively brought the consequent alterations in the region. Despite slow development but continuous impact of the modern technological advancements in networking and communications, has led the people, particularly the youth to gradually move away from their traditional occupations and its practices.

People are consciously aware of the threats of the new developments and the prospects of the threats to the customary occupational practices and usages of the inherent indigenous knowledge in protecting themselves. They are increasingly realizing that only the traditional preventive measures may not be enough and that there is need for judging their old culture-bound practices of food preservation from scientific preservation point of views. This will inevitably be helpful in understanding future potential of the resources, which are locally available but in insufficient supply.

In view of above cultural and environmental backdrop this study focuses on the traditional economic institutions, food types in use, the types of the indigenous technology in use and other indigenous practices, which are on a verge of extinction in the Lahaul valley.

Study Area

The cold desert in the northwestern Indian Himalaya, mainly the Lahaul & Spiti regions in Himachal Pradesh state extend between 31°44′34" N and 32°59′57" N latitude and 76°46′29" E and 78°41′34" E longitude[2], and covering a geographical area of 6244 km^2 in the Lahaul valley. It forms an elevated vibrant area for indigenous knowledge and its practices. In order to collect data for this study, Kuthar (2600 m amsl), Hinsa (2700 m), Jahlma (3000 m) and Khoksar (3200 m), four revenue villages located at different altitudes are selected, who represent the entire Lahaul valley were selected for study (Fig. 1). During long winter period, the Lahaul valley remains cut-off from rest of the country due to heavy deposits of snow on the Rohtang Pass (3978 m), for more than five to six months. The valley is cold, arid and it receives just about 25 mm an average rainfall and about 4530 mm snowfall[3].

Methodology

An extensive survey was conducted in the four selected villages to assess the status of the indigenous knowledge systems pertaining to bioresources uses. The information about storage of food grains, vegetables, fruits, fodder, fuel wood, use of indigenous containers were gathered by recording the responses of the villagers through structured questionnaire. More than 90% of households were interviewed in all four villages. The obtained data were also verified by the authors through personal / participant observation of the various uses of bioresources. The first hand data about traditional use of human excreta, total production of night-soil compost (NSC), agriculture area covered by NSC and animal dung for manure were obtained through direct interviewing of the family heads. The information was also gathered from secondary sources.

Results

The people in the Lahaul valley practice a number of indigenous techniques for the storage, use and management of their local resources. The storage of the yields from the cultivated crops for diverse use is one of the major activities. Some of the indigenous practices for storage of cultivated crops (i.e., food grains, vegetables, fruits), fuel, fodder and several other uses of remaining bioresources are described below.

Storage of Food Grains

The major crops under cultivation in this mountainous cold desert are cash crops (peas (Pisum sativum Linn.), potatoes (Solanum tuberosum Linn.) and hops (Humulus lupulus Linn.), traditional crops {barley (Hordeum vulgare Linn.), wheat (Triticum aestivum Linn.), maize (Zea mays Linn.), and varieties of buckwheat (Fagopyrum esculentum Moench. and Fagopyrum tataricum Linn.)}, and medicinal plants like kuth {Saussurea costus (Falc.) Lipsch.} and manu (Inula racemosa Hk.f.)[4-8]. Inhabitants in the Lahaul valley by nature make applied use and exercise their in-depth knowledge for the storage of these crops to meet their requirement results during the winter period. These techniques are simple and low cost demanding. The unique knowledge of the indigenous people is reflected particularly in terms of techniques employed in storage of potato, vegetables, meat and vessel/container. Generally foodsgrains and others food commodities are stored in the small and big sized wooden boxes, which are made up of willow (Salix alba Linn. and Salix fragilis Linn.). Willow is a multipurpose agroforestry tree. The other tree species used as raw material for similar boxes are junipers (Juniperus macropoda) and poplar (Populus balsamifera)Linn and (Populus nigra Linn.).

Storage of Vegetables

The vegetables are grown but not in large scale as there remains a very short growth season (April-August) under the xeric and cold desert conditions. Along with high fluctuations in seasonal temperature (high in short summer and below zero in winter), there are very scanty rainfall and high snowfall prevailing in the Lahaul valley. The crop cultivation during winter season is not practised due to such unfavourable climatic conditions. Therefore, the local people store some of the vegetables for meeting the requirement during off-season period.

Potatoes are stored in the sub-soil underground pits prepared in agricultural fields for off-season use. The pits with 4m x 4m x 4m dimension are dug and potatoes are stored after covering the pits with soil (Fig. 2a).

The covered area with soil is slightly raised from the surface so that in later stages these pits could be recognized easily. Under these traditional practices, it is observed that the potatoes, which are stored, remain as fresh as if freshly brought from the field, just after the recent harvesting. Such technology thus helps the people to use stored potato for consumption even after about 5-6 months. Some of these potatoes are also used as seed for the cultivation in the following year. Thus we notice that by applying indigenous technology the people get the dual benefits, using the conserved potato as food item as and when required and also keeping the best quality seed by such storage practice.

Like potatoes many other fresh vegetables such as cabbage (brassica oleracea var. capitata) etcetera are also stored in the pit, covered by sticks. Cabbage is stored along with roots during early winter for short duration before snowfall starts. But in case of storing leafy vegetables {radish (rhaphanus sativus), spinach (spinacia sp.)}, the farmers cut fresh vegetables into small pieces and are dried under sun (Fig. 2b). In this way these dried vegetables are stored in the dry containers for use in the winter season, when the agricultural activities are stopped due to heavy snowfall.

Goats and sheep are the important sources of meat in the cold desert valley of Lahaul & Spiti. Meat is considered as one of the major sources of energy to fight against the biting cold during extreme winter months in the cold desert valley. The villagers store meat it through cutting flesh into pieces and then dried up in the living room temperature conditions (Fig .2c).

Storage of Fruits

Dry fruits like thangi (Corylus jaquemontii Linn), walnut (Juglans regia Linn.) and akhorot (Prunus Armeniaca Linn.) are stored in the living room itself but fruits like apple (Malus Baccata Linn.), khumani (Prunus armeniaca Linn.) and plum (Prunus communis Huds.) are stored on the floor of the summer room only (especially designed within a living room on first floor for hot summer). Seabuckthorn (Hippophae spp.), the multipurpose nitrogen fixing trees/shrubs containing medicinal properties have a pivotal role in the traditional agroforestry systems in the study area[9]. The syrup prepared from its fruits is used for various treatments such as blood pressure, cardiovascular diseases, gastroenteritis ulcer, etc. and they are stored in an air tied container for use in future for a prolonged duration.

Indigenous Container

Different types of indigenously made containers are used to store a variety of crops and food items in the Lahaul valley. Some of them are turmeric, salt, pulses and various other food materials, which are kept in the wooden boxes made up of Salix spp. These boxes include salghuri (container of salt), okhal (container of spices), phenja (basket used for keeping bread and vegetables) and kunpad (vessel made from stone). These containers have been in use since an early time in the Lahaul valley.

Storage of Fodder, Fuelwood and Leaf Litter

In the harsh cold desert conditions of the Lahaul valley, fodder, fuel and leaf litter are essential requirements of the local people. Fodder (leaves, barks and branch of a willow tree) and litter (pine needles and other trees) are available only for a few months of the year. Fuel woods are therefore collected from the nearest forest areas during and after completing agricultural activities in the season. Kuthar (2600 m), Hinsa (2700 m) and Khoksar (3200 m) villages used to collect fuelwood from nearby forest regions but in case of Jahlma village, fuelwood collection is no more possible in absence of trees, and at the same time there has been continuous awakening of the local communities to protect the rare available species since the last few years. The indigenous methods, which are in use particularly for storing fodder, fuelwood, and leaf litter, are described in brief as under:

Fuelwood Storage

The fuelwood is collected just after agricultural works are completed and the winter season starts, i.e., September-October. The collected fuelwood for use during winter is stored in living room and also on roof of the cowshed.

Fodder Storage

The grass and hay for livestock requirement are cultivated in the sloppy area of the margins of cropland and sometimes in crop fields depending on the demand of livestock population with a farmer. In view of overall scarcity of fodder and in fulfilling this important requirement for feeding the domestic animals, grass cultivation is fully taken care of after plantation of cash crops before and after a crop season gets over. During September-October, the planted grass is cut and spread for drying for almost one week. Thereafter, grass in small bundles are made (~5-8 kg^{1}) and stored in a cowshed roof and/or a living room roof (Fig. 2d). But villagers in Kuthar either store these grasses on trees in a conical shape or in a house roof. Based on the affordability of a farmer, these grasses are also sometimes covered by waterproof tent to protect from precipitation and to prevent from decaying under wet conditions.

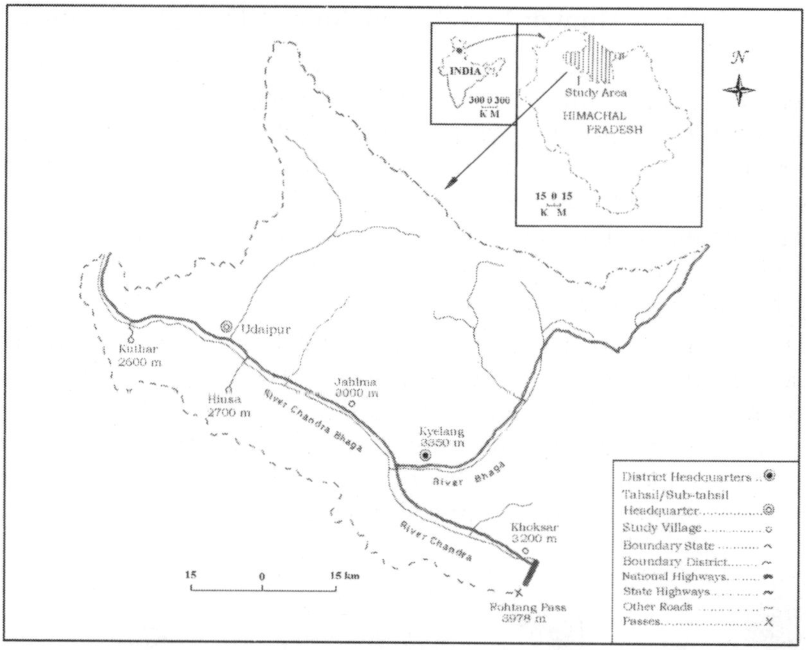

Figure 1: Geographical Location of the Villages under Study in the Lahaul Valley

Figure 2: Storage of (a) Potato and (b) Vegetables Drying up under Sunshine, (c) Meat under Room Temperature, and (d) Fodder on Roof. Photo: Santaram S. Oinam

Traditional use of Human Excreta and Animal Dung for Manure

There is great difficulty in managing the irrigation water because of unfavorable geographical terrain and adverse climatic conditions in the region. With the increasing scarcity of rainwater and high melting rate of glaciers, there are not favorable conditions to support the use of inorganic fertilizers in the cold desert farming in the Lahaul valley. So keeping in mind sustenance of the soil fertility and crop yields, the farmers developed some indigenous biocomposting techniques at their own level based on using human excreta as soil conditioner.

The high demand for manure in the Lahaul & Spiti district is supplemented through recycling night-soil[10-11]. The villagers using traditional toilets are attached with their living rooms on the first floor of the house (Fig. 3a). These toilets are the sources of freely available raw materials to practice biocompost. With the help of a rectangular hole (12" x 6") constructed on the toilet floor itself, the night-soil during defecation naturally drops on

Figure 3: Some of the Traditional Products Developed with Traditional Knowhow Techniques: (a) A View of Traditional Toilet Attached with Living Room, (b) Carding and Cleaning Wool, (c) Pula (Indigenous Shoes) and (d) Wooden Articles. Photo: Santaram S. Oinam

the ground floor and keep on depositing in layers with a conical shaped heap. After defecating, the villagers use to drop some other relevant materials known as 'fot' (mixed up of leaf litter, dung of cattle, sheep and goat) to cover the night-soil in layers one after another. The normal composting process for traditional farmyard manure (FYM) in this way takes time from 6 to 8 months to decompose completely. The night-soil compost (NSC) from compost room is emptied normally two times in a year. First in October/ November and second in March/April. Kilta (made up of from Salix denticulata Andress) is a basket which is used to unload night-soil in the agricultural fields. The unloaded biocompost in this way is piled in a series of different rows in agricultural fields to scatter properly all around in these fields after the snow is melt and a new crop season starts every year. About 15.44 % of the total agricultural land is covered through NSC in Hinsa village; whereas in Jahlma village the area by NSC could be covered as well as 6.41% of the total agricultural area (Table 1).

Table 1

Cropped Area Covered through Night-soil Compost (NSC) within the Agricultural Land in the Lahaul Valley

	Kuthar (2600 m)	*Hinsa (2700 m)*	*Jahlma (3000 m)*	*Khoksar (3200 m)*
Total agricultural area (ha)	6.03	20.34	36.01	6.64
Total production of NSC (MT)	–	25.24	16.69	–
Area covered by NSC (ha)	–	3.14	2.31	–
Per cent area covered by NSC of the total agricultural area	–	15.44	6.41	–
Per ha NSC use (MT) in crop land	–	8.04	7.22	–

The traditional farmyard manure is also used as a soil conditioner. It is a mixture of cattle dung, urine and plant materials (mainly the leaf litter). The plant material is specifically used for cushioning the cattle in their sheds. This material from the cowsheds is removed after every week and its mixture after decomposition is dumped into open, close to the cattleshed and ultimately is carried and applied in the agricultural fields.

Indigenous and Traditional Woolen Goods

The forefathers of the villagers in the Lahaul valley made various indigenous clothes from the wool of their sheep to protect themselves from severe cold (Fig. 3b). Some indigenous woolen clothes have been in use are patu (a kind of garment worn by women), choolu (garment worn by men), pajama (trouser worn by both men and women) and jeraf (sock). The other goods such as planza (cushion stuffed with pieces of clothes and shoot of buckwheat), thobi (matting woven with yarn made of goat and yak hair), and tuk (carped) were made from wool for their domestic uses. The ropes from wool were also made for various agricultural activities.

Uses of Bioresources

Besides, the local people also use their locally available other important bioresources to meet their routine based household needs. Some of the products they use are more concerned with the parts of the locally available plants. Some of the examples of bioresource use are as under:

Pula, the indigenous shoes are made from buckwheat and locally produced wool. This product is in wide use in the Lahaul valley since time immemorial (Fig. 3c). It is considered very comfortable and warm in wearing. Besides, its domestic utility, these are also produced for sale so that the villagers could also earn some income.

Some other products derived from well known bioresources belonging to wooden goods are thapaki (used for washing clothes), thog (a circular plate like structure with a long nose and a small hole in centre, used for distillation of the local wine), takali (spindle), lwarend (a small size tub used for mixing local dishes childra), thombu/dau (wooden ladle used in serving meals), doee (a wooden ladle used in serving wine), dhanu (a wooden rod used for making milk-butter), gogdum (a wooden rod used for removing husk), neukcha (a handle of knife), ren (a wooden vessel used for measurement of cereals produced at village level), brooms and walja/ jable (a long and flat in the head wooden log made of willow tree and is used for snow clearing and throwing during winter season). Kilta (a basket) is made from Salix denticulata Andress and is loaded with materials on the back for carrying domestic goods.

Some other indigenous products which are used by the villagers on routine basis are thoma (big spoon made up of wood), dhumbu (instrument made up of wood for making salty tea), thok (instrument made up of wood and used to make local wine), ghuluru (instrument made up of wood and used to make curd) (Fig. 3d), and thultan (mats filled with straw and used for seating). The mattresses produced from plant materials were commonly used for bedding and/or resting purposes. The buckwheat straw filled in a cloth cover is also used by the old people to prepare mattresses.

Conclusion

In essence, the people of the northwestern Indian Himalaya region practice a variety of indigenous practices to conserve their food and other items by way of indigenously developed storing techniques by using their locally available resources. Some of the techniques applied under these practices such as storage of potato in the sub-soil underground pit, drying up of meat and its storage in living room, storage of food grains in wooden box, and uses of buckwheat fibers in making shoes, are very 'unique' and distinctive compared to other parts of the country or elsewhere. Such various traditional uses and applications are derived after using natural resources for sustenance; and by judging the capability of all plant parts based on assessing overall resource availability. More studies and documentation in this regard are required for conserving indigenous knowledge of the hill people before it is lost forever from the knowledge of old generation. The study shows the types and manner the local bioresources are being put to use routinely. The present study not only reveals the authenticity of traditional knowledge of the ethnic people but also indicates the urgency to keep them in sustainable mode. Indigenous knowledge if not conserved properly will be seriously threatened under pressure of modernization and especially on account of the apathy among new generations.

Acknowledgements

The authors are thankful to the Director, G. B. Pant Institute of Himalayan Environment and Development, Kosi-Katarmal, 263 643 Almora (U.A.) for providing necessary facilities to complete the present work. The Indian Council of Social Science Research (ICSSR) is also highly acknowledged for granting financial assistance to carry out this study.

References

Rawat, D. S. & Joshi, R. (2000), Indigenous Methods for Storage and Use of Bioresources: Case Study, *Indian Central Himalaya*, Ambio, 29(6): 356-358.

Aswal, B. S. & Mehrotra, B. N. (1994), Flora of Lahaul Spiti (A cold desert in the northwest Himalaya), (Bishen Singh and Mahendra Pal Singh, Dehradun, India), 761.

Kuniyal, J. C., Vishvakarma, S. C. R. & Singh, G. S. (2004), Changing Crop Biodiversity and Resource use Efficiency of Traditional versus Introduced Crops in the Cold Desert of the Northwestern Indian Himalaya: A Case of Lahaul Valley, Biodiversity and Conservation, 13 (7):1271-1304.

Rawat, Y. S., Oinam, S. S., Vishvakarma, S. C. R., Kuniyal, J. C. (2004), Saussurea Costus (Falc.) Lipsch: A Promising Medicinal Crop under Cold Desert Agro-Ecosystem in North Western Himalaya, *Indian Journal of Forestry*, 27(3):297-303.

Kuniyal, C. P., Rawat, Y. S., Oinam, S. S., Kuniyal, J. C. & Vishvakarma, S. C. R. (2005), Kuth (Saussurea lappa) Cultivation in the Cold Desert Environment of the Lahaul Valley, Northwestern Himalaya, India: Arising Threats and Need to Revive Socio-economic Values, Biodiversity and Conservation, 14(5):1035-1045.

Oinam, S. S., Rawat, Y. S., Khoiyangbam, R. S., Gajananda, K., Kuniyal, J. C. & Vishvakarma, S. C. R. (2005), Land use and Land Changes in Jahlma Watershed of the Lahaul Valley, Cold Desert Region of the Northwestern Himalaya, India, *Journal of Mountains Science*, 2(2):129-136.

Rawat, Y. S., Oinam, S. S., Vishvakarma, S. C. R., Kuniyal, C. P. & Kuniyal, J. C. (2006), Willow (Salix Fragilis Linn.): A Multipurpose Tree Species under Pest Attack in the Cold Desert of Lahaul Valley, Northwestern Himalaya, India, Ambio 35(1): 43-48.

Oinam, S. S., Kuniyal, J. C., Rawat, Y. S., Vishvakarma, S. C. R. and Pandey, D. C. (2007), Disrupting Land use Changes Cause Land Degradation in Fragile Cold Desert Ecosystems: A Case of the Lahaul Valley in Northwestern Indian Himalaya. *Journal of Water and Land Use Management*, 7(2): 197-217.

Kuniyal, C. P., Vishvakarma, S. C. R., Kuniyal, J. C. & Singh, G. S. (2002), Seabuckthorn (Hippophae L.)-A Promising Plant for Land-restoration in the Cold Desert Himalayas, Proceeding of International Workshop on Seabuckthorn, New Delhi. 1-6.

Oinam, S. S., Rawat, Y. S., Kuniyal, J. C., Vishvakarma, S. C. R. and Pandey, D. C. (2008), Thermal Supplementing Soil Nutrients through Biocomposting Night-Soils in the Cold Desert of the Lahaul Valley, Northwestern Indian Himalaya. Waste Management 28(6): 1008-1019.

Oinam, S. S. (2008), Traditional Night-soil Composting Continues to Bring Benefits. Leisa Magazine 24(2): 25-27.

INDIGENOUS TRIBAL ART:
Strategy for Conservation and Promotion

Somnath Chakraverty*

In India, the earliest evidence of visual art tradition is the prehistoric rock art. In the prehistoric art galleries, the depictions of early tribal life and lore as well as other symbolic representations are predominant. Therefore, for reconstruction of tribal history in India, the pictorial evidences of rock art can be regarded as more dependable and authentic source. Some other forms of archaeological data, such as the study of tools and other artifacts, may involve some conjectures. In case of tribal art or the prehistoric rock art we face no such predicament. From the global ethnographic records on tribal art it is revealed that their visual art tradition is mostly inspired by the aspirations common to the people and it reflects their attitude, need and sentiment towards both internal and external world as also beyond it, i.e. the supernatural domain. In India, selected tribal groups practice their traditional form of art. The traditional tribal artists express aesthetics and creativity instinctively. Commercialization of the tribal art and crafts is a later phenomenon and mostly induced by outsiders. In the long existing tribal art tradition of India, so called artistic expressions are regarded as a cognitive mode of communication between members of a community within a particular time period or as a form of message passing from early ancestors to its successive generations. In this study data from thirteen different tribal communities are used for analyses of visual art tradition. In addition, a strategy and action plan for conservation and promotion of tribal art is also recommended.

Among the tribes of India, Art is more conspicuous among the shifting hill cultivators and marginal cultivators. On the contrary, visual art tradition is seen in lesser number among the hunter gatherers. The Onges of Andaman have body decoration. The Shompen at the little Andaman have totem poles and some other minor wood carvings. Birhor, Chenchus or Irulas are hunter-gatherers but they do not practice any significant visual art tradition. On the other hand, the art practice among the Nagas, (Konyak), Kuki Adi and such other Mongolian shifting cultivators of North East India; Santal of Jharkhand, Juang and Hill Bhuiyas, Lanjhia Saoras and Khonds

* Project Director, Asiatic Society, Kolkata, *E-mail: somraja@vsnl.net*

of South Orissa, Gond, Maria Gond, Murias and Korkus of Madhya Pradesh, Worli or Warli of Maharashtra, Pithoras of Gujarat is prominent. All the above mentioned tribal communities are inheritors of their art tradition. Their basic sustenance pattern is either depending on shifting hill cultivation or they are incipient and marginal-level plain land cultivator. Art is practiced by them as an integral part of ritual and other religious performances. It is mostly related to the belief for receiving a good harvest and in bringing overall security and prosperity of the individuals through a supernatural means. To the majority of the tribal communities, the concept of art characterizes a mode of visual expression for non-verbal communication, which essentially comprises an inherent aesthetic idiom.

The shifting hill cultivators with their crude type of implements as well as technique are more dependants on nature. Thus the feeling of insecurity is evident in their conventional art. The Lanjhia Saoras of Koraput and Ganjam district of Orissa use art to control the supernatural forces, to avert disasters and with a view to bringing prosperity.

In the present study, traditional art practices of selected tribal communities in India are being reviewed. The study is being based on first hand data collected empirically. Each of the tribal art tradition was separately studied by the author individually. During collection of field data, special emphasis was given on four distinct aspects i.e. 1. Recording of the tribal art motifs in its eco-cultural setting. 2. Studying significance and meaning of art. 3. Their traditional process of maintenance, training, and 4. new changes.

The Santal of Jharkhand, Juang of Keonjhar and Dhenkanal districts, Lanjhia Saora tribe of Ganjam and Koraput district of South Orissa and the Korkus of Chhindwara, Betul and Hoshangabad in Madhya Pradesh are among the selected tribes. Santals are mostly settled cultivators and unskilled labours engaged in agriculture and in industries. The other three communities are mostly shifting cultivators and seasonal food gatherers.

Wall painting, clay bas relief and wood carvings are frequently witnessed in Santal villages. The wall embellishments are seasonal in nature and generally executed during 'Bandna' or 'Sohorai' festival held on the night of 'Kartick Amawasya' (new moon night during October-November). In eastern limit of Chhotanagpur plateau, in Jharkhand, especially in the industrial zones the festival is usually deferred until the end of 'Poush' (January) at the end of harvest.

The Santals as well as other indigenous communities celebrate the festival with a belief that on the dark night of new-moon, the supreme god

Art & Material Culture in Juang Household
District : Keonjhar, Orissa

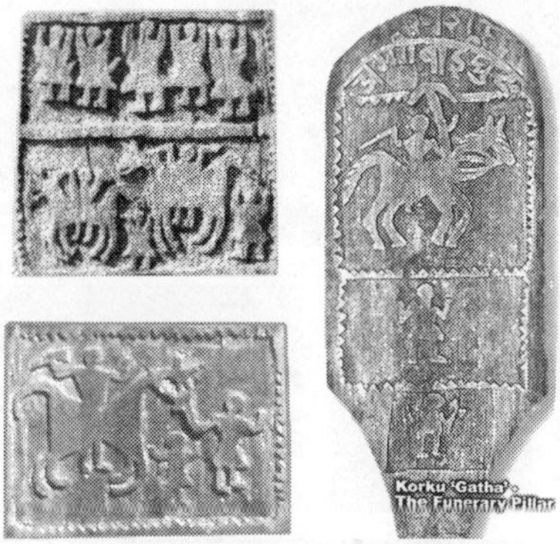

Korku Tribal Wood Carvings
District : Hoshangabad, Madhya Pradesh

Santal Wood Carving

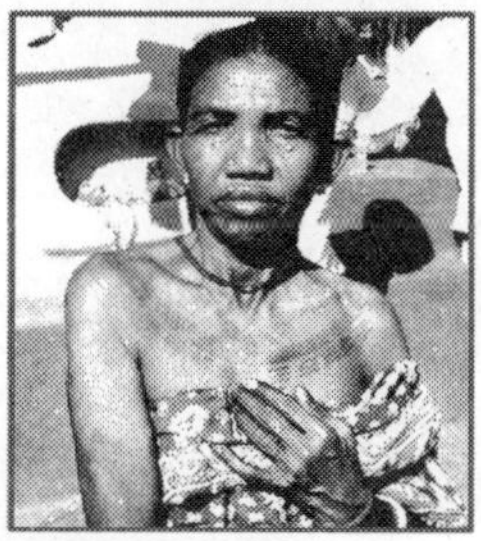

Body decoration among Santals : Tattoo

Murals in Santal Household

Tribal Art in Hazaribagh, Jharkhand

Naga Arts & Crafts

Warli Art, Maharashtra

Pithora Art

Saora Art Orissa

Bhil Art

Gond Art

Khond Metal Art Orissa

will visit the cattle-shed of every household in disguise. The houses are cleaned and plastered by mud in the beginning of the celebration. The artistic embellishment on the walls signify prosperity and success of the family and their thrust for seeking supernatural blessing is indirectly expressed in the motifs of art. Aesthetic purpose is apparently dominant in the Santal art. The tangible function is deeply rooted , however, in the intangible subconscious level of the artist as well as of the society. The function is primarily to render safety and security to life.

In Santal society, art is practiced in the individual households. But it is a symbolic expression of a spontaneous cultural practice which the whole community celebrates. The decorative linear designs, floral motifs and depictions of both wild animals and domesticated animals are frequent in the Santal murals. Santals living in remote forest areas paint figures of elephant and tiger to prevent any aggression of those animals. Indeed the village settlement patterns, location of Jaharthan, the sacred place and the very house-construction of the Santal displays glimpse of unique architecture.

Wood carving is a languishing craft tradition in Santal society. In earlier wood carvings, battle scenes between Santal archers and British troupe were frequent theme. In earlier Santal art, they identified themselves as men holding bow and arrow in hand and having a tail at the back. The protesting elements in the Santal art are not rare. Their self awareness and search for identity as emerged historically through conflict against outsider exploiters or 'diku' is still being retained through their oral literature and art. In certain areas, through the conscious effort of the Santal elites, tribal people are becoming more involved with the local problems related to deforestation and land alienation etc. Such awareness is increasingly reflected in their art. Their search for identity is more conspicuous in the art of forthcoming generation. Through symbolic use, tribal art is a successful mode of communication of ideas in a society where literacy rate is even at the minimum level.

The Juangs of North Orissa are largely dependent on shifting hill cultivation. They are also seasonal food gatherers as well as hunters. Juang art is principally related to their traditional dormitory system. The 'mandaghar' or 'darbar' is the male bachelor's dormitory whereas 'dhangri-ghar' is the traditional female dormitory of the tribe. In the dormitory, the youthful people learn wood carving and clay bas-relief work through practices. Each of the Juang dormitories contains various carved figures on its wooden structure. The maximum numbers of Juang art are represented in clay bas-relief and wood carvings.

The major theme of Juang art is - anthropomorphs representing their hero cult figures, supreme God and Goddess named 'Rushi' and 'Rushini'. Types of wild animals and figures of birds represented in Juang art are varied in type and available in that particular forest habitat.

Tattooing on the body is a favourite to the Juang women. Beside aesthetic purposes, the tattooing or 'Khada' is believed to have a great role in protecting them from evil eyes. They strongly believe that the tattoos prevent certain diseases like headache and certain chronic pain. They believe that presence of a distinct tattoo-design in both sides of eyes can protect a man from lightning and thunder.

In Keonjhar district, most of the old dormitories which were traditional art galleries containing the works of several generations have already been demolished by the contractors. They were appointed by the Juang Development Agency for the resettlement of the Juangs. So far, the dormitory art provided the source of inspiration to the younger generation. Now it is being replaced by the modern small permanent structures which can not provide a minimum amount of space to its members. The degeneration of the traditional dormitory system caused changes in their social structure. Their traditional art related to the dormitory system is endangered due to induced cultural changes.

The Korku tribe living in the Hoshangabad and Betul districts of Madhya Pradesh largely practice wood carvings which are in the form of funerary pillars known as 'gatha'. Thus Korku art is largely ritualistic and related to magico-religious belief. It is also connected with the concept of after life and transmigration of soul. The art also reflects the tribal belief in the concepts of 'Karma', rebirth and hierarchy existing in the Korku society. One year after the death of an individual, his near relatives can arrange 'Sidoli' ceremony. This is post cremation green funeral in type. The near relatives of the deceased appoint one expert craftsman for carving the funerary pillar. The pillar is called 'gatha'. It is either carved on stone or on a wooden platform. Through prolong rituals and ceremony the wood is collected from the teak (Saguan) tree and ultimately a wooden plaque is prepared. A figure of an 'Ojha' or sorcerer is first carved at the bottom of the wooden tablet. The belief is, if the supernatural force of a sorcerer be appreciated properly, he can not do any harm to the ceremony.

Among the Korkus carved figures on the 'gatha' vary from person to person. It is determined by the sex, occupation of the deceased and his/her social position. Horse riding man holding bow and arrow, spear or even guns in hand indicate the gatha offered in memory of a man who was of a socially higher in position. Elephant riding figures are rare because it represent a very rich man or a tribal chieftain. The most common feature in gatha is of male representing a man holding agricultural implements in hand, hunting posture or as cowherd woman are generally represented in dancing mood or engaged in household work.

Among the Korkus all the wooden gatha ought to contain the symbolic celestial figures of Sun and Moon on the top. The Sun and the Moon are regarded as the supreme God and Goddess to Korkus. After the Sidoli ceremony, the gathas are ultimately placed in a particular sacred grove or in a mango tree near the forest. Korkus have several territorial clans and members of the each clan have their separate sacred groves which are the final resting place of the ancestral spirits. The family members sometimes visit the grove and offer tobacco or 'bidi' there to their ancestral spirits.

The Lanjhia Saoras living is remote mountainous areas of Koraput and Ganjam districts of Orissa are considered as a 'primitive tribe'. They are largely dependent on shifting hill cultivation. In their households they paint 'Idital-Anital' or Ikon by way of their urge for a better harvest, for treatment of diseases and for avoiding disasters. The paintings represent large panels on the walls inside the room. Rice flour, ash, ocher or other rock minerals are generally used by the painters. The painters are generally divine experts, spirit-possessed men or sorcerers who are appointed by the clients. The painters paint whatever they visualize in their dreams after being possessed. The pictographs represent large number of motifs of men, animals and anthropomorphic figure of supernatural beings.

The Lanjhia Saoras identify the supernatural sources for their respective problems by employing the sorcerers. In case of any acute problem they try to find supernatural ways for solving it. The artist's perception as well as the tribal world-view is largely expressed in the pictographs. During mango-festival, the tribal people offer their collected first fruit to the icon and keep it in an earthen pot hanging over the painted wall. The harvested grain, millets and seeds are stored within those pots so that it could be protected by the supernatural being when kept under their custody.

On analyzing a cross section of the data on visual art practiced by all tribes, it is understood that tribal art is largely utilitarian and has significant religious significance, at least among more 'primeval people'. The tribal groups like the Santals who are more exposed to the external world have "art for arts" sake. Tribal art studies reveal the emergence and genesis of art style. The changing pattern of art style, form and contain provide a major clue for analysis and periodization of Rock Art of unknown date and origin.

Tribal art is not homogenous in its form and content. The level of change or drift in tribal social organization and culture is never universally uniform. Therefore within the category of tribal art, a range of variation exists. The tribal art of the foragers, hunter – gatherers and nomad pastoralists differs from the settled cultivators. The life-opportunities, environmental setup and chronological experiences influence on the art practices among tribal communities. Therefore, a universal feature of tribal art is rather a complicated endeavour to discern. But analyses of the limited data on tribal art of the selected groups determine some basic concepts to identify the tribal art.

Some of the crucial distinctivenesses of particular art traditions are as follows:

- The art motifs are composed of minimum or essential use of lines, both straight lines, curved lines and dots etc.
- In both Figurative and non-figurative motifs, repetitions are frequent. Variations of forms are limited. Permutations and combinations of selected number of elements are prevalent.
- Absence of realistic details in paintings, and use of shading technique is almost absent.
- Uses of bright, primary colours are more frequent without any combination and alteration. Sometimes crude pigments are directly applied.
- Individual motifs are more frequent. Composition of several diverse types of figures or motifs in aggregate to represent a visual narrative is rare.
- The life opportunities as well as day to day activities, world view and pattern of belief are largely depicted in content.
- Art seems purposive and communicative, sometimes aimed to convey messages for consecutive generations.
- Art works are broadly impressive and usual expressions are voluntary, spontaneous and followed by tangible inspirations.
- Technique is basically crude and it is not regarded as a specialized skill for any occupation that an artisan group usually considers.
- In representation of animals, profile views are relatively more conspicuous.

Many socio-economic factors, degeneration and decay of tribal art are also influenced by their conversion or transformation to other religious faith.

The art of tribal communities and other indigenous populations due to its simplicity in representation provide us certain indications to understand their aspirations and obsession. The tribal artist is conditioned by his social cultural matrix. Thus the work of an individual tribal artist largely represents the idea, belief and sentiment of the society.

Basic Programmes for Promotion of Tribal Art

Proper measures should be taken to protect the age old art tradition of the tribal communities. The tribal people should be made aware of their rights to protect their own art and culture. Moreover, protecting the art tradition will also help them in restoring their identity.

The national rural and tribal policy, when implemented, should give importance to promotion of tribal art through launching income generating projects. Improvisation of the craft and designs for a national and global market should be encouraged, with care, as a policy. The market oriented commercial production may be one of the methods for preservation and restoration of the languishing tribal art and crafts. But the confidence building programme among the tribal artists and craftsman is more important in the initial level.

There is need for launching an action-oriented programme for promotion of the languishing tribal art. The field workers during his / her visit to tribal villages may approach the villagers and their grass root-level organizations such as the tribal club, local panchayat to convey the importance of art in particular. Special drive need to be in place to grow awareness on art. During field visit group interview, organizing of workshops, video-show, slide-shows on tribal art (of the same tribe) may be arranged. Display of albums containing photographs of tribal art may be arranged during field visit. Other effective programmes may include exhibition of posters on the village road or during market day, in fairs and festivities. Regular encouragement to the master-craftsman and their trainee disciples is also useful for sustenance of tradition. The researchers/ fieldworkers will emerge as a facilitator to resolve the emerging issues related to preservation and continuity of the art tradition. Designing of awareness and other feed-back programmes, can be formulated according to the local needs and emerging necessities arises in particular situation. The researcher should volunteer himself to act in a mediatory role in connecting tribal people with the proper agencies for rendering benefits through a comprehensive development programme. Such action oriented research is urgent for promotion, conservation, preservation and revitalization of languishing tribal art.

Specific Proposals for Promotion of the Languishing Tribal Art

1. Involving tribal clubs, associations, panchayat and local museums for arranging of regular displays, campaigning through awareness building programmes in preservation and promotion of tribal art and crafts.

   Encouragement to the tribal artists through organizing workshops, search of tribal talents through village-level art-contests, regular campaign through art-fairs and exhibition in the village fairs, festivals and in weekly markets. A set of photographs on tribal art and culture need to be prepared and arranged for regular exhibition in rural, urban and semi-urban areas to attract both tribal and non-tribal visitors including common people as well as tribal elites.
2. Preparation of an exhaustive database including a catalogue on various tribal art forms with visual imagery. The social relevance and symbolic meaning of art are to be recorded. Entire process of manufacturing of art and artifacts will be recorded and would be preserved in a computer-generated database.
3. To install a website with exhaustive information on the particular tribal art and its uniqueness in the perspective of salvaging cultural heritage of Indian civilization to attract the global interest and to harness proper appreciation and recognition.
4. Development of several interactive compact discs (CD); video-documentation (digitalized) of the particular tribal art tradition, genesis of art and introducing several contemporary talents in particular tribal art tradition.
5. The talented tribal artists are to be awarded for necessary encouragement during the state- level exhibitions and as a part of other promotional programmes.

Tribal art represents both verbal and non-verbal form of inner sentiments of the group. Therefore tribal art study could be a source for understanding their emotion as also their grievances. In India, for reconstruction of a more dependable tribal history and ethno-history in general, art could be a reliable source.

Through launching of appropriate projects the craft may emerge as an alternative source for employment. Through involving more tribal artisans in manufacturing more improved varieties from their traditional items of craft, a subsidiary source of occupation could be developed. The data - repository on tribal art and the catalogue containing the basic design elements could be a source for organizing further economically beneficial programmes.

Table 1
Tribal Art in India: A Comprehensive View

Tribal community	*Distribution in State*	*General Economy*	*Art Types/ Forms*	*Thematic representations A wide*	*Significance / Role of Art*	*Observation Related to*
LANJHIA SAORA	Koraput, Ganjam & Gajapati districts, Orissa	Shifting-hill cultivators	Wall Paintings	range of pictographic & figurative representations on tribal life, myth and aspirations related to supernatural world.	To render material benefit by appeasing/ controlling the supernatural forces, curing diseases, safe child-birth etc.	magical belief and rituals.
JUANG	Keonjhar district, Orissa	Shifting-hill cultivators	Clay bas-relief and carvings on wood, bamboo	Individual figurines representing animals, celestial beings, mythical characters and episodes.	Primarily associated to their youth dormitory system. Unconscious effort of tribal youths during their informal training & process of socialization before puberty.	Apparently decorative designs associated to tribal youth dormitory.
BHUINYA (PAURIA, HILL)	Keonjhar & Sundargarh districts, Orissa	Shifting-hill cultivators	Clay bas-relief and carvings on wood, bamboo	Individual figurines representing animals, celestial beings, mythical characters and episodes.	Primarily associated to their youth dormitory system. Unconscious effort of tribal youths during their informal training & process of socialization before puberty.	Apparently decorative designs associated to tribal youth dormitory.

Table 2
Tribal Art In India : A Comprehensive View

Tribal community	*Distribution in State*	*General Economy*	*Art Types/Forms*	*Thematic representations*	*Significance / Role of Art*	*Observation*
ORAON	Jharkhand	Settled cultivators, skilled & unskilled labourers.	Wall Paintings	Individual figurines representing animals, celestial beings, mythical characters and episodes	Apparently decorative designs. But the symbolic representations are vestigial degenerated forms evolved from earlier magical and supernatural belief and practices.	Apparently decorative designs associated to tribal youth dormitory.
MUNDA	Jharkhand	Settled cultivators, skilled & unskilled labourers.	Wall paintings	Individual figurines representing animals, celestial beings, mythical characters and episodes. Engraved anthropomor-phs on burial stone.	Apparently decorative designs. But the symbolic representations are vestigial degenerated forms evolved from earlier magical and supernatural belief and practices.	Apparently decorative designs associated to tribal youth dormitory.
SANTAL	W. Bengal, Jharkhand & Orissa.	Settled cultivators, skilled & unskilled labourers.	Wall paintings, clay bas-reliefs, wood-carvings, tattoo-marks, puppetry, jewellery or ornaments etc.	A wide range of figurines in the form of individual figurine & visual narratives. Myths & historical accounts are depicted frequently.	Apparently decorative designs. But the symbolic representations are vestigial degenerated forms evolved from earlier magical and supernatural belief and practices.	Art as a symbolic icon to strengthen group solidarity.

Table : 3
Tribal Art In India : A Comprehensive View

Tribal community	*Distribution in State*	*General Economy*	*Art Types/ Forms*	*Thematic representations*	*Significance /Role of Art*	*Observation*
KHOND	Orissa	Shifting-hill cultivators	Designed textiles and metal/bronze figurines representing individual figures. Made by Pano– an artisan group as well as a Scavanger caste.	Figurines representing animal, man and artifacts in activity common in tribal experiences.	Particular art objects are intimately related to household rituals and icon of 'Dharni Penu' is related to their earlier ritual of human sacrifice.	Art made by specialist artisan caste.
KORKU	Madhya Pradesh	Shifting-hill cultivators	Carvings on stone and wooden tablets/platforms.	Human figurines in activity to represent and recognize the occupation of the dead ancestors, both male & female.	'Gatha' or memorial stone/wooden tablets prepared for final funeral ceremony in memory of departed soul of ancestors.	Magical significance.
MARIA GOND & OTHER GOND– speaking tribes.	Madhya Pradesh & Chhatisgarh.	Shifting-hill cultivators	Wood carvings and sometimes murals on household walls.	Individual figurines representing animals, celestial beings, mythical characters and episodes.	Primarily associated to their youth dormitory system. Unconscious effort of tribal youths during their informal training & process of socialization before puberty.	Dormitory & household art.

The action-oriented research programme should also include developing a guideline and strategy to revitalize the languishing tradition of tribal art. The documentation and restoration of the languishing art is necessary process requiring immediate measure to motivate the tribal groups. This is also an attempt for keeping their discrete cultural identity unaffected. Through providing economic benefit to the tribal craftsmen, the traditional art could be restored from its inevitable degeneration.

References

Anderson, Richard I. (1979), Art in Primitive Societies. Englewood Cliffs: Prentice - Hall.

Archer, W. G. (1947), The Vertical Man : A Study in Primitive Indian Sculpture London : George Allen and Unwin Ltd.

Boas, Franz (1955), Primitive Art. New York : Dover Publication.

Chakraverty, Somnath (1987), Tribal Murals of Chhotanagpur. The India Magazine. 6 (2) : 20-27.

Chakraverty, Somnath (1995), Isco : Rock Art Site in Hazaribag. In Recent Perspectives on Prehistoric Art in India and Allied Subjects. Edited by R.K.Sharma and K. K. Tripathy, pp. 74-99. New Delhi : Aryan Books International.

Chakraverty, Somnath (2004), Mystical Icons of Lanjhia Saoras : A Primordial Tribal Art Tradition of India. In New Discoveries, New Interpretations, New Research Methods. pp. 155-163. Brescia : Centro Camuno di Studi Preistorici.

Chakraverty, Somnath (1995), Rock Art and Ethnographic Data Retrieval in India. In Rock Art vis-à-vis Ethnography. Edited by Rabindra Nath Agrawal. Nagpur, Maharastra : Gupta Publishers.

Chhattopadhyay, K. P. (1943), Korku Funeral Customs and Memorial Posts. *Journal of the Royal Asiatic Society of Bengal*, 9 (2) : 201-209.

Dalmia, Yashodhara (1988), The Painted World of the Warlis : Art and Rituals of Warli Tribes of Maharastra. New Delhi : Lalit Kala Akademi.

Das, A. K. (1979), Tribal Art and Craft. NewDelhi. Agam Kala Prakashan.

Das, A. K. (1992), North East India, in Tribal India : Ancestors, Gods and Spirits. Pp. 3-22. Bombay. Marg Publications.

Dattå, Kalikinkar (1905), The Santal Insurrection of 1855-57. Calcutta.

Elwin, Varrier (1948), Notes on the Juang. Man in India. 28 (1-2) : 1-182.

Elwin, Varrier (1951), The Tribal Art of Middle India : a Personal Record. Bombay; Oxford University Press.

Elwin, Varrier (1955), Religion of an Indian Tribe. Bombay : Oxford University Press.

Elwin, Varrier (1959), The Art of North - East Frontier of India. Shillong : North - East Frontier Agency.

Firth, Raymond (1951), The Social Framework of Primitive Art. In Elements of Social Organization. Edited by R. Firth., pp. 155–182. London : Watts.

Firth, Raymond (1992), Art and Anthropology, in Anthropology, Art and Aesthetics. Edited by Coote, J. and A. Shelton , pp. 15 - 39. Oxford : Clarendon Press.

Fischer, E. and Haku Shah (1971), Mogra Dev : Tribal Crocodile Gods. Ahmedabad : Gujarat Vidyapith.

Fischer, J. L. (1961), Art Styles as Cultural Cognitive Maps. American Anthropologist. 63 : 79–93.

Ghosh, Asok K. and Somnath Chakraverty (1988-89), Genesis and Changes of Tribal Art - Examples from West Bengal. Indian Museum Bulletin : 23 & 24 :136-141.

Ghosh, A. K. and Somnath Chakraverty (1995), Rock Arts of Eastern India and their Bearing with local Tribal Arts : A Cross-sectional Study on Continuity in India at the Down of History in *India At the Down of History* Edited by Asok Datta, Asok K. Ghosh and C. Margabandhu. Delhi : Agam Kala Prakashan.

Gordon, D. H. (1936), Korku Memorial Tablets. Man. 36. (19–52) : 17–19.

Gulshaw, W. J. (1949), Tribal Heritage : A Study on Santals. London.

Haddon, Alfred C. (1895), Evolution in Art. London., Walter Scott Ltd.

Haselberger, H. (1961), Methods in Studying Ethnological Art. Current Anthropology. 2 : 341–384.

Jain, Jyotindra (1984), Painted Myths of Creation : Art and Ritual of an Indian Tribe. NewDelhi : Lalit Kala Akademi.

Jayakar, Pupul (1981), The Earthen Drum- an Introduction to the Ritual Arts of Rural India. New Delhi : Publications Division, Government of India.

Layton, Robert (1991), The Anthropology of Art. Cambridge : Cambridge University Press.

Orans, Martin (1965), The Santal, a Tribe in Search of a Great Tradition. Detroit: Wayne State University Press.

Troisi, Joe (1976), The Santals -a Classified and Annoted Bibliography. New Delhi. Manohar.

WOMEN'S NUTRIBUSINESS COOPERATIVES IN KENYA: An Integrated Strategy for Sustaining Rural Livelihoods

Audrey N. Maretzki*

With funding provided by the Center for Higher Education of the United States Agency for International Development, The Pennsylvania State University and Tuskegee University collaborated with the University of Nairobi in establishing women's NutriBusiness Cooperatives in the Rift Valley and Central Provinces of Kenya. Between 1992 and 1999, the cooperatives were established, facilities and equipment were supplied and extensive participatory training was provided by university-affiliated investigators and project staff. This initiative enabled approximately 2500 rural Kenyan women farmers to add value to their crops by processing and locally marketing nutritious, convenient, culturally-appropriate weaning food mixes. Implementation of the NutriBusiness model is described and challenges of cultural engagement are highlighted.

(J Nutr Educ Behav. 2007; 39: 327-334)

Introduction

In much of the developing world, social progress has occurred, and living standards have risen. However, the conditions associated with human development in sub-Saharan Africa have deteriorated since 1990, and the region as a whole is unlikely to reach any of the targeted millennium development goals by 2015.[1]

In 1992, The Pennsylvania State University (PSU), in collaboration with Tuskegee University (TU) and the University of Nairobi (UoN), was competitively awarded a University Development Linkage Program (UDLP) grant by the United States Agency for International Development (USAID) to establish 2 women's nutribusiness cooperatives in Kenya. As defined by Norge Jerome, then Director of the USAID Office of Nutrition, a nutribusiness involves "activities that address nutritional needs by providing quality foods and food products at affordable prices through

* Emeritus Professor of Food Science and Nutrition, Department of Food Science, The Pennsylvania State University, USA

small-scale private sector approaches. The nutribusiness concept also incorporates environmentally regenerative production, storage and distribution techniques that avoid pollution and inappropriate or excessive use of energy and other natural resources."2 This article describes how rural poverty and human development issues were addressed through implementation of the nutribusiness concept in 2 rural Kenyan communities.

The Nutribusiness Project

Project Sites

In 1992, the NutriBusiness Project began in 2 Kenyan sites: Bomet District in the Rift Valley Province and Murang'a District in the Central Province. The NutriBusiness Project continued through 1999. The 2 project locations, though agronomically similar, are culturally different. The residents of Bomet are primarily Kipsigis, a Nilotic culture of settled pastoralists, whereas the residents of Murang'a are mostly Kikuyu, a Bantu culture with a long agricultural history. In both areas, however, women are subsistence farmers, and many belong to 1 or more village women's self-help groups. Women's groups are organized at the village level and have successfully created small-scale entrepreneurial opportunities for many rural Kenyans. Involvement in these incomegenerating groups protects the money women earn through collective activities from appropriation by other family members. From the UoN agricultural campus, it took nearly 8 hours, on unpaved roads for the last 2 hours, to reach the Bomet site, whereas it took less than 90 minutes, largely on a paved highway, to reach the Murang'a site. Neither location had a public water supply or electricity. Climatically, the areas are quite similar. They are at comparable elevations, with seasonal rains and occasional droughts, but in most years, rainfall is adequate to produce crops without irrigation.

What was Originally Proposed

The original UDLP proposal included a research design that involved 4 adjacent, but politically distinct, sublocations in Bomet and the same number in Murang'a. Based on random assignment, one of the sublocations in each district was to become the site of a small-scale food processing facility, enabling shareholders from that sublocation to form a nutribusiness cooperative that would produce and regionally market a nutritious, culturally acceptable weaning food made from crops grown locally by the women on their small plots of land, called "shambas." A second sublocation would receive an intensive nutrition education program to teach local women how to prepare nutritious food for young children using locally available ingredients. In a third sublocation, the intensive nutrition education strategy would be combined with access to the cooperative's weaning food. The fourth sublocation would serve as a control.

The Reality of Project Implementation

News travels quickly in rural Kenya, and before any decision could be made about where to site the processing facilities, it became apparent that, for political and social reasons, it would not be possible to treat the sublocations differently, and furthermore, that community leaders would be very actively involved in any decision-making that involved facilities. This reality led to a decision to use existing women's groups as a basis for organizing the cooperatives.

The logic for enrolling women's groups, rather than individual women, as members of the nutribusiness cooperatives was that these groups were already engaged in projects to generate income, and therefore the members were likely to be familiar with conducting meetings, making collective decisions, and keeping fiscal records, as well as generating written minutes of their meetings. Each of the women's groups had 15 to 20 members who lived in close proximity and respected the cultural practice of decision making by the group's most senior members.

It soon became apparent that the poorest women in a village were not likely to be members of any women's group. Consequently, a decision was made to ask respected community leaders in each area to identify approximately 20 able-bodied women who they believed could not afford to join a women's group. Personal interviews were conducted with these individuals to assess their economic circumstances and their interest in being part of the NutriBusiness Project. Subsequently, a "needy" women's group was established in each area and project funds were set aside to assist the group in establishing its own income-generating project. The Murang'a group chose to raise pigs, and the Bomet group chose to raise chickens. This strategy enabled economically disadvantaged women to achieve a degree of social and economic equity with their more affluent neighbors and to participate as equals in the NutriBusiness Project.

NutriBusiness Field Coordinators

The NutriBusiness Project employed a field coordinator in each area who reported administratively to the UoN principal investigator (PI) through a project manager in Nairobi. On a daily basis, the field coordinators reported to the chairwoman of the board of directors for the cooperative in their assigned area. The full-time field coordinator positions were fully project-funded for 1 year, with the understanding that each cooperative would annually absorb a larger proportion of the coordinator's salary until, at the end of 5 years, the field coordinator would be employed full-time by the cooperative as the manager of its processing facility. During the early phase of the NutriBusiness Project, providing technical support and training for the "needy" women's groups was a very time- and energyintensive task for the field coordinators.

NutriBusiness Project Reconceptualization

It quickly became apparent that receiving nutrition education was much less appealing to rural Kenyan women than becoming shareholders in a cooperative business venture. Consequently, an intensely participatory strategy was initiated to enable the women farmers in each of the project sublocations to add economic value to the crops they grew on their shambas by processing and marketing a weaning food that could improve the nutrition of their own children and increase the availability of convenient, affordable, culturally appropriate weaning food in regional peri-urban markets. By directly linking the development of women's agribusiness knowledge and skills to the improved health of children, the project addressed the interrelated issues of poverty and human development by building multiple forms of capital (social, financial, human, physical, and natural)[3] in these rural Kenyan communities, using women's intimate connections with food and family as the medium through which to promote development.

What was conceived as a community research and development project was rapidly transformed into a participatory learning initiative for both university investigators and rural community residents. Early in the life of the project, it was hypothesized that if the nutribusiness model could be successfully implemented in Bomet, an area isolated from the market economy of Nairobi and with a population that was poorly educated, it could be replicated by women in many other rural Kenyan communities. Conversely, if the nutribusiness model was found to be unworkable by women in Murang'a, who were more educated and familiar with the way businesses operate in an urban metropolis, it was not likely to succeed elsewhere. As a result, the decision was made to provide similar project facilities and training in Bomet and Murang'a and to observe the respective strategies used by the women for making decisions, managing resources, capitalizing on opportunities, overcoming obstacles, and moving toward the goal of establishing a sustainable business venture.

Initial Activities in the Communities

An early project activity was exchange visits between women leaders from Bomet and Murang'a. This exchange helped to establish a shared identity with the NutriBusiness Project and created strong bonds of friendship between women from ethnic groups that were at times rivals in the heated Kenyan political climate of the early 90s. The visits had the added effect of promoting friendly competition between the 2 cooperatives.

The exchange visits were followed by field trips to Bomet and Murang'a by a multidisciplinary faculty team from the participating universities. The purpose of these faculty visits was to conduct an informal participatory rural community appraisal focused on household composition; child and community health; economic and social activities of women's groups; local activities of governmental, religious, and civil society organizations; specific activities engaged in, and decisions made by, adult men and women, youth, and the elderly; child rearing and feeding practices; crop and animal production, household use, and sales; and household food acquisition, preparation, and consumption practices. During these visits, women were observed as they prepared food for, and fed, their young children. Samples of these locally prepared children's food items were collected for nutrient analysis in the UoN food science laboratories.[4]

The information gathered in the field became the basis for future community workshops.

Participatory Workshops in the Communities

Several months after the rural appraisal was undertaken, a 3-day workshop was conducted in each area. For this workshop, laboratory-generated information on the nutrients in a typical serving of each locally prepared infant food item was shown as a bar graph that compared the food item with a young child's daily nutrient needs. The bar graphs represented the nutritional quality of traditional weaning food items the women themselves had prepared, and the information was accessible even to those who were illiterate. What distinguished this activity from a typical nutrition education lesson was that the women were members of a cooperative that was embarking on the development, production, and eventual marketing of a weaning food product. By the end of the presentation, the nutritional superiority of traditional mixed dishes over the popular weaning gruel (uji) containing only a single grain had been clearly illustrated.

The next phase of the 3-day workshop involved the assignment of participants to teams made up of several individuals from each of the participating subdivisions in the area. The task of each team was t2o "prepare a good food for a young child" from crops that were grown on their shambas. In preparation for this activity, the field coordinators secured grains as well as other indigenous and exotic food items that were grown locally. For each of these items, a colorful nutrient bar graph was created on a large sheet of newsprint. The graphs were grouped into grains, dried beans, leafy green and yellow vegetables, and "other" vegetables, fruits, and tubers. The actual food item was placed on the newsprint beside its graphic representation. After viewing the display of ingredients, each team selected what they would like to use in their cooperative's weaning food product (Figure 1). Equipped with a knife and a single cooking pot placed on 3 stones over an open fire, they cooked their dish for all the workshop participants to sample. An animated critique of each dish followed the tasting. Without the provision of specific instructions on how to make nutritional decisions, each group had combined 1 or 2 grains, beans, a leafy green, and 1 or more "other" items. By the conclusion of the cooking, tasting, and critiquing process, the group had identified the key ingredients to be included in their weaning food product. In Bomet the key ingredients were finger millet, maize, beans, pumpkin, and pumpkin leaves. In Murang'a the key ingredients were bananas, maize, beans, carrots, and amaranthus leaves.

For the second cooking activity, teams were structured by sublocation. This time each team was instructed to prepare a dish combining all of the key ingredients, but the amount of each ingredient and how the dish would be prepared was left to the discretion of the group. An observer/recorder was assigned to each group to record the amount of each ingredient used and how the dish was prepared. Aliquots of the finished products were packaged for transport to the UoN for analysis, after which the products were sampled and evaluated for taste, smell, texture, and consistency by the participants.

On the final day of the workshop, the participants were divided into 2 teams, and individuals from the sublocation that had prepared the best-liked product on the previous day provided "expert" instructions on how the dish should be prepared. The final products were sampled and critiqued by all the workshop participants before being served to a number of village children between 6 months and 3 years of age who were brought to the workshop site by their mothers.

The workshop participants anxiously watched as each mother first tasted the 2 samples in random order and then fed them to her child. Participants who were able to write, carefully recorded the reactions of the

Figure 1: NutriBusiness Workshop Participants Prepare their Group's "Good Food for a Young Child"

mothers and their children. After the mothers and children departed, the discussion was particularly lively. The women had come to recognize that these tasters were their potential consumers whose acceptance or rejection would spell the success or failure of their entrepreneurial venture into the world of food processing and marketing.

Nutritional Optimization and Shelf-life Testing

Knowing the proportionate amount of each key ingredient in the weaning food items prepared in the workshops enabled project nutritionists to use African food composition tables[5] to calculate the approximate nutritional composition of each product and to adjust the formulations to meet, as closely as possible, the Codex Alimentarius standards for a supplemental, cereal-based food item for older infants and young children.[6] None of the key ingredients was eliminated from either Tupcho (which translates as 'working together'), the name given by the Bomet women to their weaning food product, or from BASCOT (a novel word incorporating the first letter in the name of each ingredient in the Murang'a product). Both of the optimized formulations, however, included carrots and/or pumpkin marrow and pumpkin leaves and/or amaranthus leaves. These modifications allowed each group some opportunity for seasonal ingredient substitution without affecting the nutritional composition of their product.

After the weaning food formulations had been optimized, both the Bomet and Murang'a products were processed in the food science laboratory at the UoN in sufficient quantity to conduct accelerated shelf-life studies. These studies indicated that the dry weaning food mixes could be stored in sealed plastic bags for up to a year at ambient Kenyan temperatures. A sufficient amount of the Bomet formulation was also processed to conduct a controlled feeding trial.

Preparing Optimized Formulas in the Communities

The individual ingredients for each mix were processed, dried, and milled into flours in the university laboratory. These flours and the combined mixes were subsequently used in sublocational workshops held in each area (Figure 2). In these workshops, representatives from the participating women's groups first prepared their optimized product from fresh ingredients and then created their dry mix by weighing out and mixing the separate flours in the correct proportion and cooking the product according to preparation instructions that would appear on the package. When they compared their weaning food prepared from raw ingredients and from a dry mix, the women clearly understood that their Nutri-Mix (as the products were eventually labeled) was nutritionally superior to the uji that most weaning-age children in Kenya were receiving. The representative from each participating women's group left this workshop with a packet of their Nutri-Mix and written instructions they were to follow in preparing the product for all the members of their group to sample. This preliminary product distribution to about 80 women's groups was the first opportunity for the approximately 2500 women who were associated with the Kenya NutriBusiness Project to actually see and taste the products they had been hearing about for several years.

Organizing the NutriBusiness Cooperatives

Organizational development training was conducted in each area to illustrate how the nutribusiness cooperative would be structured. Subsequently, a full-day meeting was organized at a local hotel to select the executive committee for each cooperative. The organizational workshops involved the designated representatives and alternates from participating women's groups and were held in each of the 4 project sublocations in Bomet and in the 3 Murang'a sublocations. The number of participating women's groups varied by sublocation from 5 to 15. At these workshops, the responsibilities of the nutribusiness representatives, alternates, and officers were discussed. Subsequently, each sublocation elected its own nutribusiness officers from among the designated women's group representatives in attendance. Following local custom for the number of officers elected by a women's group, the Tupcho NutriBusiness Cooperative in Bomet had 16 members on its board of directors, and the Murang'a NutriBusiness Cooperative had 9.

Figure 2: NutriBusiness Workshop Participants Learn the Importance of Accurately Measuring the Amount of Liquid to be used in Preparing their Nutri-Mix Product

Cooperative Management and Leadership

Once the nutribusiness boards of directors in Bomet and Murang'a had duly elected their officers, the project manager began the process of registering the cooperatives with the Kenyan Ministry of Cooperatives (MOC). Subsequently, the 2 boards were brought together in Nairobi for 3 days of intensive, hands-on cooperative management and leadership training. The training was conducted in English, with translation into KiSwahili as well as into Kikuyu and Kipsigis, as necessary, to accommodate the language skills of all participants. The field coordinators, who took an active part in planning and conducting the training, were expected to assist their board members in providing follow-up training for the cooperative members in each location. It was also expected that, once the cooperatives were officially registered with the MOC, additional training as well as monitoring and oversight of financial records would be provided by MOC officials assigned to the Bomet and Murang'a district offices. This expectation was not fulfilled, and eventually the project was obliged to contract with a nongovernmental organization to review the records of one of the cooperatives and provide both the project staff and the cooperative itself with an independent assessment of the various financial and other record-keeping systems that needed to be in place to achieve the desired level of transparency.

Product Marketing

A challenging part of establishing a nutribusiness was to effectively engage the cooperative's rural shareholders in the marketing of their value-added food product. Rural Kenyan women were accustomed to selling their agricultural produce in local markets, where the price fluctuates seasonally with supply. They were also familiar with selling a commodity such as maize to a government marketing board or selling milk to a national dairy cooperative. However, the task of selling a multi-ingredient, shelf-stable convenience item with a unique nutritional profile designed for a specific market segment was a totally new concept to them. Preparing members of the cooperative to make rational decisions about marketing such a product required innovative training that took place repeatedly during the project.

Marketing workshops were conducted for members of the board of directors and other shareholders from each cooperative. Role playing and a variety of hands-on activities were employed to illustrate the importance of the 3Ps (product, placement, and pricing) to the success of their enterprise. The need for product quality assurance, through the application of simplified hazard analysis and critical control point (HAACP) methods, as well as the importance of worker supervision and inventory management to prevent pilferage, were addressed. The need for planned sourcing of raw ingredients, accurate weighing and measuring, appropriate product labeling and dating, protective packaging, care in the storage and handling of ingredients and safety precautions that needed to be taken at each stage in the product processing, as well as distribution issues, were also addressed in these sessions. Eventually, each cooperative arrived at a wholesale as well as a retail price for its Nutri-Mix product that reflected a reasonable projection of its ongoing business costs and anticipated sales volume. Shareholders in the cooperatives, as well as receiving payment for the raw ingredients they provided, had an expectation that they would annually share in any distribution of the cooperative's profits. In addition, members were able to purchase the Nutri-Mix at the wholesale price, either for their home use or for resale at the retail price in their community. This marketing strategy was popular with the shareholders.

Facilities and Staffing

The NutriBusiness Project funded construction of the facility for each cooperative and purchased the essential processing equipment. A small truck with a capped bed was also supplied to each cooperative. The trucks were fitted with bench seats for transporting people, but their main use was for transporting raw ingredients and fuel for the hammer mill and dehuller with which each facility was equipped. The project vehicles were badly abused by their male drivers, who used them for various types of for-hire transport. Costly vehicle repairs were soon needed, and the cooperatives' members learned that owning a vehicle could be a liability as well as a convenience and a very visible status symbol.

Each of the cooperatives employed a young man to operate its hammer mill and grain dehuller. In addition to producing the various flours for the weaning food mixes, these pieces of equipment were operated on a fee-forservice basis to process grains for home use. Milling and dehulling fees were paid either in cash or as a portion of the grain to be milled. Profits to the cooperatives derived from the milling and dehulling operations included the sale of accumulated grain as well as the sale of by-products, which were used for animal feed. The mills also served as popular meeting places for residents of the village, and the prestige associated with their ownership was very important to the women.

Solar Dryers

The most technically challenging element in the processing of the Nutri-Mixes was the design and construction of a solar dryer capable of handling the year-round drying of cooked beans quickly enough to prevent the growth of mold and mold toxins (such as aflatoxin) during the seasonal rains. After determining that the solar dryers being marketed and used in Kenya at the time were not adequate, the task of designing a dryer for the NutriBusiness Project was undertaken locally. A design was created for a solar dryer equipped with solar panels and a storage battery. This system stored enough energy during daylight hours to power a fan that significantly increased air circulation in the drying chamber and permitted drying to continue after sunset by pulling heat into the drying chamber from the base of crushed rocks on which the dryer was constructed. The solar battery also permitted the use of a mechanical device to securely seal the plastic bags in which the Nutri- Mix was packaged for retail sale. This dryer design allowed a single layer of cooked beans spread on 24 wire mesh trays, each measuring 3 feet by 3 feet, to dry in approximately 9 hours. Drying the other ingredients for the mixes required considerably less time and posed fewer safety risks. The solar dryers designed for the NutriBusiness Project were fabricated by the Nairobi-based Kenya Industrial Research Development Institute (KIRDI) and transported by truck to the processing sites.

Other specialized food processing equipment was also designed for use at the rural nutribusiness sites and fabricated by skilled Kenyan "jua kalis," small, independent metal and wood crafters, who were grateful for the business the project provided.

Additional studies were undertaken through the Nutri-Business Project to develop a unique animal-source food product that could be safely processed under the drying conditions obtained in the project's solar dryer.7,8 This dried product, called a "Chiparoo," combined rabbit or chicken meat with white or sweet potatoes to produce a crispy, shelf-stable product that could be crumbled into cooked porridge for infants or eaten as a snack by older children.[9] Chiparoos were successfully taste-tested in a rural Kenyan community, but project funding terminated before their production could be integrated into the nutribusiness operations.

Product Processing Workshop

After the first dryer was installed in Bomet, a 3-day processing workshop was conducted, to which the field coordinator, the board of directors, and other members from the Murang'a NutriBusiness Cooperative were invited. During this workshop the participants were taken through every step of the Nutri-Mix production process, from receiving the raw materials through packaging and dating of the finished product. In the nutribusiness operation, most raw ingredients are delivered to the processing site by cooperative members, who receive immediate payment. This is an important consideration for women who have very little cash available. After being received, perishable commodities (bananas, pumpkins, carrots, amaranthus, and pumpkin leaves) are cleaned and sliced as needed and then blanched prior to drying to preserve color and nutrients. Beans are soaked and their external hulls removed prior to being boiled for 45 minutes to inactivate antinutrient factors. Maize is dehulled in a domestically fabricated dehuller to reduce its fiber content before milling. Finger millet is soaked and deglumed prior to drying. This process of removing the millet hull increases shelf life and decreases fiber. After drying and subsequent milling, each ingredient is stored separately in large, tightly covered plastic bins until the porridge mix is prepared. The process of weighing and mixing the separate flours to achieve a consistent product was demonstrated during the processing workshop, as was a packing, sealing, and labeling process that assured that each bag of Nutri-Mix contained 500 grams of porridge mix and carried the date on which the mix was packed. The retail price of Nutri-Mix in 2000 was approximately $1.00 (US) per package.

Evaluating the Porridge Mixes

The principal difference between the Bomet and Murang'a formulations was that the Bomet product contained finger millet, an ingredient that Kipsigis women have traditionally considered to be the most important weaning food for young children, whereas the Murang'a product contained bananas, a fruit widely grown in the central region and used both fresh and dried in preparing traditional Kikuyu weaning food items. Both the Bomet and Murang'a products contained maize as an inexpensive energy source, beans as a source of protein, and carrots or pumpkin marrow and amaranthus or pumpkin leaves as alternative sources of provitamin A. A sample of the dry porridge mix from each location was sent to an independent laboratory in the United States for nutrient analysis. This information was used to create a nutrient label, reviewed and approved by the Kenya Department of Health, for each product. Though few of the women in either group were initially aware of nutrition labels, they were insistent that their weaning food's label should include nutrition information as well as the required ingredient listing and preparation and storage instructions. They also agreed to include on the label a statement that this product was appropriate as a supplemental food for children 4-6 months or older and that it was not a substitute for breast milk.

After the product formulations were established, a controlled feeding trial was conducted in a rural nutrition rehabilitation center. The children received either the institution's normal cereal-based gruel or the Bomet porridge mix for 6 weeks. Weight gain and hemoglobin status were monitored. Children receiving the Tupcho Nutri-Mix showed improved iron status and a greater weight gain when compared with children who received the rehabilitation center's regular diet.[10] The cost of conducting a similar study using the Murang'a formulation was beyond the scope of the project budget. However, the comparable nutrient composition of the 2 Nutri-Mix formulations suggested that the Murang'a product would produce similar results.

Discussion

Problems Encountered

After receiving initial training and technical assistance on the use of its dryer, the Bomet cooperative began processing the Tupcho Nutri-Mix and was very successful in selling it in local villages. Members were elated when the Tupcho NutriBusiness Cooperative received an award of distinction in a regional small-business exhibition. Within a short time, however, the cooperative's manager, a single mother with several school-aged children, succumbed to acquired immunodeficiency syndrome (AIDS), and the very popular field coordinator left the project. Shortly before the cooperative was forced to deal with these problems, the UoN PI died unexpectedly, and the women in Bomet were left without the professional and personal support of a highly respected member of their ethnic group. Although the UoN agreed to continue its technical assistance to the Bomet cooperative, regular visits to the distant Rift Valley were difficult to schedule, and the alternative arrangements that were made to provide support on an as-needed basis were hampered by poor communications between the field and the UoN campus. When a broken part for their solar dryer was taken to Nairobi for repair and not returned, it meant that the cooperative could no longer process its porridge mix. Given the reality of their situation, the Bomet women decided to use their mill and dehuller to process maize and millet on a fee-for-service basis, and they transformed their building into a facility for storing grain that they bought and sold locally when the seasonal price was favorable.

In contrast to Bomet, the Murang'a NutriBusiness Cooperative received continuing technical and marketing support from the UoN and, after the UDLP project ended, was able to market its Bascot Nutri-Mix to local health centers as well as to individual consumers in the area. The capacity of its processing facility was not reached, however, before a severe drought in Central Kenya temporarily halted production of the porridge mix. The drought forced the cooperative to rely solely on revenue generated by fee-forservice milling and dehulling of grain until members were once again able to provide sufficient raw ingredients to resume production of their BASCOT Nutri-Mix.

In 2005, Touchstone Consultant Services, a marketing firm with close connections to the UoN's College of Agriculture, approached the Murang'a NutriBusiness Cooperative with a proposal to reinvigorate its product marketing by renaming the product, redesigning the packaging, and repositioning the product as a nutritional food supplement rather than as a weaning food. The marketing strategy employed was to target the 2 national supermarket chains in Kenya as well as health centers, schools, and organizations involved in the provision of food supplements to persons with AIDS and other conditions requiring nutritional support. A business plan has recently been developed to expand marketing and technical services to the Murang'a NutriBusiness Cooperative and possibly to the Tupcho NutriBusiness Cooperative in Bomet, as well (written communication with Anne Tei Mukunya, March 2, 2007). Touchstone consultants will also provide services to 2 additional nutribusiness projects that were developed between 2001 and 2005 in Kenya's Eastern Province with financial support from the United States Agency for International Development's program in Kenya (USAID/Kenya). These nutribusiness sites, like Murang'a, are communities that are accessible to urban markets, and through their proximity to, and connections with, the university, they should be able to receive technical support not only from UoN, but also from the Kenya Agricultural Research Institute.

Implications for Research and Practice

The relevance of the nutribusiness concept is as a comprehensive, local development strategy targeting women. In rural African communities, change occurs at a pace that reflects the dynamic interplay between indigenous and external knowledge systems. Institutional change agents have initiated a wide range of evidence-based outreach programs to address the plethora of problems standing in the way of the achievement of national development goals in rural Africa. However, these change agents often fail to perceive the importance of creating an opportunity for communities' indigenous knowledge systems to effectively meld with the Western ways of knowing that are embraced by the change agents.[11] Hassel has termed the process of interaction between academic scientists and indigenous people "crosscultural engagement," where the cultures to be crossed are those of indigenous communities on one hand and the community of Western science on the other.[12]

In the NutriBusiness model, rural women's traditional knowledge and skills are valued and integrated with a local development strategy, through which they gain and apply new knowledge and skills while developing confidence in their ability to collectively make decisions and accept the consequences of these decisions. At their own pace, and in their own cultural and ecological reality, nearly 2500 women in 2 Kenyan communities were "engaged" with change agents and with the novel nutribusiness concept of processing and marketing unique food products that are convenient, healthful, and appropriate to their culture. These women appear to be confident that their cooperative initiative and effort will, over time, enable them to not only "do good" for others but also "do well" for themselves. The Kenya NutriBusiness Project is an example of change that has occurred because the unique cultures of campus and community are effectively engaged in activities to simultaneously reduce poverty and promote human development.

Acknowledgment

This project was funded by University Development Linkage Program Grant #PCE 5063-A-00-2043-00 through The Center for Higher Education, U.S. Agency for International Development.

Supplementary Data

Additional photos from the NutriBusiness Project accompany the on-line version of this article (available at *http://www.jneb.org*).

Notes & References

1. United Nations Development Program. *Human Development Report* 2005: International cooperation at a crossroads. Aid, trade, and security in *an unequal world*. New York: United Nations Development Program; 2006.
2. Jerome N. *Nutribusiness. FrontLines,* Washington, DC: U.S. Agency for International Development; 1991: p. 1.
3. Scoones I. *Sustainable rural livelihoods: A framework for analysis*. Institute for Development Studies Working Paper #72. Available at: *http://www.ids.ac.uk/ids/bookshop/wp/wp72.pdf. Accessed April 13,* 2007.
4. Muroki N, Maritim G, Karuri E, et al. Involving rural Kenyan women in the development of nutritionally-improved weaning foods. *J. Nutr Educ.* 1997; 29: 335-342.
5. U.S. Department of Health, Education and Welfare and Food and Agriculture Organization. *Food Composition Tables for Use in Africa*. Washington, DC: U.S. Department of Health, Education and Welfare and Food and Agriculture Organization; 1968.
6. FAO/World Health Organization. *Codex Alimentarius. Standard for processed cereal-based food for infants and young children*. Codex Alimentarius STAN 74 Vol. 4: 1981.
7. Kieras SJ. *Safety assessment and sensory analysis of a meat-based dried snack food for children in sub-Saharan Africa* [master's thesis]. University Park, Pa: Pennsylvania State University; 1999.
8. Kieras S, Mills EW, Knabel S, Maretzki AN. Validation of pathogen destruction during manufacture of a meat-based potato snack (Chiparoo). *J. Food Proc Pres.* 2003; 26: 385-399.

9. Maretzki AN, Mills EW. Applying a NutriBusiness approach to increase animal source food consumption in local communities. *J. Nutr.* 2003;133:4031S-4035S.

10. Kulwa K. *Effect of Tupcho mixed porridge on the nutrition of malnourished children (6-36 months) in an urban slum, Kibera, Nairobi* [master's thesis]. Nairobi, Kenya: Applied Nutrition Program, University of Nairobi; 2000.

11. Semali LM, Maretzki AN. Valuing indigenous knowledge: Strategies for engaging communities and transforming the academy. *Journal of Higher Education Outreach and Engagement.* 2005:10:89-106.

12. Hassel CA. The craft of cross-cultural engagement. *Journal of Extension.* 2005;43:6.6FEA1. Available at: *http://www.joe.org/joe/2005december/a1.shtml. Accessed April 13, 2007.*

TRADITION AS A MODERN STRATEGY:
Indigenous Knowledge as Local Response to Globalization in Africa

Geoffrey I. Nwaka*

The paper considers the relevance of Indigenous Knowledge, and how it relates to Modern Science, and to conventional development practice. Indigenous Knowledge is used to refer to the vast and largely undocumented body of knowledge, wisdom, skills and expertise which a given community has developed over time, and continues to develop as it grapples with the challenges of its environment, with outside ideas, and with constantly changing conditions. Indigenous Knowledge represents the heritage of creative thought and practical everday life which is passed on orally or through experience from one generation to the next. Indigenous Knowledge is dynamic, and is not really in conflict or in competition with modern sicence or modernity. Following the tenets provided in the World Bank volume - Indigenous-Knowledge: Local Pathways to Global Development -this paper sees indigenous knowledge as a model for rethinking and redirecting the development process, and as a way to involve, enable and empower local actors to take part in their own development. This tendency, as is well known, has been reinforced in the UNESCO sponsored 'World Decade for Cultural Development' (1988-1997), the UNESCO Declarations on Tolerance, Cultural Diversity and Dialogue Among Civilizations; the UN International Decade of the World's Indigenous Peoples (1995–2004), and other global initiatives and debates which have stressed the cultural dimension of development, and the need to take local knowledge and practice fully into account in the development process (UNESCO, 1995). This paper ponders the challenges of Africa in coping with globalization in a way that is compatible with local values and priorities; and which strikes the right balance between global and local cultures in national governance and development. This paper thus considers how indigenous knowledge and native practice can be put to good use in support of local governance and development in African countries; how development policies and programmes can be made to reflect local priorities, and build upon and strengthen local knowledge, capacity and organization, especially in such vital areas as agriculture and natural resource management, law review and conflict resolution, education, health care and poverty alleviation. Brodly pursuing the view of Marshall Sahlins when he invokes the peoples "to indigenize the forces of global modernity, and turn them to their own ends", since the real impact of globalization depends largely on the responses

* Professor of History, Abia State University, Uturu, Nigeria

developed at the local level, this paper acknowledges the renewed interest in Indigenous Knowledge and institutions which are in line with the current advocacy of the minimalist state and the 'enabling approach' as condition for good governance.

Globalization is now widely perceived in Africa as a new version of earlier forms of external domination and exploitation. Its economic and welfare benefits and opportunities appear to be unevenly shared, and which bypass or adversly affect many countries of the developing world. But Marshall Sahlins has rightly emphasized the need for all peoples "to indigenize the forces of global modernity, and turn them to their own ends", since the real impact of globalization depends largely on the responses developed at the local level.

The challenge for Africa is, therefore, how to engage and cope with globalization in a way that is compatible with local values and priorities; how to strike the right balance between global and local cultures in national governance and development.

For a long time African customs and traditions were misperceived as irrational and incompatible with the conventional strategies of development. But the economic crisis and policy failures of the 1980s and '90s, and the current threat of global recession have exposed flaws in the Western, neo-liberal, 'external agency' model of development imposed from the top by national governments and international development agencies. The undue emphasis which this pattern of development places on purely qantitative economic growth is now blamed for the worsening problems of environmental degradation, widespread poverty, widening inequalities within and between nations, and the undermining of those values and institutions which promise to hold these negative forces in check. Because of growing concern about these problems, there is renewed interest in an alternative approach to development which emphasizes the cultural dimension of development, and the often overlooked potential of indigenous knowledge as "the single largest knowledge resource not yet mobilized in the development enterprise".

This paper considers how indigenous knowledge and native practice can be put to good use in support of local governance and development in Nigeria and other African countries; how development policies and programmes can be made to reflect local priorities, and build upon and strengthen local knowledge, capacity and organization, especially in such vital areas as agriculture and natural resource management, law review and conflict resolution, education, health care and poverty alleviation.

The World Bank has recently published an impressive collection of essays aptly titled: *Indigenous-Knowledge: Local Pathways to Global Development.* Following the examples set in this volume that this paper sees indigenous knowledge as a model for rethinking and redirecting the development process, and as a way to involve, enable and empower local actors to take part in their own development.

Critics of African development compare the current pattern of development in the continent to building a house from the roof down:

> *... all the institutions of modern urbanization are in place – the banks, the factories, the legal system, the unions, etc; but all these appear to be suspended over societies that have no firm connection to them, and whose indigenous institutions, even when oriented in the right direction, lack the necessary scaffolding to connect them to their modern surrogates (Mabogunje, 1992).*

Mamadou Dia of the World Bank also blames state failure and the development crisis in Africa on the–

> *"structural disconnection between formal institutions transplanted from outside and indigenous institutions born of traditional African cultures" (Dia, 1996).*

To explain the poor performance of public sector management in Africa, Professor Ekeh also argues that the modern political and administrative structures and institutions which we now operate - the civil service, the police, the judiciary and other state institutions - were created by the alien colonizers who neither sought nor won the affection of the people. These institutions inherited from the colonial period have continued to be regarded as alien and oppressive, to be avoided, resisted or opposed if possible. There is general apathy and cynicism towards government, and some ambivalence about accountability in governance. By contrast, the general attitude of the people to the primordial traditional institutions and organizations are much more selfless and transparent because of the cultural norms, obligations and sanctions that come into play (Ekeh, P. 1975; cf Honey, Rex and S. Okafor eds., 1998). The argument is that these traditional values, attitudes and institutions should be consciously harnessed and brought to bear on national governance, development and public affairs.

The renewed interest in indigenous knowledge and institutions is in line with the current advocacy of the minimalist state and the 'enabling approach' as condition for good governance in a period of structural adjustment and public sector reform. Governments in developing countries are urged to reduce their role to what their dwindling resources and capacities permit; to decentralize the structure of governance, promote genuine partnership, and enlist the broad participation of non-state actors and stakeholders, including traditional institutions and other organizations of civil society. This trend has been reinforced by the UNESCO sponsored *'World Decade for Cultural Development'* (1988–1997), the UNESCO *Declarations on Tolerance, Cultural Diversity and Dialogue Among Civilizations*; the UN *International Decade of the World's Indigenous Peoples* (1995–2004), and other global initiatives and debates which have stressed the cultural dimension of development, and the need to take local knowledge and practice fully into account in the development process. (UNESCO, 1995).

The main body of the paper considers the meaning and relevance of Indigenous Knowledge, and how it relates to Modern Science, and to conventional development practice. We use Indigenous here in a more general sense to refer to the local, the traditional and the endogenous in Africa, as opposed to the alien ideas and institutions of modernity which came with European colonial rule and Christian missionary influence. At the same time, the term Indigenous Knowledge is used to refer to the vast and largely undocumented body of knowledge, wisdom, skills and expertise which a given community has developed over time, and continues to develop as it grapples with the challenges of its environment, with outside ideas, and with constantly changing conditions. It represents the heritage of creative thought and practical everday life which is passed on orally or through experience from one generation to the next. Indigenous Knowledge is dynamic, and is not really in conflict or in competition with modern sicence or modernity. Very few, if any, serious scholars now consider indigenous knowledge to be a viable alternative to modern science and technology; but we must acknowledge that the exclusive use of modern science in itself is not enough for the complex task of achieveing Sustainable Development in diverse cultural and ecological contexts. The real challenge is to recognize the strenghts and limitations of both indigenous knowledge and modern science, and explore how the two knowledge systems can complement each other.

The paper then tries to relate Indigenous Knowledge to good governance and poverty alleviation in Nigeria since the United Nations considers good governance as "perhaps the single most important factor in eradicating poverty and promoting development". Much of the current literature on good governance in Africa has tended to focus attention at the national and state levels, and on such general issues as human rights, civil service reform, electoral and judicial reforms and so on. The major gap in the good governance agenda appears to be at the local level where the major isssues of poverty reducation, popular participation, and support for an active civil society remain largely under-researched and unaddressed.

Recent studies have rightly questioned the undue emphasis which scholars place on centralized state systems and bureaucratic institutions in the study of public administration in Africa. The poor performance of these states in the 1980s and, 90s has increased the interest in the study of local self-governing and self-organizing capacities, and in indigenous non-state structures of governance (the clan, emirates, village, age grades, credit and mutual aid institutions, etc) which have sustained the people when states and governments have failed. This approach is particularly needed in Nigeria because of widespread disenchantment with excessive centralization that has been brought about by the long period of military dictatorship between 1966 and 1999. The details of the patterns and challenges of local governmental reforms in Nigeria since 1976 are presented in this paper to show how best to integrate Indigenous Knowledge and Traditional Institutions into modern governance.

The study also considers the implications of the Indigenous Knowledge Movement for development assistance. Hitherto, donor agencies have tended to engage numerous outside consultants and experts who sometimes assume a knowledge or capacity vacuum among the people they seek to assist, instead of seeking to identify and tap into existing local capacities, institutions, skills and practices. Increased emphasis on the indigenous appears to be a more promising way to enhance local ownership, sustainability and impact of aid and development partnership. When technical assistance underrates and overlooks local knowledge and expertise, it reinforces the problems of dependency and underdevelopment instead of reinforcing and building upon existing local capacity.

The paper concludes with some general reflections on the Indigenous Knowledge Movement as an appropriate local response to Globalization and Western Knowledge Dominance, and as a way to promote Cultural Identity and Inter-Cultural Dialogue at the wider arena and in the context of African Development. With the increasing tempo of globalization, Africa cannot now opt for an insular and entirely home grown approach to its development, but must follow a pattern of development which recognizes the merits and limitations of both local knowledge and global science, and explores how the two can best complement each other. Like the Japanese and the rapidly developing countries of Asia, Africa must aspire to achieve endogenous development which has a distinct African cultural fingerprint.

Note

This is a shorter version of the full paper on the theme. The author will provide a larger version of this paper which we will include in the forthcoming issue of the Journal of *Social Anthropology. – Editor.*

References

Adedeji A. and B. Ayo eds (2000), *People-Centred Democracy in Nigeria* Spectrum Books Ibadan.

Ake, Claude, (1988), "Building on the Indigenous", in Fruhling, P. ed., *Recovery in* Africa: *Challenge for Development Cooperation in the 90s* , Stockholm, pp. 19-22.

De Soto, Harnando, (1989), *The Other Path-Invisible Revolution in the Third World,* NY;

Dia, Mamadou (1996), *Africa's Management in the 1990s and Beyond-Reconciling Indigenous and Transplanted Institutions,* World Bank, Washington DC.

Ekeh, P. (1975), "Colonialism and the Two Publics in Africa - A Theoretical Statement" *Comparative Studies in Society and History,* Vol. 17 (1) pp. 91-112.

Haverkort, Bertus, *et al.* (eds.), (2002), *Ancient Roots, New Shoots-Endogenous Development in Practice,* London: Compas/Zed Books.

Honey, Rex and S. Okafor (eds.) (1998), *Hometown Associations - Indigenous Knowledge and Development in Nigeria,* London, IT.

Hopper Anthony, ed. (2000), *Culture and Sustainable Development in the Pacific,* Asia Pacific Press Canbarra, Especially Chapter 3 by Marshall Sahlins.

Mabogunje, Akin L. (1992), "A New Paradigm for Urban Development", Proceedings of the World Bank Annual Conference on Development Economies, 1991, Washington DC, pp. 191-219.

Mutuma, Gumisai (2007), "Africa's Indigenous Peoples Fight for Inclusion" *Africa Renewal,* Vol. 21, No. 1, pp. 6-8.

Semali, L. M. and Joe L. Kincheloe, eds. (1999), *What is Indigenous Knowledge? Voices from the Academy.* Falmer Press, London.

Seragaldin, Ismail and J. Taboroff, eds. (1994), *Culture and Development in Africa.* Proceedings of World Bank Conference, Washington DC.

SDC (Swiss Agency for Development Cooperation) (2003), *Culture is Not a Luxury: Culture in Development Cooperation,* Bern.

UNESCO, (1995), *Our Creative Diversity-Report of the World Commission on Culture and Development,* Paris.

Warren, D. Michael, L. Jan Slikkerveer and David Brokensha, eds. (1995). *The Cultural Dimension of Development-Indigenous Knowledge Systems,* London, IT.

World Bank, (2004), *Indigenous Knowledge: Local Pathways to Global Development,* WB Washington DC.

SAHLINS' *TRIBESMEN* (1968) RECONSIDERED: Tribes of Highland Orissa in Perspective

Georg Pfeffer*

When dealing with hill peoples in South and Southeast Asia we seem to sense a good number of structural commonalities, but perhaps we need to clarify these issues. Anthropological research, in my opinion, does imply comparison and generalization, but with regard to tribal societies, the viable attempt of a general outline seems to be Sahlins' book *Tribesmen* -1968 – small in size but far-reaching in content. I would like to investigate the extent to which his findings can be applied to highland Orissa i.e., not just those people defined as *Scheduled Tribes* by the Indian administration.

By saying "Modern civilization knows no borders" Sahlins begins the tenor, decades before the term globalization had been invented. Europeans, he continues, had changed the societal setup of the world within the short span of 500 years. Tribesmen, on the other hand, had been "rapidly colonized, baptized, and culturally traumatized". Thereafter, Sahlins concludes, "civilization allows itself the luxury of an intellectual digestion: the primitives are largely anthropologized" (1968: 1). We are conducting an inquest, even if the corpse, at least partially, continues to show signs of life.

India

The above impressive vision of history is, in my opinion, is not entirely applicable to India, colonized by Europeans but a civilization in her own right and a state that had always encompassed many millions of tribesmen. True, the British turned the present Jharkhand Province – the major tribal region in Chota Nagpur - into the industrial heartland of India and after independence this policy was continued with and extreme impetus after the liberalization of the Indian economy in the 1990s. Further south, the

* Freie Universität, Berlin, Germany

Sundargarh and Sambalpur Districts of Orissa were developed by gigantic and ecologically devastating industrial projects–a process now progressively extended southwards-so that the tribal "household economy" (1968: 74ff) has, in many cases, been reduced to the habitation in 'urban slums'.

So far less has changed to the south of the great river, the Mahanadi dividing the province. The British did fight so-called *Meriah* wars against the populous Kond people then practicing 'human sacrifice', but - there being little revenue in sight - stayed away from the region for most of the time. The peasant subjects of the lowlands - until the present day - only very partially and gradually moved into the southwestern tribal zone from the adjoining strip in coastal Orissa.

Modern Development

Only in the nineteen-seventies did the provincial government establish *ashram* or boarding schools for tribal students who, in fact, ran away whenever they could. The vast majority of the youths failed to enroll from the beginning[1] and to this day, schooling is not a general feature of the tribal areas. More important were special "development agencies" created for Juang and Bhuiya[2], Kuttia and Dongria Kond, Saora, Bondo and Koya[3]. These seven had been declared *Primitive Tribal Groups* or *PTG* in the nineteen-seventies and each subjected to the efforts of a "special officer" of the provincial administrative service who was supposed to invest major amounts of public money for the "uplift" of the respective tribe. In fact, the tribal people were saved from the onslaught. The major portions of such budgets are alleged to have been consumed or embezzled by some members of administration. General administrative corruption to this day is the guardian of tribal existence.

Wherever this was not the case and public funds were actually invested in development projects, crops and livestock of the tribal people were improved by additional varieties and marketing facilities. Such a benevolent government policy of "protective discrimination" directly contradicted the efforts of another administrative department that of the Forestry as founded by the British-Indian concepts. The colonial power had declared all Indian forest to be property of the state and made it a point to keep the tribal people, their animals and their slash-and-burn cultivation, out of the "Reserved" and "Protected Forests"[4]. No major policy changes have been introduced in independent India. Thus on the one hand, the swidden cultivators must raise improved varieties of crops and animals in the forest - in the manner they have practiced for millennia - whereas on the other hand, the foresters disallow woodcutting. Thus in reality, as everybody knows, these officials derive a considerable extra-income from the tribal recipients of development aid. Yet a controversial government policy has been activated in recent decades, that of tourist promotion. While some developers insist on changing the tribal way of dressing and dancing to conform with the style of the lowland peasants and whereas forest officers prohibit tree-cutting and swidden cultivation, the departments for tourist promotion advertise large pictures of "naked Bondo", "tribal dances" and hoe-cultivation to attract foreign tourists who keep searching for "exotic" objects of photography.

In practice the tribal economy had changed very little under the long-term impact of the colonial power. New hazards have appeared in the form of foresters, policemen, tourists and schoolmasters, but old ones, such as the marauding Maratha army and other soldiers of fortune, have disappeared in turn. Before the European colonialists, the agents of the Indian civilization used to search for elephants, diamonds and other valuables in "forest land" (Jharkhand), just as tribal territory, over the millennia, had been the hideout for all sorts of armed forces defeated in the lowlands.

Today India makes every effort to be a modern nation state, but most[5] of the above mentioned seven tribes live as they used to do hundreds of years ago. In 1980, I have seen the "special officer" of the Kuttia Kond intervene very little. In fact, he had never visited a Kuttia village at all and spent most of his time at the provincial capital of Bhubaneswar lobbying for an extension of his lucrative posting. Setting up a huge administrative apparatus for their "uplift", the state does take cognizance of these tribes but does not really make serious effort to transform them. The ghastly European inclination to improve everything and everybody is absent in 'Hindu Orissa'.

Peasants and Tribes

What about the other tribal communities of Orissa[6] i.e., those beyond the category of certified primitives? Most have since long adopted the plough and outwardly cannot be distinguished from the peasants of the caste society in the lowlands, except perhaps for certain specialties in dress and appearance. The social structure of these tribes is different, however. Where exactly lies the difference, compared to the *Chasa* and the other peasants of the plains?

India is a land of peasants. This is the term for a rural population, not just the cultivators that form a part of a larger, more complex society. Both peasants and tribes have always been involved in external exchanges beyond their own settlements, but Eric Wolf (1966) rightly tells us that the character of this involvement is different. Tribesmen control their means of production, their land and their labour, and exchange work and products for culturally defined equivalent goods and services of others. Peasants, however, must transfer their surpluses to a dominant segment of society that uses them both to underwrite its own standard of living and to channel the remainder to groups that do not farm (Wolf 1966: 3/4). No culturally *equivalent* goods and services are exchanged in this manner.

In my opinion, the cultivators in much of the old[7] tribal districts of Phulbani, Kalahandi, Ganjam and Koraput continue to control much of their own labour, even if, temporarily, they are forced to involve themselves in various jobs for wages. Sahlins is writing on an ideal type. When looking at reality, we must consider a proportional approximation to the model. Relatively speaking, I think, alienation of labour power is not a major issue in those tribal districts. Similarly superior layers of non-cultivating owners do not claim the land of the tribal people. In contrast to lowland Orissa, tribal cultivators are not expected to pass on a major portion of their crop to others. They are not even expected to pay revenue, because their income is considered to be too low to be taxed. Whereas in the coastal Puri District, for example, a *Potha*, or the letter of ownership awarded by the land registration officer, may contain six or seven names in a ranked order, the *Potha* for tribal land will only mention the cultivator.

The state has "settled" the landed property in all of those regions where the plough is applied to both wet rice and dry rice farming i.e., the state has certified ownership by superior official right. This is not – or not yet – the case in the swiddens of the "primitive seven". The state has also intervened in many other ways e.g., by raising cashew nut and other cash-crop plantations and by organizing transport and communication, or by selling cheap rice to the "*bpl*[8]", for example. Mere market *places*, i.e. weekly markets, have changed in the sense that they have gained access to the national and world market. Tribal men and women - wielding plough *or* hoe in the course of cultivation – raise turmeric, rape-seed, chillies, bananas and other cash-crops to be sold by intermediaries on the national and international market.

Yet this is a gradual change. Much of the market *place* – where buyers may simultaneously be sellers – is still concerned with the use value rather than the exchange value of the items. People buy commodities, such as cheap mill-made textiles and agricultural implements, but they also buy and sell cattle to sacrifice and earthen pots to worship their gods and to initiate seasonal changes. Numerous other items of the sort cannot really be called "commodities". Rural cultivators or craftsmen exchange them within the local domain of the weekly market. Similarly priests and temples have not yet made it to tribal villages. The old religion continues to be in force. Peasants, in short, are subjected to *distinct* spiritual, political and economic forms of leadership whereas tribal people are not.

War and Peace

"Civilization" says Sahlins "is an advance in organization, a qualitative transformation of the cultural type.... In the broadest terms, the contrast between tribe and civilization is between War and Peace" (1968:4). War, in the tribal case, is spelled in the Hobbesian style of *Warre* and meaning the constant danger to peace. What does "War and Peace" mean in highland India?

The Bondo and the Dongria Kondh in a somewhat different manner - serve to exemplify *Warre,* and Elwin, in a descriptive account, wrote on "Maria, Murder and Suicide" (1943). Later others followed plagiarizing his title for their respective study in one tribal community or the other. Death has been a conspicuous subject. Those of us, who have done fieldwork in Orissa, have observed how murders-let alone other offences - were systematically withheld from the police, the agency of the state. But then the same is true in peasant communities of the lowlands; just as tribal and non-tribal people are observed to have called in the police in efforts of private vengeance. The police have become an instrument of *Warre*. Most 'Indianists' are aware of the fact that the formal forces of law and order are, in fact, frequently the greatest danger to law and order. Murder, rape and extortion in Indian police custody are too regular a feature to be worth mentioning. Indian 'civilization', it seems, does not stand for Peace - spelled with a capital *P* in Sahlins' argument.

Peasants suffer under the police, and so do tribal communities to an increasing degree. It should be remembered, however, that police rarely tour the tribal villages. Tribes live in the "remote area" and can-for all practical purposes-be left alone by the police, while police stations are a regular hazard among the peasants of the lowlands. Hindu civilization has always had governments with official "public authority ...over all persons and groups as such-by virtue of residence in the domain". This has been lacking in tribal areas and is only very gradually entering them at present. Tribal people are not in practice "subject to the sovereign, to its jurisdiction and coercion." (Sahlins 1968: 6). Government appears and has always appeared - as an intruder, best to be avoided. The European efforts to pacify tribal India in the19th century, on the other hand, had been met by spontaneous resistance called "The Great Kol Rising" in the history books, with the Kol being substituted the Kondh or the Ho in other regions or the Santal *hul* to be remembered to this day, as is the revolt led by Birsa Munda. While the peasants of the lowlands allowed the colonial rulers to substitute Indian regimes, all tribal people rose in open resistance against the outsiders brought into their lands under European leadership.

Levels and Sectors

In the Sahlins' model, tribal anarchy is based upon two foundations. One is the multivalence of institutions, the generalized structure. "Production, polity and piety" (1968:15) are not separated, but different functions of the same institutions. The second foundation is the inclusive series of group membership. "From one vantage...the tribe presents itself as a pyramid of social groups....We speak of a 'segmentary system' not simply because it is built of compounded segments, but also because it is only so built." (1968:15). Viewed from a different angle,

> *"the tribe is divided into concentric circles of kith and kin: the household in central position, a circle of lineage kinsmen surrounding it, a wider circle of village relations, and then furthermore the tribal and inter-tribal spheres. Each sphere, otherwise a level of organization, becomes in this perspective a sector of social relations, relations become increasingly broad and dilute as one moves outward from the familial navel.... Now the strength of a tribe is generally in homestead and hamlet..."*
>
> **(Sahlins 1968: 15/16).**

These extensive quotations of the central message on "levels" of organization within the segmental pyramid and on "sectors" of social relations as a concentric model do apply to tribal India. In the field of religion, for instance, the question of the number of souls assigned to an individual, is really a matter of segmentary levels (1968: 18) and so is economic cooperation or support in gift exchange and raiding. The household is the major multivalent institution: Sahlins speaks of the "familial mode of production" (1968: 75). Household loyalties are central in contrast to the fuzzy borders of the tribe, the latter level or sector having least importance. The outstanding importance of the smallest sector is the indicator of the 'primitiveness' of the tribe as well as of the tribal power of resistance in the face of the civilized onslaught.

Descent in Tribal Orissa

When comparing this tribal design with conditions in Orissa, certain obvious questions arise: Sahlins' concept of a segmentary lineage system was adopted from Evans-Pritchard's African Nuer (1940) and is not quite applicable to Orissa, as I have shown elsewhere (Pfeffer 2001). Pedigrees of the Nuer type are not in use; ancestors are forgotten and not instrumentalized for the segmentary pattern. Other ways and means are found to oppose segments, techniques differing in detail but employing the senior/junior opposition of a general "middle Indian type" (Pfeffer 1997:13/14).

Accordingly, Clanship in tribal Orissa offers food for thought. Moving through the Kuttia Kond territory, one can notice the common sacrificial pole of adjoining villages marking the same clan. Niggemeyer (1964: 47) has even drawn a map uniting various villages of the Kuttia Kond in Territorial Clans, but his drawing covers only a small portion of the Kuttia land. Majumdar (1950) similarly finds territorial clans within the great Ho tribe, just as Bailey (1960: 73) for the Kondh of northwestern Phulbani, does notice this institution, even if the latter is supposed to be in a status of "decay" (1960: 69), a statement I dare to question after a recent tour of the region. Obviously, far too little overall research has been conducted in this field. During my visits to about 30 different tribal communities of Orissa, positive proof of the existence of territorial clans could be found in the Kond region[9] whereas elsewhere, descent and territory do not coincide in such an obvious manner.

Regarding the composition of villages, everywhere an affinal minority is tolerated or even invited to complement the body of mutual agnates within a settlement, but again the latter may be viewed from different angles. We may find a single clan dominating a single village. This may or may not be a clan also represented in the neighboring villages. The Koya case, however, is clearly different: several phratries settle in a single village. Then - by contrast to most other tribal communities - intermarriage *within* the village is not only allowed but also expected, and this may also be a general pattern for the other Gondi tribes.

Thus in many or most tribal societies of Orissa we find dispersed clans, in Koraput and in the northern districts of Sudargarh, Sambalpur and Mayurbhanj and even dispersed tribes with certain residential centers of gravity. None of these clans or tribes would ever assemble in joint action. There being no lineages in the African sense, but only "local lines" at the village level, chances of predatory expansion - Sahlins (1961) favourite subject - are very limited. This aspect of Sahlins' argument does not at all seem to be applicable in highland Orissa.

What appears to be a general pattern is the *composite clan*, a descent category, not a group, that is united by a common totemic emblem but not by detailed - known or invented-genealogical links. In Koraput-and perhaps elsewhere-this clan-membership transcends tribal units. In that southwestern region-as in the northern Chota Nagpur complex of Kharia, Munda and Oraon in tribal Jharkhand or among Santal and Bhumia of Midnapur in West Bengal and adjoining areas - the mythemes - if not whole mythical accounts-are the same: Members of neighboring tribes are never strangers-or non-humans-but involved in the same mythical dramas. Sometimes these dramas account for the inter-clan relations, but then, as usual, we lack data.

Discussion

Most inhabitants of Orissa's southwestern districts live in tribal societies, because these are not differentiated into functional institutions and have avoided government institutions, the market, and the temple as best as they could. The familial mode of production rules these societies, higher levels of organization becoming increasingly irrelevant, wider sectors of social relations unknown. All tribesmen of highland Orissa can name individuals supposed to be their "priests" and secular "leaders", but the latter are petty chiefs (Sahlins 1968: 21) and the former work in the fields and involve themselves in segmentary confrontations like anyone else. They operate as "sorcerers (1968: 109) or communicate with the dead.

Tribesmen today do ride buses and sell turmeric to agents of the Indian government, just as they pray to Siva whenever their schoolmasters 'ask' them to do so. They may avail of these opportunities whenever these innovations have been introduced by outside forces that control the benefits. Hill society, however, is not made or unmade by such intrusions.

Notes

1. Children of settlers and of the client weaver Scheduled Castes are usually enrolled today in the limited number of schools.
2. Juang and Bhuiyan live in the northern District of Keonjhar but away from the industrialized zone.
3. I use the administrative tribal names, even if the people understand respectively themselves to be remo or koitor, i.e. "humans" in contrast to settlers from the lowlands.
4. In 'Reserved Forests 'trees must not be cut, whereas in' Protected Forests' only a variety of high quality timber is tabooed.
5. A visit 1983 indicated that many of the 500 000 members of the Sora tribe had been forced to leave their land and their religion (see Vitebsky 1992). Furthermore the newly built highway between Mumbay and Kolkota cuts

through the Juang territory and much of the Koya land has been given to the Bengali refugees of the 1971 crisis in Bangladesh.

6. About half of Orissa's 40 million population lives in a tribal society, even though only about a quarter officially belongs to the Scheduled Tribes. The other highlanders have been assigned to the Scheduled Castes or the Other Backward Classes or none of these "protected" categories at all.
7. The old districts were subdivided into new ones in 1995.
8. The abbreviation for people who are said to exist "below the poverty line" is "the bpl". Government trucks tour the tribal areas selling rice at a nominal rate mostly to women of the–landless–craftsmen and cattle-herders, the clients of the landed tribes.
9. This confirms R. Hardenberg's recent (2001) observation among the Dongria Kondh.

References

Bailey, F. G. (1960), *Tribe, Caste, and Nation. A Study of Political Activity and Political Change in Highland Orissa.* Manchester, Manchester University Press.

Elwin, Verrier (1943), *Maria Murder and Suicide.* Bombay, Oxford university Press.

Evans-Pritchard, E. E. (1940), The Nuer: A Description of the Modes of Livelihood and Political Institutions of a Nilotic People. Oxford, Oxford University Press.

Majumdar, Dhirendra Nath (1950), *The Affairs of the Tribe. A Study of Tribal Dynamics.* Lucknow, Universal Publ.

Niggemeyer, Hermann (1964), *Kuttia Kond. Dschungelbauern in Orissa.* München, y Renner.

Pfeffer, Georg (1997), The Scheduled Tribes of Middle India as a Unit: Problems of Internal and External Comparison. *In* Pfeffer, Georg & Deepak Kumar Behera (eds.); *Contemporary Society: Tribal Studies* Vol. 1. New Delhe, Concept pp. 3-28.

Pfeffer, Georg (2001), The Structure of Middle Indian Tribal Society Compared. *In* Pfeffer, Georg & Deepak Kumar Behera (eds.); *Contemporary Society: Tribal Studies* Vol. 5. New Delhi, Concept (*in print*)

Sahlins, Marshall D. (1961), The Segmentary Lineage: an Organization of Predatory Expansion. *American Anthropologist* 63: 322-45.

Sahlins, Marshall D. (1968), *Tribesmen.* Englewood Cliffs, Prentice Hall

Wolf, Eric R. (1966), *Peasants.* Englewood Cliffs, Prentice Hall

BIODIVERSITY, ANTHROPOGENIC PRESSURE AND CONSERVATION: The Case of the Khangchendzonga Biosphere Reserve

Umesh Kumar*

The Khangchendzonga Biosphere Reserve is one the fourteen declared biosphere reserves in India. Located in the picturesque state of Sikkim in the Eastern Indian Himalayan Region and named after the world's third highest mountain peak, Mt. Khangchendzonga, it covers an area of 2619.92 sq.km. The Biosphere Reserve has been witness to increasing conflict between the Native People and the Protected Area regulation, providing the challenges in the sphere of participatory sustainable resource management and conservation of genetic resources with an appeal for ecosystem. In any exercise meant to address this issue there is urgent need to consider the human dimension of Biosphere Reserve from the very outset and to survey stockholders' attitudes about conservation in order to take into account the inherent traditional dependence of people on forest resources. The study reveals that in the societal perception of space there is a sequential evolution of the conception of sacred landscape with sacred species and sacred- stone at the bottom, and the mighty Guardian deity Khangchendzonga on the top. It is revealed that the people are not lacking in the knowledge about the conservation of the environment, which is in their own interest. There are many dimensions to it; including the sacred/ ritual dimension and which find expression in rites and rituals of the local communities. Nevertheless, in recent times mounting population pressure and increased Himalyan visitation have resulted in the degradation of the ecosystem. The causative factors, in addition to above, being the ever-increasing dependence of human populations on forest for fuel, fodder, timber and non-timber forest produce. An attitude survey done by applying contingent valuation method shows that people are indeed concerned about the conservation of the forest resources, even though their helplessness in succumbing to misusing the forest is too evident. The result of attitude-survey, no doubt, is emphatically affirmative. It has shown the willingness of the people to accept the conservation concerns and also to pay for it. It is, therefore, sine-qua-non that socio-economic concerns of the people need to be addressed properly, mainly in terms of facilitating alternative livelihood options and involving the stakeholders in the conservation efforts.

Keywords: *Khanchendzonga Biosphere Reserve, conservation, eco-system, attitude survey, contingent valuation method, willingness-to-pay, willingness-to-accept, people's participation, sacred landscape.*

* Anthropological Survey of India, 27, Jawaharlal Nehru Road, Kolkata-700 016, India, *E-mail: raghuvanshiuk@rediffmail.com*

The environment, which is rich in biological diversity, offers the broadest range of options for people to rely on for the fulfillment of human survival. Loss of biodiversity influences the local area and its economic bases and social fabric. The experiences of the past few decades have shown that as industrialization and economic development take place in the society, the patterns of production, consumption and the needs change, and they pressure on people to alter their responses to ecosystems. Conservation and sustainable use of biodiversity, hence, are fundamental to Sustainable Development. This aspect is important for us as an assessment of biological diversity at world level reveals that Asia is the most threatened continent (Hannah & Lohse, 1993, Mittermeier, 1988). Perhaps, the best approach to understand biodiversity is to look at it in a hierarchical manner in which biological organisms are organized. The smallest unit starts from the diversity contained in the genetic material of individual organisms and then goes on to encompass the biological communities in which species are organized and then to cover the wider ecosystem in which they exist.

Biodiversity is recognized at three levels viz., genetic, species and ecosystem levels (Fig. 1). In all these levels of biodiversity, the components are dynamic in space and time. The genetic composition of species changes over time in response to natural and human induced selection process. The ecosystems strongly respond to external dynamics and internal stresses.

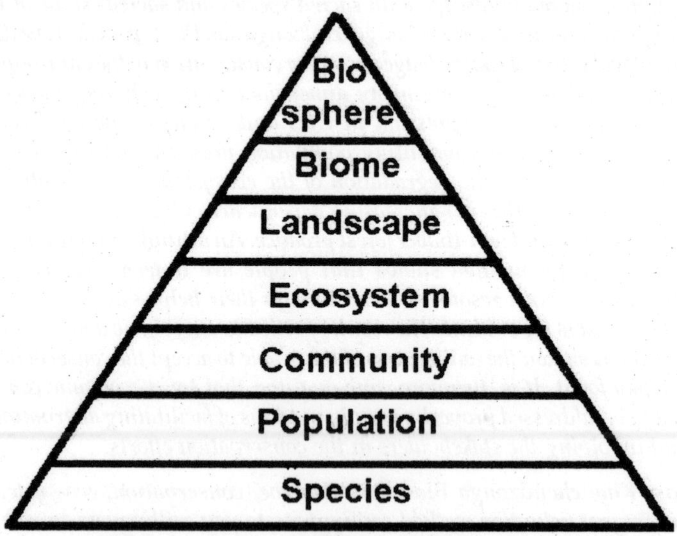

Figure 1: Hierarchy of Biological Organization

Based on IIRS Report on Biodiversity Characterisation at Landscape Level, 2001

Ecological systems do not exist as discrete units but represent diverse parts of a natural continuum in the form of landscapes. While biodiversity is usually measured at the species level, maintenance of biodiversity requires management at higher levels of organization, particularly at the landscape scale, which effectively includes human beings also. The ideal is to preserve overall ecosystem vigour, including species diversity. It can be best accomplished by integrating it into the fabric of social, environmental and economic contexts. Here lies the immense implication of the concept of the sustainable development where the issues of the man and environment are integrated together, for a better future for all the living being.

This viewpoint of man - environment linkage needs to be critically seen in the milieu of the Biosphere Reserve. The commencement of Biosphere Reserves goes back to the "Biosphere Conference" organized by UNESCO in 1968. This was the first inter-governmental conference organised to resolve the conservation issue and need for judicious use of natural resources, thereby predicting the present-day notion of sustainable development. This Conference resulted in the launching of the "Man and the Biosphere" (MAB) Programme of UNESCO in 1970. It aimed to facilitate resolution of increasing conflict between the people and the Protected Areas.

The UNESCO's agenda stipulates that Biosphere Reserves should be representative of a bio-geographic province and should have appropriate zoning system with legally constituted and minimally disturbed core zone. In addition, the site should conserve unique and pristine biodiversity, ecosystems and landscape suitable to explore and demonstrate approaches to sustainable development and should be of appropriate size to serve three crucial functions, viz., Conservation, Development and Extension of logistic support. It is proposed to bring at least one representative site within each bio-geographic province of any given country under the network of Biosphere Reserves. All the more, Biosphere Reserves are designated to deal with important questions of reconciling the conservation of biodiversity, the pursuit of economic and social development and maintenance of associated cultural values. Consequently the Government of India, through the Ministry of Environment and Forest, launched in 1986 the Biosphere Reserve Programme. At present there are 14 recognised Biosphere Reserves in India.

Forest dwellers vis-a-vis Biosphere Reserve Management

In the context of India, human populations living within the Biosphere Reserves have always been seen as a permanent threat involving conflicting interests and debate. The continuous discord on the issue at international level, prompted the UNESCO (1996) to move away from the earlier held view of concentric rings of core, buffer and transition zones, and to adopt a more flexible way of looking upon the local needs and situations. Thus grew the approach of flexibility and creativity within the Biosphere concept, which was suitably widened particularly in view of the constraints posed by the need to see both biodiversity as well as the cultural diversity symbiotically. The advantages of cultural diversity at societal level are felt to be comparable to those accruing from the biodiversity. However, the question remains that while the issues of biodiversity have been addressed at length and caught attention widely, the important theme of cultural diversity has not been touched upon for serious analysis.

The Biosphere Reserves of India are the abode of many indigenous/ traditional communities who remain integral part of the ecosystem, living close to the Nature. Living in the areas rich in natural resource, indigenous/ traditional communities fulfill many of their livelihood requirements from the rich biodiversity around them. The ecosystems such as forest not only meet a variety of livelihood needs of the forest dwelling societies, through products such as timber and non-timber forest products, but also sustain traditional shifting cultivation and other agricultural practices contributing to the food security of the people within the Biosphere Reserves. In general, included within the management efforts of the Biosphere Reserves are protection of natural resources within Biosphere Reserves from the outside intrusions, and also restricting the use of its resources by the local communities, residing in the Biosphere Reserve and nearby. The concept of sustainable use of resources is being introduced in some areas but due to lack of information and regulations appropriately and also on account of location specific misunderstanding there are obstacles to handle the issue of resources utilization.

Of late emphasis is laid on the involvement and cooperation of the local forest dwellers in eco-development by way of community participation in forest eco-system management/ rehabilitation programme. In this respect there has been thinking for linking eco-development issue with the traditional institutions and customary system of land/ forest - based activities based on the traditional value system of local communities. The Biosphere Reserve management, therefore, necessitates not only understanding of ecological issues but also the social customs and economic practices including the cultural patterns. In order to achieve this, conservation-linked development strategy has to be based on a value system that people can understand, appreciate and accept. Therefore to ensure peoples' participation properly there is need to employ a 'bottom-up approach'.

The description below is devoted to comprehend the impediments faced by the Khangchendzonga Biosphere Reserve, mainly on account of the anthropogenic pressure around it and also to depict the present status of the forest resources, including the responses of the people and their attitude in the context of conservation efforts.

The Study Area

The present study pertains to the Khangchendzonga Biosphere Reserve in Sikkim (Figure 2), where 14 revenue villages lye in the periphery of the Reserve zone in West District. Out of these fourteen villages, two villages -Yuksam and Dubdi - were selected for collection of data. Further, for comparative purposes, Lachen, Gnon-Samdong and Lyngzah villahges were selected from North District, for investigation. There is preponderance of Bhutia community in Yuksam while the Nepalese are a major community in Dubdi revenue village. The Lachen village is inhabited primarily by Bhutia, who call themselves Lachenpa. The other two villages namely Gnon-Samdong and Lyngzah fall within the Dzongu reserve area and are uni-ethnic, inhabited by the Lepcha community.

The principal occupation of the people living in these villages is agriculture supported by animal husbandry. The agricultural pursuit is of subsistence level. With flourishing of tourism in Yuksam and Lachen some people have been engaged in this industry. There is also increasing involvement of local people in the hotels and transport sectors. As a result today only a few villagers pursue traditional occupation.

Methodology of Research

Both primary and secondary data have been used to fulfil the objectives of the study. In order to gather the primary data field investigations were carried out in two phases- November to December 2006 and April to May 2007. Remote Sensing (RS) and Geographic Information System (GIS) tools were used to retrieve data on land use and land cover of the area. The data pertaining to fuel wood consumption was culled by adopting a weight survey method based on fuel consumption over a period of 24 hours. In all 55 households were intensively surveyed. During the survey the each sample stakeholder was visited and the head of family was requested to monitor the amount of fuel wood that would be burnt during that particular day. The wood was weighed by spring balance before its use. On the next day, the remaining wood was weighed and deducted from the original

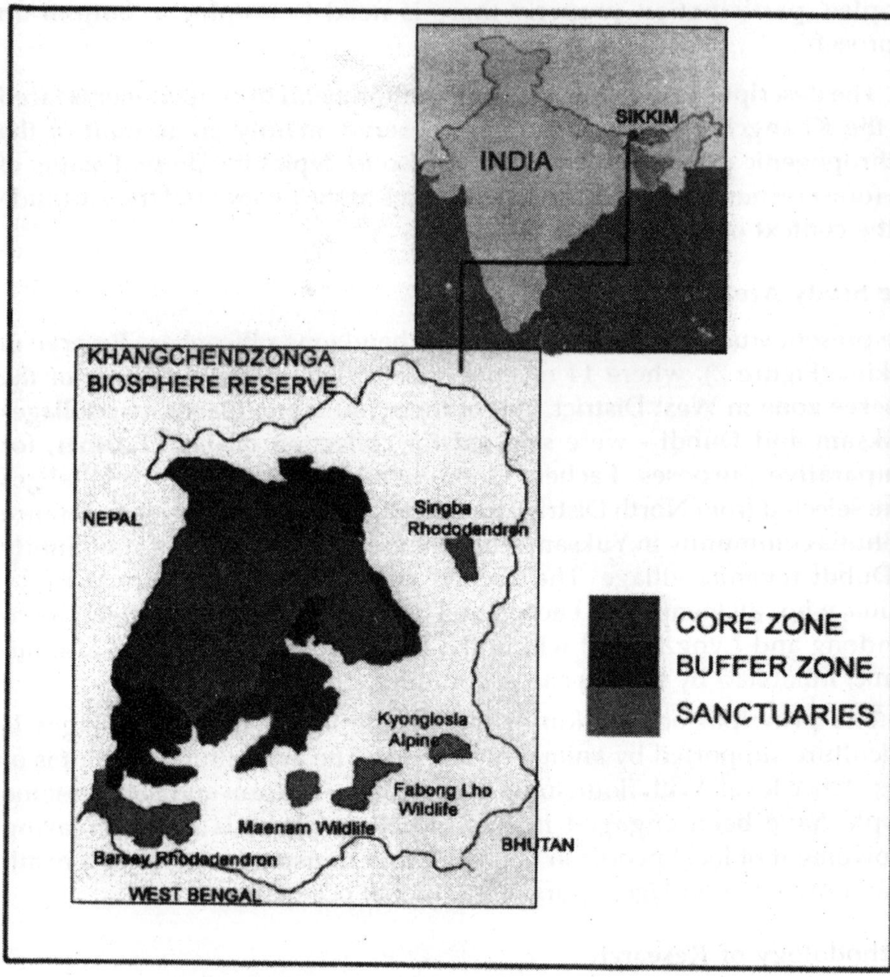

Figure 2: Khangchendzonga Biosphere Reserve

bundle to calculate the actual consumption per day. Time spent for fuel wood collection was noted when the members of the households went to the forests. Participatory Rural Appraisal (PRA) technique was also used to collect the information on preferred species for fuel wood consumption, timber and fodder. Paired resource ranking method was adopted to find out the availability of natural resources and preference in the use of resources.

Based on observation on human needs and biosphere interference, a conservation attitude survey (CONVT) was conducted in some of the important fringe area settlements falling in the North and West Sikkim.

Contingent valuation method (CVM) within the ambit of ecological economics with emphasis on willingness-to accept (WTA) and willingness-to-pay (WTP) approach was adopted for these settlements located crucially in respect of Khangchendzonga Biosphere Reserve. This was done to understand the level of concerns of population or the stakeholders pertaining to the environmental conservation activities. The basic premise of the this valuation is that the environmental conservation costs of enforcing Biosphere Reserve principles through restrictions of the use of natural resources shall also be borne by the local populations or the stakeholders within their socio-cultural field and economic framework of subsistence. To organise the data and to interpret the possible underlying issues, the entire responses to the questionnaire were further categorized into: conservation driven concern, socio-economic driven concerns, willingness-to-accept (WTA) and willingness-to-pay (WTP) concerns and participatory concerns in the Biosphere Reserve concepts. In addition, some qualitative information was gathered on the roles of NGO in conservation efforts through observation and discussion.

Land Use and Land Cover

Satellite imagery (1:50000) IRS-1A, LISS-II, FCC of bands 2, 3 & 4 were interpreted for forest cover and other land-use employing a photo interpretation techniques for the year 1999, in conjunction with the Survey of India topographical maps (Chhetri *et al.*, 2002). The interpretation of the imagery shows that 30.55 per cent of the area is under snow cover. It is followed by Fir-Rhododendron forest, dense mixed forest and alpine pasture, which occupy 20 per cent, 16 per cent and 12.49 per cent of the area respectively (Table 1).

Table 1
Areas under Biosphere Reserve and Land use/cover of Khangchendzonga Biosphere Reserve

Sl. No	*Land use/cover*	*%*	*Area km²*	*NDVI values*
1	Dense mixed/conifer forest	16	419.19	more than
2	Open mixed/conifer forest/silver fir-Rhododendron forest	20	523.98	0.2-0.27
3	Degraded mixed/conifer forest	7.14	187.06	0.12-0.19
4	Scrub land/forest blank	2.63	68.9	0.05-0.11
5	Alpine scrub/pasture land	12.49	327.24	
6	Alpine barren land/barren land	9.92	259.9	0.01-0.04
7	Snow cover/glaciers	30.55	800.38	
8	Rivers/streams/lakes/exposed soil	1.27	33.27	less than 0.01
	Total	100	2619.92	

Source: Report of Maharana, I., Rai, S.C., Chettri, N., and Sharma, E. 2000

Availability and Preference of Species

Population living close to Biosphere Reserve is highly dependent on forests in the buffer zones, mainly for non-timber forest products (NTFPs), including extraction of medicinal herbs, litter, wild edible fruits, and other minor forest products (MFPs). Although the timber cutting is strictly prohibited, it seems difficult to stop the collection of fodder and fuel wood such as rhododendrons- a keystone species acting as biodiversity indicator of the region. Keeping in mind the aforementioned need of the villagers a study on the availability and preference of resources for fuel, timber and fodder was carried out in the month of November- December in Yuksam and Dubdi villages while in Lachen, Linzah and Gnon-Samdong it was carried out in the months of May and June. Analysis of data and interpretation are provided below.

Status of Fuel Wood: Species Under Pressure

Fuel wood provides the major proportion of household's energy consumption in the domestic sector, while commercial alternative energy sources contributed very little. The consumption of fuel wood varied amongst stakeholders with respect to different physical and economic factors. Pair-wise ranking of species used as fuel wood in Yuksam and Dubdi Blocks have been presented in the Table 2. There are altogether 13 species used as fuel woods. The availability of status of this 13 species suggest that Uttis is most widely available fuel wood followed by Bans, Bajrant, Mahua, Uttis and Assare. The other species are available less widely. But the preference wise, Bajrant is the most preferred fuel wood species followed by Jat Katus, Phalanth, Jhinguni and Asare. The least preferred species is Panyun. A co-relation between the availability and preference shows that except Bajrant, Assare and Jhinguni, the other species, which are in high in preference list, are not abundantly available. Moreover, Jat Katus is the second most preferred fuel wood species but is least available in the open forest. The above analysis reveals that except Bajrant, the other preferred species are less in number. It means that in order to procure these species they have to depend on the reserve forest. Secondly the excessive exploitation of this species is expected to reduce their availability in the open forest.

In Gnong- Samdong and Linzah villages of Dzongu area there are altogether eleven species identified by villages as fuel wood (Table 3). Interestingly Chilloni, Uttis, Lapsi and Mahua are among the most preferred species. Among the least available species are Tooni, Kaulo, Saur and Malato. Other species are moderately available. Seen from the view of the

Table 2
Pair-wise Ranking of Species used as Fuel Wood in Yuksam and Dubdi Villages

SN	*Local Name*	*Scientific Name*	*Availability*	*Preference*
1	Bajrant	Quercus lamellosa	11	13
2	Jat Katus	Castanopsis hystrix	01	12
3	Phalanth	Quercus lineata	05	11
4	Jhinguni	Eurya acuminata	07	10
5	Asare	Viburnum codrifolia	09	09
6	Bans	Dendrocalamus sp.	12	08
7	Mahua	Engelhardtia spicata	10	07
8	Uttis	Alnus nepalensis	13	06
9	Pansi	Sorbus sp.	02	05
10	Kharane	Symplocos ramisissima	04	04
11	Argali	Edgeworthia gardeneri	08	03
12	Tusare		03	02
13	Panyun	Prunus cerosoides	06	01

Table 3
Pair-wise Ranking of Species used as Fuel wood in Dzongu

Sl.No.	*Local Names*	*Scientific names*	*Availability*	*Preference*
1.	Chilloni	Schima wallichii Chis.	11	11
2.	Phalant	Quercus lineate	6	10
3.	Katus	Castanopsis hystrix	7	9
4.	Saur	Betula cylindrostachys Wall	3	8
5.	Panisas	Tectona myriocarpaHeurue & Muell	5	7
6.	Utis	Alnus nepalensis	10	6
7.	Mahua	Engel hardtia Spicata Bl.	8	5
8.	Lapsi	Spondias axillaries	9	4
9.	Malato	Macaranga pustulata	4	3
10.	Tooni	Cedrela Toona roxb.	1	2
11.	Kaulo	Machilus edulis	2	1

preference the Chilloni ranks the first followed by Phalant, Katus, Saur, Panisas, Uttis and Mahua. A co-relation between availability and preference shows that Chilloni is most widely available as well as most preferred fuel wood species. But other species, which though rank high in the preference list, are either moderately available or least available.

Fuel Wood Consumption Pattern

In order to find out the consumption pattern of fuel wood 45 households were taken as sample, and the data collected from them, details of which are given in the Table 4. In the Yuksam Block only those settlements were considered which were dependent on Khanchendzoga Biosphere Reserve for fuel wood consumption. These settlements are Tshoka, Geychen,

Norbugang, Khongtay and Yuksam. The settlements, which are not dependent on Khanchendzoga Biosphere Reserve, are Kopchey, Mantabong, Topsing, Gofa Danra, Dostang and Mangsabong.

Table 4
Fuel Wood Consumption Pattern in Different Villages

Settlement	*Number of households*	*Total Population*	*Sample Size*	*Fuel wood consumption pattern Kg/captia/day*	*Mg/yr*
Yuksam	364	1951	15	4.73	3368.303
Dubdi	69	402	10	3.5	513.555
Lachen	1609+12	2955	5	5.0	5334.475
Linzah	80	397	5	3.8	550.639
Gnon-Samdong	66	401	10	3.6	526.914

The consumption pattern of fuel wood is estimated to be 3368.303 Mg yr-1.in the village of Yuksam dependent on KNP corridor. In case of Dubdi it is 513.555 Mg yr-1. The consumption pattern of fuel wood in Lachen, Linzah and Gnon-Samdong is 5334.475, 550.639 and 526.914 Mg yr-1. The average consumption of fuel wood in Yuksam and Dubdi Blocks together is 3881.858 Mg yr-1 while in two villages of Zongu, the average consumption of fuel wood is 538.776 Mg yr-1.

Status of Timber and Fodder: Species Under Pressure

The inventory of resources used for fuel wood at low and high altitudes showed that the trees surrounding the village vicinity, irrespective of species have the maximum pressure of fuel wood extraction. Nevertheless certain species are preferred over others for the fuel use because of their better burning quality. Bajrant (Quercus lamellose), Chilloni (Schema wallachi), Jat Katus (Castanopsis hystrix), Phalant (Quercus lineate), Jhinguni (Eurya acuminate), Katus (Castanopsis hystrix) and Aassare (Viburnum codrifolia) are the most preferred species at low altitude. At high altitude Rhododendran spp., Quercus lineta, Quercus lamellose, Betula alnoids and Magnolia spp. are the preferred species, which are used as firewoods. But the availability of these preferred species in the forest is facing tremendous pressure. The settlements at high altitude viz, Tshoka, Lachen and Thangu are the major consumers of fuel wood. Many species from natural forests especially Rhododendron arboretum, R. barbatum, Magnolia spp. are cut for use as fuel by these settlements.

The above discussion shows that the people in the surroundings of the forest area tend to collect fuel wood repeatedly from the same patch of the forestland. The forest cover in close proximity to the settlement and camping sites thus experienced maximum pressure. After the supply from the closer points decline, people penetrate further and further into the forest widening the area of impacted zone. In addition, the other factor that has put continuous pressure is the selective use of specific species as choice for fuel. In recent years therefore the existence of fire wood trees have become sparse. As a result the people have adopted the alternative variety but the quality of now available fuel wood is poor and the shortage of good quality has led to widespread switching over to inferior quality fuel wood. The area severely exploited and time devoted in collection of choicest fuel wood from surrounding forest is resultant indicator of fuel wood scarcity. High pressure was observed in Monastery forest at Dubdi and trekking corridor Yuksam-Gochala. It is apparent that if the harvested quantity exceeds the production capacity, one would not lose the growing stock. It in turn it hugely affects adversely the biodiversity also. Thus the fact remains that the large scale felling of trees and shrubs along the trek route and camping sites is the accelerating the degradation process. Forest is becoming thinner, leading to erosion of topsoil and disturbing the ecology of the area.

The present practice of fuel wood extraction is injurious to the eco-system. If this practice continued it would adversely affect the ecosystem structure and function. Extraction of fuel wood were slightly reduced after the intervention of Sikkim Biodiversity and Ecotourism Project, but the negative impact of extraction would still be substantial because much of the extraction is concentrated in the forest surrounding settlements and trekking corridor. It is presumed that promoting use of alternative fuel resources can minimize the impact of fuel wood extraction on biodiversity.

Indeed the Sikkim biodiversity and Ecotourism project promotes alternative use of firewood through various awareness programmes and capacity building training. Several Lodge operators in Yuksam are now using alternative energy like kerosene and LPG for tourist purposes. Porters are now able to hire blankets while on treks to minimize use of firewood for heating. A code of conduct has been developed by a Yuksam based NGO named Khangchendzonga Conservation Committee (KCC) for visitors. The travel agents association of Sikkim has also adopted a code of conduct whereby alternative energy utilisation on treks has become mandatory.

The PRA conducted in Yuksam and Dubdi Blocks with respect to the timber used by the villages reveals that there are eight species of timber woods, which are preferred by the villagers. Of these preferred species Uttis, Siris, Katus, Okhre are abundantly available while Kaulo, Tooni, Tarsingh and Chanp are least available (Table 5). Though the Chanp wood species is least available but it is the most preferred one. Katus, Okhre, Kaulo, Uttis, Tooni, Siris and Tarsingh follow it. Thus we find that except Katus, Okhra and Uttis other species are not available in abundance. As such in order to procure these species the local people depend on the buffer forest of Khangchendzonga Biosphere Reserve.

Table 5
Pair-wise Ranking of Species used as Timber Wood in Yuksam and Dubdi Villages

S. No.	*Local Name*	*Scientific Name*	*Availability*	*Preference*
1.	Chanp	Magnolia sp.	1	8
2	Katus	Castanopsis hystrix	6	7
3	Okhre	Litsae citrate, Juglans regia	5	6
4	Kaulo	Machilus edulis	4	5
5	Uttis	Alnus nepalensis	8	4
6	Tooni	Toona ciliata	3	3
7	Siris	Albizzia lebbeck Benth	7	2
8	Tarsingh	Beilschmiedia sikkimensis	2	1

Table 6
Pair-wise Ranking of Species used as Timber Wood in Dzongu

Sl. No.	*Local Names*	*Scientific names*	*Availability*	*Preference*
1.	Chanp	Magnolia sp.	2	8
2.	Malagiri	CinnamomumCecidodaphne Meeissn	1	7
3.	Kimbu	Morus indica L.	4	6
4.	Okhare	Litsae citrate, Juglans regia	3	5
5.	Katus	Castanopsis trixhys	5	4
6.	Kaulo	Machilus edulis	7	3
7.	Utis	Alnus nepalensis	8	2
8.	Tooni	Toona ciliate	6	1

In case of the two villages of Dzongu namely Gnong-Samdong and Linzah there are eight timber species preferred by the villages. These are Chanp, Malagiri, Kimbu, Okhare, Katus, Kaulo, Utis and Tooni (Table. 6). Among these species the Uttis is most widely available followed by Kaulo, Tooni, Katus. The least available species are Malagiri and Chanp. Interestingly the least available of species like Chanp, Malagiri, Kimbu and Okhare are the most preferred ones. This co-relation between availability preferences suggests that in the want of preferred species in the open forest the people depend on the buffer forest of Khangchendzonga Biosphere Reserve.

In all the studies area the people rear cattle, which include sheep, goat, cow, ox and dzo. In order to feed them they require fodder, which includes the leaves of trees and grasses. In Yuksam and Dubdi area there are 13 species of grasses, which are used as fodder (Table 7). Among them the most widely available grasses are Gaglatu, Banmara, Rattnoli and Elame. The least available grasses are Duari, Kurkuro, Mirre, Bans, Chiple and Kamle. But preference wise the most preferred species is Amliso followed by Bans, Kurkuro, Chiple, Kamle and Galatu. The least preferred are Elame, Banmara, Mirre and Rattnoli.

Table 7
Pair-wise Ranking of Grass Species used as Fodder in Yuksam and Dubdi Villages

S No.	*Local Name*	*Scientific Name*	*Availability*	*Preference*
1	Amliso	Thysanolaena setosum	08	13
2	Bans	Dendrocalamus sp.	04	12
3	Kurkuro		02	11
4	Chiple		05	10
5	Kamle		06	09
6	Gaglatu		13	08
7	Phultarul	Diascorea sp.	07	07
8	Kurro		09	06
9	Duari		01	05
10	Rattnoli	Polygonum molle	11	04
11	Mirre		03	03
12	Banmara	Eupatorium adenophorum	12	02
13	Elame		10	01

Table 8
Pair-wise Ranking of Grass Species used as Fodder in Dzongu

Sl. No.	*Local Names*	*Scientific names*	*Availability*	*Preference*
1.	Chiple (Kuhlonpe)	Bucklandia populnea Biosphere Reserve	1	22
2.	Thotne(kundyyum)	Polygonum molly Wright	5	10
3.	Unieu (tongtok)		11	9
4.	Piray Unieu (Lukship tongtok)		7	8
5.	Banso (Bamboo)	DendrocalamusHelmintonii Ness, Arn & Sikkimensis Gamble	10	7
6.	Ratnaulo	Polygonum molle	9	6
7.	Amliso	Thysanolaena maxima	8	5
8.	Okhare	Juglian regia L.	6	4
9.	Banmara	Eupatorium Adenophorum Spreng.	2	3
10.	Tetepati	Artimesia indica	3	2
11.	Dhokrephal (Domari reep, onlyfor goat)		4	1

In Dzongu there are 11 species of grasses, which are used to feed cattle (Table 8). Among them the most available species are Unieu, Banso, Ratnaulo, Amliso, Piray Unieu. The least available species are Chiple, Banmara, Tetepati, Dhoakrephal and Thotne. But the preference for the species suggest that Chiple is the most prefers species but it is least available. Thotne, Unieu, Piray Unieu and Banso follow it while the least preferred species is Dhoakrephal followed by Titepati and Banmara.

In Yuksam and Dubdi blocks there are 18 species of trees, leaves of which are used as fodder (Table 9). Among them the most visible species are Billoni, Nibara, Gugun, Dudilo and Asare. The least available species are Titepati, Dudilora, Chindde, Khosmiri and Pipale. Preference wise, the most preferred species is Dudilora followed by Bad, Dudilo, Nibara, Gugun, Phuto and Tooni. The least preferred species are Billoni, Titepati, Asare, Bajrant and Jhinguni.

In the Gnon-Samdong and Lyngzah villages of Dzongu, there are 15 species of trees, the leaves of which are used as fodder (Table 10). Among the most utilised species are Nibara, Dudilo, Baral, Lali, Bar and Gagun. The least utilised species are Titepati, Jhinguni, Kutemero and Katus. Interestingly in the Dzongu area the most available species are the most preferred species.

In the last ten years the population of Sikkim has increased by approximately 33% (Census of India, 2001). Thus, it can be easily ascertained that greater pressure is put on resources. In the fringe areas, the traditional agriculture and pastoralism exist as the traditional economic pursuits. While the agriculture is at subsistence level, there is high dependency on natural resources in the surrounding forest. The practice of livestock rearing to supplement agriculture and generate direct income is reasonably prevalent. Open grazing (eg, yak grazing on alpine pastures) is practiced for the most part of the year, with limited stall-feeding. In order to meet the fuel timber and fodder needs, the villagers are largely dependent on the Buffer zone forest of Khangchendzonga Biosphere Reserve. The area is likely to face long-term impact, adversely particularly on habitat in Khangchendzonga Biosphere Reserve. Increased habitat degradation will positively lead to serious undesirable effect on rare and endangered species.

Conservation Attitude Survey

People's participation in conservation efforts related to Biosphere Reserve is very important. Equally important is sticking to some disciplines including some obligations, which need to be enforced by the people themselves, as certain actions of the people are unfavorable to preservation

Table 9
Pair-wise Ranking of Species used as Fodder (Except Grasses) in Yuksam and Dubdi Villages

S. No.	Local Name	Scientific Name	Availability	Preference
1	Billoni	Mae chisia Don.	18	01
2	Nibara	Ficus hookeri Mig	17	14
3	Gugun	Saurauria nepaulensis	16	13
4	Dudilo	Ficus nemorates Wall	15	15
5	Asare		14	02
6	Bad	Banyan	13	16
7	Bajrant	Quercus lamellose	12	03
8	Payale		11	11
9	Tooni	Toona ciliate	10	08
10	Phuto		09	12
11	Kaulo	Machilus edulis	08	09
12	Khanyu	Ficus cunia Ham.	07	10
13	Jhinguni	Eurya acuminate	06	04
14	Pipale	Piper longum	05	07
15	Khosmiri		04	06
16	Chinde	Pentapanax leschennaulti	03	05
17	Dudilora		02	17
18	Titepati	Artemesia vulgaris	01	(Used by goats)

Table 10
Pair-wise Ranking of Species used as Fodder (Except Grasses) in Dzongu

Sl. No.	Local Names	Scientific names	Availability	Preference
1.	Nibara	Ficus hookeri Mig	15	15
2.	Dudilo	Ficus nemorates Wall	14	14
3.	Baral		13	13
4.	Lali	Amoora wallichi	12	12
5.	Bar (banyan)	Terminalia bellirica	2	11
6.	Gagun	Saurauria nepaulensis	1	10
7.	Khanyue	Ficus cunia Ham.	10	9
8.	KaBiosphere Reservea	Ficus infectoria	11	8
9.	Labar	Ficus elastica Roxb	8	7
10.	Chulitaro	Biosphere Reserveassiopsis mitis	5	6
11.	Phalant	Quercus lineate	6	5
12.	Katus	Castanopsis trixhys	7	4
13.	Kutemero	Litsea polyantha	9	3
14.	Jhinguni	Eurya acuminate	3	2
15.	Titepati (Bush)	Artemesia vulgaris	4	1

of the eco-system. Imposition of Biosphere regime in terms of conservation entails certain restrictions on the use of Biosphere resources and it turns into some costs, which people have to bear. In order to know the people's response towards such restriction a Conservation Attitude Survey (CONAT) of approximately 20 % of the households was carried out in the selected fringe settlements of West Sikkim to determine how local communities and stakeholders perceive the situation and express their concerns about environmental conservation. Contingent valuation method (CVM) within the ambit of ecological economics with emphasis on willingness-to accept (WTA) and willingness-to-pay (WTP) approach was adopted for these settlements located crucially with respect to Khangchendzonga Biosphere Reserve. This was done to understand the manner through which the concerned population or the stakeholders express their environmental conservation concerns. The issues, which are important both for the policy makers and stakeholders, were considered for CONAT. The basic premise of the this valuation was that the environmental conservation costs of enforcing Biosphere Reserve principles of restrictions on the use of natural resources shall also be borne by the local populations or the stakeholders within their socio-cultural and economic framework. To interpret the possible underlying issues, the entire responses of the query were further categorized into: conservation driven concern, socio-economic driven concerns, willingness-to-accept (WTA) and willingness-to-pay (WTP) concerns and participatory concerns in the Biosphere Reserve concepts.

Table 11.A
Conservation Attitude Survey

Village name	*Sample size*	*Conservation Concern (%)*	*Socio-economic fuelled concern (%)*	*WTA driven concern(%)*	*Participatory concern(%)*
Yuksam	10	90	80	100	100
Norbugang	06	67	30	85	90
Khongtay	07	85	57	100	100
Tsong	37	76	62	95	100
Mangtabong	30	73	56	90	100
Khecheopalri	07	85	71	100	100
Rambyathang	05	60	20	84	90

Table 11.B
Statistical Derivation

Response Category	*Mean*	*Variance*	*Std. Deviation*
Conservation concern	76.57	116.94	10.81
Socio-economic Concern	53.71	396.27	19.91
WTA Concern	93.43	047.95	06.92
Participatory Concern	96.43	033.67	05.80

Table 12C
Correlation of Responses of Different Categories

(A)	WTA and Participatory Concern	- 0.9090
(B)	WTA and Socio-Economic Concern	- 0.9341
(C)	WTA and Conservation Concern	- 0.9751
(D)	Conservation and Socio-Economic Concern	- 0.9313
(E)	Conservation and participation Concern	- 0.8465
(F)	Socio-Economic and Participatory Concern	- 0.9180

The socio-economic status and the ecological indicators of the settlements covered in this study were ascertained through the survey (Table 11A). The six settlements selected for the study positioned in the buffer zone of Khangchendzonga Biosphere Reserve. CONAT interviews were carried out with random sampling framework in these settlements. For covering a total of approximately 433 households belonging to these settlements, 102 households were actually surveyed. Settlement wise overall positive conservation responses in the categories A, B, C and D were derived (Table 11.B). The average positive ratings obtained ranged from 40 to 100 per cent. The general positive responses were observed to be high except within the category B (Table 11.B) with high standard deviation (19.91) and variance value (396.27). This points to the fact that the "socio-economic driven concern" expressed by the respondents are weaker compared to responses under other categories. The correlations of responses of different CONAT categories were established and compared. The best correlation was observed between WT/WTP and conservation concern (Table 12C).

The results show that the people are aware of the dangers to the eco-system and they are willing to accept as well as pay for the sake of the conservation because they are worried about the adverse impact of the degradation of forest cover on the overall biodiversity. People also felt that the need is to consider the alternative economic avenues. People are happy that at least the growing tourism industry has come as a respite, and more and more villagers are now revolving their economic activities around tourism. These feelings and deductions are procured also in the results of the WTA/WPA and socio-economic survey. The social and economic driven concerns are worth correlating to the data of WTA/WTP, and to findings of the conservation and participatory concerns. Therefore, despite best of conservation attitude initially, socio-economic conditions of the people play a crucial role in shaping and maintaining the conservation attitudes of the community living close to Biosphere Reserve area.

The study has revealed that conflicts of interest did arise particularly when the real pressure of conservation restrictions begin to affect socio-economic conditions of people living in fringe area settlements, in the absence of viable alternatives to their traditional dependence on Khangchendzonga Biosphere Reserve resources.

The key to resolution of all conflicts over biosphere reserve resource use lie in the social, economic and environmental agendas prepared by keeping the people's basic concerns in mind. This perception takes us to the area of the sustainable development. Discussions and observations recorded in the field situations suggest that the policies for Khangchendzonga Biosphere Reserve should give careful attention to the participation of stakeholders as well as their perceptions, in the sphere of recently implemented joint forest management strategy. Such an approach, it seems may ensure that stakeholders do not become antagonists, instigating conflict in Khangchendzonga Biosphere Reserve areas.

People's Participation, Sacred Landscape and Conservation

A participatory approach involving stakeholders is essential for effective management of natural resources and ecosystem conservation in Biosphere Reserve zones. Such an approach must involve recognition and appreciation of the people's traditional knowledge and traditional ecology-preservation strategies in the management of Biosphere Reserve resources. For example, in certain parts of North Sikkim, close to the Biosphere Reserve, local communities have a system known as Zumsha, which is concerned with the social and environmental issues of local significance. The local governance system of Lachen valley is unique. This system is called the Dzumsa system. The literal meaning of this is 'gathering of people'. It is the traditional institution entrusted with task of administering and organising activities within a given territory. The general council of the Dzumsa is composed of household heads. The head of the Zumsha is known as Pipon. This system of self-governance was initially established during the first half of the 19th century in order to provide balanced cohesion to the societies. In the year 1970s, when the Indian Government initiated the reorganisation of the Sikkim's administration and when the necessity arose to introduce the Panchyatiraj system, the Dzumsa was officially recognised as the appropriate system of self-governance in place of Panchyatiraj. This system thus continues to function even today in Lachen and Lachung. The Zumsha system prescribes and regulates activities such as grazing, tree felling and ensures conservation and production of medicinal plants and herbs, by using the traditional ecological knowledge and through imposing penalties for violations. Grazing is permitted only when complete care is taken to retain the regeneration capacity of rangeland. This includes demarcating a particular piece of land for grazing, determination of the number of the cattle allowed to graze, guidelines about the correct season, and suggestions concerning the times when cattle should be allowed inside and outside the Biosphere Reserve zone and other areas of the forests. Granting by the zumsha of the right to fell the trees and collect medicinal plants and herbs, with the recommendation of Pipon, is also based on judicious decisions and using the traditional ecological knowledge, which prompts towards conservation in true spirit.

In the granting the rights to people for collection of appropriate forest produce and specialised medicinal plants, with specified quantity, types of species etcetera the factors of individual family's socio-economic status and needs of the members are taken care of. In doing so the issue of ecological regeneration is also taken into account.

Sikkim is known as 'Demazong', which means, "hidden valley full of treasure, fruits and flowers". It is the land of hydraulic culture where almost every water body, be it small or big, is treated as sacred. In fact the sacredness begins at species level and reaches up to the landscape level with the Mountain Khangchendzonga acting as guardian deity (Fig.3).

The Khangchendzonga Biosphere Reserve people maintain a symbiotic relation between their sacred belief and the surrounding biosphere ecology. This linkage prompts them to venerate and propitiate their deities at both the local level and higher level. The local deities are related with nature and its components. Because of this symbiotic linkage there are festivals and rituals related to the environment and which are observed during the year. In the month of August, 'Panglhabsol' festival is celebrated in Biosphere Reserve zone and Buddhist lamas perform rituals and offer prayers in the name of the Mount Khangchendzonga. The monk and devotees go up to Dzongri 'Dhaplha gang' to offer prayers to Mount Khangchendzonga and other deities for good crop and bumper harvest and to make the whole region free from diseases and natural disasters. There are altogether 109 known large and small lakes in Sikkim regarded as sacred by the people. Besides, the rivers and springs are also regarded as sacred. People dare not pollute these water bodies. In fact the people of Sikkim also apprise the outsiders about the sanctity of these water bodies and the danger of the nature's wrath they might face if they pollute the water bodies. Of these 109 lakes, seven lakes are considered most holy and believed to be encompassing the power to fulfil the wishes of the people. Therefore, they are also called as Wishing Lakes. These seven holy Wishing Lakes are Khecheoparli, Kathok Tso, Bar Cho Marpu, Phu Cho Karpu, Ka Bur La Tso and Dafuk Yum Tso. These lakes are considered as seven offering bowls of the sacred Mount Khangchendzonga. In addition, there are four holy caves in the four directions of Sikkim, viz, Lhari Nying Phu in the North, Dechen Phu in the west, Khandu Sang Phu in the south and Bas Phu in the east direction. These caves are religiously protected and people do not disturb the flora and fauna of these areas.

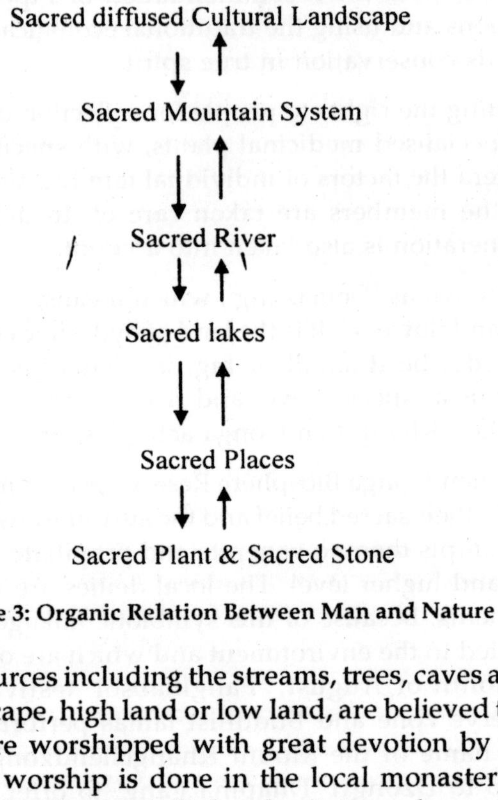

Figure 3: Organic Relation Between Man and Nature

All natural resources including the streams, trees, caves and mountains, indeed every landscape, high land or low land, are believed to be the abode of deities, which are worshipped with great devotion by the people. In some cases special worship is done in the local monastery, often in the morning rituals. This religious belief and religious observances are noted at each meso and micro levels.

Every human habitation and places, which have the footprints of human being, are decorated with 'Wheel of Life', eight lucky signs, Prayer Flags. The religious 'stupas' called Chorten dot the whole of Sikkim. The prayer flags can be seen almost everywhere in Sikkim- on hills, along the water bodies, beneath big trees and on housetops.

The sacred shrines, gompas, monasteries, and temples, big and small, followed by different communities, are located in whole Sikkim. The entire state reverberates with the hymns of Buddhism, which has pervaded the life of the people. The religion is not an external element to the people but it encompasses the ecology, people's worldview and their sacred symbiotic linkage with the mountain and the whole Biosphere Reserve region. Consequently it has led to emergence and articulation of organic relationship between man and the nature (Fig. 3). This relation is apart from the any reductionist approach, which puts emphasis on the importance of parts. It is, on the contrary, it is a holistic relation wherein man interacts with nature with respect and treats it as a sacred living entity.

Conclusion

Embedded in the Himalayas, the Khangchendzonga Biosphere Reserve Zone requires appropriate management in terms of both natural ecology and cultural landscapes. The communities living in and around Biosphere reserve zone do not necessarily damage the environment. However, the increasing population and demands of livelihood sometimes prompted the people to overuse the surrounding regions, rather unintentionally. The people pursue agriculture rather at subsistence level. The practice of livestock rearing to supplement agriculture and generate direct income is quite prevalent among the communities living close to Khangchendzonga Biosphere Reserve. They are highly dependent on forests in the buffer zones, be it for timber or non-timber forest products. This situation indeed calls out for an effective conservation strategy based on provision of alternative livelihood options and additional resources, to reconcile the pressure and dependence in the Biosphere Reserve resources in appropriate manner. The efficient management of the ecological resources is expected to lead to conflict prevention, at various levels. This can be achieved by founding capacity building amongst the local communities. Increasing the awareness and introducing the alternative livelihood options will ensure reducing dependence on biosphere resources that are necessary for the ecology conservation. Nevertheless, the most important initiative to be implemented concurrently for ecosystem protection has to be based on participatory approach wherein community is given responsibility for effective monitoring and exercising judiciously their traditional rights of resource use. The ideal is to preserve overall ecosystem vigour, including species diversity. It can be best accomplished by integrating it into the fabric of social, environmental and economic contexts. Here lies the immense implication of the concept of the sustainable development where the issues of the man and environment are integrated together, for a better future for all the living being.

Acknowledgement

The author is thankful to the Director, Anthropological Survey of India, for making the research work possible for this author in Sikkim, under the national project, wherein the author collected data, at individual level. This is the shorter revised version of the report being submitted to the ASI. The views expressed here are of the author alone. The author is thankful to Dr. N.K.Das, Editor, Journal of Social Anthropology, for offering critical comments and for editorial assistance in improving the paper.

References

Ackerman, E. A. (1963), Where is a Research Frontier? *Ann. Ass. Geogr.* 53, 429-440.

Chapman, G. P. (1970), Perception and Regulation: A Case Study of Farmers in Bihar. *Trans. Inst. Biosphere Reserve. Geog.* 62, 71-94.

Chorley, R. J. (1971), The Role and Relation of Physical Geography. In Progress in Geography. Vol. 3 (Eds C. Board *et al.*). Methun, London.

Haeckel, E. (1866), Generelle Morphologie der Organismen. 2 volumes. Georg. Remer, Berlin.

Hannah, L. and Lohse, D. (1993), Annual Report, Conservation Institutions, Washington D.C.

Krishna, Akhouri Promod *et al.* (2002), Human Dimensions od Conservation in the Khangchendzonga Biosphere Reserve: the Need for Conflict Prevention, Mountain Research and Development.

Mittermeier, R. A. (1988), Primate Diversity and the Tropical Forest: Case Studies from Biosphere Reserveazil and Madagascar, and the Importance of the Megadiversity Countries. In: E.O. Wilson (ed.), Biodiversity. National Academy Press, Washington, D.C.

Park, R. E. and Burgess, E. W. (1921), Introduction to the Science of Sociology. University of Chicago Press, Chicago.

Rai, S. C. and Sundriyal, R. C. (1997), Tourism Development and Biodiversity Conservation: A Case Study from the Sikkim Himalaya. Ambio, 26: 235-242.

Sharma, R. D. (1993), Energy Consumption Survey in the Aravalli Project Area. Survey Project Report No.3, Aravalli Project, Haryana Forest Development, Gurgaon, Haryana, 107pp.

Steward, J. (1936), The Economic and Social Basis of Primitive Bands. In R. H. Lowie (ed.), Essays in Anthropology in Honour of Alfred Louis Kroeber, pp. 31-50. Berkeley: University of California Press.

(1938), Basin-Plateau Aboriginal Sociopolitical Groups (bureau of American Bulletin 120), Smithsonian Institution, Washington, DC.

(1955), Theory of Cultural Change: The Methodology of Multilinear Evolution, University of Illinois Press, Urbana.

Stoddart, D. R. (1965), Geography and Ecological Approach. *Geography*, 50, 242-251.

Sundriyal, R. C. and Sharma, E. (1996), Anthropogenic Pressure on tree Structure and Biomass in the Temperate Forest on Mamlay Watershed in Sikkim. *Forest Ecology and Management*, 81: 113-134.

APPENDICES

Appendix-I

Villages in the Fringe Zone of Kbiosphere Reserve

Revenue Block (West Sikkim)	*Households*	*Population*
Dubdi	69	402
Yuksam	364	1951
Tsozo	89	476
Khacheopalri	114	556
Meli	116	623
Melliaching	109	589
Topung	52	286
Singrangpung	47	227
Nambu	146	859
Kongri	71	442
Labdang	80	456
Dhupidara	76	493
Narkhola	82	510
Mangnam	64	380
	1,479	8,250
Revenue Block (North Sikkim)	*Households*	*Population*
Lachen	1609	2923
Shipgyer	166	695
Tung	52	201
Lachen Forest Block	12	32
Salim Pakel	132	615
Lingthem	210	1161
Lingdem	97	542
Tingbong	164	1001
Lingzah-Tolung	80	397
Sakyong-Pentong	41	196
	2,563	7,763
Total	4,042	16,013

Appendix II
Conat Attitude Survey Questionnaire

Class	*Response Context*	*Questions asked for CONAT assessment*	*Yes*	*No*
A	Conservation related concern	1. BIOSPHERE RESERVE is important for healthy biodiversity.		
		2. Felling of trees and wildlife killing should not be allowed.		
		3. Felling of trees, wildlife hunting & grazing will adversely affect biodiversity.		
		4. BIOSPHERE RESERVE is for benefit of our future generation.		
		5. Although more land is required for agriculture / other livelihood practices, but it is necessary to protect the land inhabited by wildlife.		
		6. BIOSPHERE RESERVE is for outsiders, we have nothing to do with it.		
		7. BIOSPHERE RESERVE is also the abode of Guardian Deity and is essential for a healthy environment.		
B	Socio-Economic related concern	1. BIOSPHERE RESERVE is for outsiders and for those who enjoy nature viewing. We do not enjoy this as we have to face problem from BIOSPHERE RESERVE.		
		2. It is good if local people are allowed to hunt in the BIOSPHERE RESERVE.		
		3. It is good if local people are given free access to BIOSPHERE RESERVE for timber, fuel wood, fodder and other NTFP collection as well as for livestock grazing.		
		4. Since there is dearth of land , it would be good if some land is given with in BIOSPHERE RESERVE.		
C	WTA/WPA related concern	1. Wildlife of the BIOSPHERE RESERVE is causing us trouble, we should be allowed wildlife hunting.		
		2. BIOSPHERE RESERVE is beneficial and we are willing to pay the price in terms of conservation restrictions.		
		3. BIOSPHERE RESERVE conservation may cost us culturally also, but we are willing to accept it,		
D	Participatory concern in the BIOSPHERE RESERVE concept	1. We shall participate in researches related to BIOSPHERE RESERVE conservation		
		2. We shall volunteer for training for capacity building on value addition in NTFP, cultivation of medicinal plants, plantation work, social forestry, nature tourism promotion and conservation edication.		

TRIBES WITHOUT FOREST:
A Critique of Forest and Environmental Conservation Issues

J. J. Roy Burman*

In most parts of tribal India the tribes continue to have a symbiotic relationship with the forests. In more recent years however there are instances when the tribespeople are moving out from traditional habitat and there are many who now aspire to earn money and be part of market economy. However not all tribes depended on forest economy. Many of the nomadic tribes and transhumant populations who barely lived on forests had the tradition of trade. Multiple factors including governmental actions, introduction of new regulations, and slow penetration of industrialization, urbanization and commercialization of forests have depleted the forest resources fast and the tribes have been adversely affected. Many activists and academics are trying to focus the issues of the forest at national level and re-establish the land rights of the tribes. Likewise, many tribes are today demanding their territorial rights (which they lost in the colonial era) over the natural resources and some are even seeking the right to self-determination. In this review it is suggested what remedial actions deserve immediate action and compliance.

In most parts of tribal India the tribes continue to have a symbiotic relationship with the forests. In more recent years however there are instances when the tribespeople are moving out from traditional habitat and there are many who now aspire to earn money and be part of market economy. Not all tribes, however, depended on forest economy. Many of the nomadic tribes and transhumant populations who barely lived on forests had the tradition of trade. Multiple factors including governmental actions, introduction of new laws, and slow penetration of industrialization, urbanization and commercialization of forests have depleted the forest resources fast and the tribes have been adversely affected. Many activists and academics are trying to focus the issues of the forest at national level and re-establish the land rights of the tribes. Likewise, many tribes are today demanding their territorial rights (which they lost in the colonial era) over the natural resources and some are even seeking the right to self-determination.

* Centre for Dalit & Tribal Studies, Tata Institute of Social Sciences, Mumbai

Tribe-Forest Symbiosis

Forest is an inseparable, part of tribal life. Most of the tribal communities live in and around forests. The forests provide them with edible fruits and leaves, fruits and tubers, honey and water etc. The symbiotic relationship existing between the tribal people and the forests is not confined to the economic activities alone, but also transcends to the cultural realms (Ahmed 2004: 148). This symbiotic relation, however, depends upon the balance of their needs and the ecological status of the forests. The mutual dependence ensures sustainable protection by the tribals of all vegetation. The forests serve as the life support systems of the tribals and they take all the preventions against destruction of forest and forest wealth. Consisting of 461 groups, the tribes constitute 8.3 per cent of total population of 83,580.634 as per 2001 Census of India, with a. About 80 per cent of them live in the central belt of the country and the rest in the northeastern region and Andaman and Nicobar regions. The notion of tribe still generates a curiosity and enigma. It has been argued explicitly for long time that tribesmen in India have lived in forests and are the 'Vanyajati'. Ahmed claims that forest cover of 65.8 per cent of larger forest cover of country is in tribal districts. Thus, Ahmed ((2004: 145)) states that tribal socio-economic life is intimately connected naturally with forest ecology. The folklores of the tribes remind them of the benefits by living in harmony with forest and the consequences of any harm done to it. The forests reinforce their close linkage with and peaceful harmony with nature. Geeta Menon (1988: 175) similarly views that there is a close relationship between nature and culture, which in turn ensures a balance between human beings and nature. The tribals used the forests in quite a judicious manner and preserved them as a resource for posterity. They thus had a constructive dependence on forests and other natural resources. KS. Singh too endorses the views about the tribe-forest symbiotic relationship,

> *"Forests are still lifeline of most tribes-their economy, their culture, their belief system.... Tribes had and still have natural rapport with their environment. Even in reclamation of land, a tribal shows sensitivity and tenderness which is uniquely his own. He would not destroy a tender plant. He would not fell a fruit-bearing tree or trees considered sacred; he would not take for a toothbrush a twig from a young and tender sapling but from an old twisted tree. Traditionally tribes have never exploited or over-exploited forest resources and have always made judicious use or have been economical in the use of resources"* (K.S. Singh (2004: 42).

Through their innumerable writings B. K. Roy Burman (1982), L.K Mahapatra (1997) have pursued similar viewpoints. Guha and Gadgil argue that economies of the hunting-gathering tribes including shifting cultivators were stable and based on prudent use of nature. The tribes exploited forests based on limited needs (as needed for small population) and through highly regulated socio-cultural practices. Indeed the scholars have appreciated the ethno-environment management institutions of the tribes like the sacred groves, numerous taboos and other practices that regulated the prudent use of nature.

Tribes without Forest: Tribes and Non-forest Reliance

Although it is a fact that most tribes from ancient times had lived in forests and edified a close linkage with nature, there are other viewpoints, which critique the equilibrium model and speak of extra-forest economy of tribes. There were many tribes who lived out of forests. Mallinowski studied the tribes of Western Pacific who indulged in a network of gift giving, barter and trading relations forming a Kula Ring. Both the Bedouins in West Asia and the Sherdukpens of Arunachal Pradesh (India) dwelt on long distance trade through land routes. The Bedouins are nomadic tribes of West Asia who mainly thrived on rearing sheep, goats and camels and trade. The Sherdukpens barter is based on exchange of items like salt, woolens, clothing, food grains and bell metals. This has considerably shrunken at present after the closure of the international border. The Adis of Siang district indulged in trade within the state and in the border markets of Assam. The main articles of barter were raw hides, chilly and in exchange. They brought down rock salt, woolen clothes, raw wood, Tibetan swords and vessels, iron utensils and brass bangles (Roy 1966). There used to be considerable trading between the Khasi, Jaintia and Garo tribes of Meghalaya with the southern plainsmen (of Bangladesh now) since ancient times. Historical records suggest that the famous silk route from central Asia passed through it. Nongbri (2006: 210-11) points out that Khasis in Cherapunjee used to extract iron Ore to manufacture swords to be traded in markets of Sylhet and Surma valley. The industry later lost out to British artifacts. The Totos of Toto para (bordering with Bhutan) in Jalpaiguri district of West Bengal carried out trade of orange and other artifacts between Bhutan and Doors for centuries. The entire social structure of the tribe surrounds around trade and is supported by social structure based on two moieties. While one carries off the goods towards the plains in the south the other did so to the hills of Bhutan to the north. Then we witness the nomadic Gujjars in the borders of Kashmir and Himachal Pradesh thriving by raising cattle sheep and goats and selling of milk products. Arora and Haldar (1994) have reviewed the situation. They opine that the nomadic communities in India sustain through various occupations. On the basis of their occupation they may be grouped in various categories, viz. hunter and food gatherers, beggars and fortunetellers, traders and hawkers, acrobats, jugglers, conjurers and showmen, labourers, makers and sellers of different articles, and as medicine-men-physicians, often almost as quack specialist.

The nomadic tribes also obtained their livelihood from various non-forest sources by engaging themselves in broker- ship, catching and selling of animals, leatherwork etcetera. There are some instances of reported prostitution too. In India we have pastoral tribes too. The Toda are small tribe of Nilgiri plateau. They practice buffalo rearing in the semi forest zones. There are several studies made on them and they are famous through monographs of anthropology. In spite of several changes the Toda dairies dot their habitat even now. Mann (1986) points out that the Ladakhi tribes mainly pursue agriculture and pastoralism. Many of them also work as daily wage labourers. In the past they were involved in trading with Central Asian countries. Many Ladakhis have now joined the service sector.

Many scholars of late have shifted their interest and are concentrating on the larger forest related issues and the predicament of the tribes today. Scholars accept that forests are no longer to be found in their pristine' form as a lot of it has been destroyed due to industrialization. There are debates about the role of the tribes in the process. Evidently there is now a shift from constructive dependence to destructive dependence. Ghate (2004) indicates that though forestry accounts for substantial part of the tribal economy, it is not enough to meet their needs round the year (particularly for the landless people) and more so as the labour work in the forestry sector is only seasonal.

How the forest dwelling tribes have been compelled to seek fortunes elsewhere in response to industrialization and depletion of forests is discussed by Patnaik (2005: 56). Patnaik writes that the Katkaris in Maharashtra had to give up their traditional occupation of making kalha under the compelling influences of dubious government policies and exploitation by the contractors. Further, they have abandoned the preparation of charcoal due to ban on felling trees. This drove them to eke out their living as agricultural labourer and daily wage labourer. Many of them now work in the brick kilns particularly during the agriculturally lean seasons. Patnaik made an occupational classification of the Katkaris on the basis of a study of eight villages of Raigad district of Maharashtra, covering 233 respondents. Patnaik found that these people were dependent on various occupations in the following order: Brick making 55%, Agricultural labour 99%, Fishing 69%, Daily labour, 99%, Forest gathering, 52% Cultivation 09%. These figures indicate that the dependency on the forest is least. The analysis of data in census of India reports suggests that at the all-India level, a fairly high percentage of tribespeople returned as agricultural labourers. The data are divided in terms of participation of ST workers by industrial categories, Cultivators Agricultural Livestock, Forestry, Labourers, Fishery & Plantations. However the fact remains that an overwhelming majority of the tribes in India are engaged as cultivators. Taken together, 87.19 per cent of the tribes are involved in above-mentioned sectors. The number of tribes depending exclusively on forestry is thus almost negligible.

In fact, the marginalisation process of the tribes is starkly evident with the rapid increase in the labour sector. Archana Prasad (2003) argues that the romantic image of tribes so depicted by the anti-modern critique implied a cultural ecology, which emphasized that cultural practices have corresponded to ecological roles. Sumit Guha (1999) too is opposed to the romantic views about tribal-forest interface. He argues that being 'far from civilization' does not amount to being close to nature. Guha avers that tribes were frontier people and they did not sustain merely on the forests, "Interaction should be seen as an adaptation and a consciously chosen strategy, to draw in resources of the open country through exchange as well as sustainable robbery" (Tribute/customs). For the Bhils of southern Rajasthan, the modes they adopted were a vital resource. During difficult times they appear to be the main resource raising wealth. Ironically, in the Khandesh area of Maharashtra, the Bhils were employed as watchmen. The District Gazetteer of Dhule district (1974) states, "The Bhils who were among the chief hill tribes and who had before lived with other inhabitants commanded the mountain passes where their power was considerable. They had worked as village watchmen and had been the great instruments of policing the area. They retired to the hills. The whole range of hill was subject to the command of their chieftains who had not only the aboriginal hill race at their command but generally a few Arab and Hindustani soldiers whom they retained to assist in enforcing contributions from merchants and travelers. Skaria indicates that the Bhils extracted kind of a tribute (From the plainsmen) - 'Haks', especially ' Giras Haks', which meant a mouthful or share, and symbolized the right to receive the due from a village. The Mahadeo Koli tribes in Maharashtra occupied the strategic locations between the Deccan and the coastal ports of Konkan upto Surat. They are known to have regularly extracted quit money from the international traders and raided the marching troops for a sum. In the border areas of Assam and Arunachal Pradesh, some tribes used to descend on the Miri settlements during the winter. They stayed in the Miri houses and forced tributes and retired to the hills with the booty. The plains people of Assam bordering with Arunachal Pradesh also paid posa to the hill tribes. However, this portion of historical account pertaining to some tribes is only one of the facets of the tribal political economy. We obviously cannot generalize the practices of the tribes of India from this perspective.

There is no doubt that large number of tribes depended on forest resources and maintained symbiotic relationship. There are also evidences from some many parts of India suggesting that tribes left their pre-agricultural activities and adopted the sedentary agricultural economy. Historical evidences reveal that in the pre-Maratha days the Gonds of Garh Mandla were dependent on plough cultivation rather than shifting cultivation. Their association with forests was thus very insignificant as they visited forests only during famine or when they needed to procure some produce. The later marginalisation of the Gonds and their venture into forest areas was the result of a two-stage process. The first was the processes of colonization of fertile agricultural lands by the caste-Hindus who were brought into the tracts by Maratha rulers. Secondly, the permanent settlement of agricultural and zamindari lands by the British ensured that the movements of tribals between the highlands and plains were stopped forever. This led the tribal people in remote forests and highlands. Prasad (2003: 3-9) cites the case of Agaria tribes who in spite of residing close to the forests, indulged in making and repairing of ploughs and sickles for their Baiga neighbours. They were also forced to work on the trade routes to fulfill their needs when they were repairing axes. Through the presence of Agarias we see the incorporation of the Baigas into a wider agrarian economy. In times of famine, the Agarias played an important part in sustaining the Baiga economy. They sold their food, oil and salt and thus provided essential everyday goods to the Baigas. Indeed there are many perspectives in tribe-forest interface. Prasad (2003: 3-9) in fact disputes the 'original' and 'well adjusted' image of tribes as forest dwellers.

J. J. Roy Burman (2003) following Kosambi's estimation revealed that there were many sacred groves distributed along several ancient trade routes leading from the Deccan Ghats to the Konkan ports in Maharashtra. Significantly, the reigning deity in many of these grove-temples was Pauna Devi - the deity of 'fulfillment of desires'. The majority of the guests in ancient days were invariably the traders - selling wares in the international markets through the ports. But they were also weary about the Ramoshis, -the 'criminal tribes' notorious for their depredations. The local villagers often hired them as guardsmen. They enjoyed a symbiotic relationship with the local people. The local villagers gained from the Pauna Devi groves where the traders rested, and who prayed for safe journey and successful trade and offered alms. The groves became source of cash income in areas that lacked centralized authority to regulate trade. Quite like the Pauna Devi groves, in Rajasthan too there existed small border level sacred groves along the roadways. The travelers and traders threw small pebbles along with some money at the groves while entering into the village territory. These groves are locally known as 'Kankarvani'. These groves, however, do not seem to have any direct bearing on forest management or environment. Even otherwise, the sacred groves have come under intense pressure due to increased theocracy and materialistic religions. In Konkans several sacred groves were felled and large temples were built, when the government, took over the lands in 1960s. In order to retain de facto control over the lands the local villagers built Temples.

Tribes and Deforestation

According to many scholars, tribal habitats are no longer in their pristine form as wanton depletion of forests has been witnessed in these areas in the last few decades. One scholar terms this as change from constructive dependence on forests to destructive dependence on forest. Bhandari and Channa (1992) too state that tribal-forest linkages have been shattered in the present time. Prabhu (1986) is of the opinion that the Imperial government allowed the tribals to live in forests as they provided cheap labour by which forests could be cut, the timber transported and readied for timber trading. The tribals thus formed an appendage to the colonial interests. The colonial interests in extracting natural resources located in tribal areas totally altered the political-economic equations. The forest buffers (where the majority tribesmen dwelt) between kingdoms too became dysfunctional with the formation of a unified political entity - the Indian nation-state, colonial and post-colonial. The need to maintain forest buffer in Burma that segregated the British and the French troops (which was based in a few South-East Asian countries) also became obsolete. The introduction of railways and roadways in the tribal areas seriously affected the trade routes.

In modern times, we witness all over India wanton depletion of forests. In most areas such as northeast India, where community control over resources was very strong, wanton depletion of forests has been witnessed in the recent years due to modernization and commercialization (Mitra 2002). The incentives provided by the State to individual- landowners have also failed in clearing of the forests (Mitra 2002: 265). Rapid deforestation is now a common phenomenon in the entire Northeast where the tribals are majority in most of the states. Without any industry worth the name, timber provides the best means of earning cash in the region. No wonder, the Supreme Court had passed strong strictures against transportation of wood within the North-East in December 1996, but the reality is different from the ideal.

Sarah Jewitt (1998) has discussed engagement of the contractors in entangling the tribes in forest destruction. This prompts tribespeople to go for 'illicit' felling of trees. Indira Munshi (1995) too indicts the Forest Department and contractors for rapid depletion of the forests in Thane district of Maharashtra. The pull from adjoining Mumbai city and commercialisation too has compelled the tribals to legally and illegally exploit the forests. The 'Development' projects in the tribal areas too had a deleterious effect on the forests and other natural resources. Scholars inform that many of the tribals displaced due to development projects like Hirakud dam and other minor medium irrigation projects have taken resort to large-scale felling of trees and selling them in the markets. One scholar states that about two lakh acres of forest lands have been released to the Dandakaranya Development Authority after deforestation in Umerkote and Malkangiri zones for resettlement purposes. Mohapatro (1997: 76) indicates that public projects alone in Koraput district have led to the destruction of forests to the tune of 98,427.85 hectares during the last four decades. Behera (2000:305) states those conditions of modernity, a higher rate of demographic growth and increased consumption goals of the people have made the traditional methods of foraging and horticulture uneconomic option even for the people engaged in them. Rath (2006:21) informs that the Juang Development Agency totally pushed out the Juangs in Orissa from their forest habitats after they were banned from pursuing shifting cultivation and virtually turned them into landless labourers. The commercial forestry that was introduced did no good to anybody. Prasad (2005: 16) indicts colonialism, capitalism and commercialization of natural resources in the tribal areas for the destruction of forests. 'Encroachment' (so-called) over forest- lands (Lands under the control of Forest Department) adjoining human settlements is a common phenomenon in India. Many poor tribals who find it difficult to earn their livelihood often intrude into the forest to eke out their living. This has also resulted in large-scale deforestation. Amita Baviskar (1998: 256) acknowledges this issue and notes more than 1000 encroachers in some areas of Madhya Pradesh. It is revealed that each household developed husbandry and long distance trade. Apart from these, for many of the tribes seasonal migration and wage earning is a common phenomenon. The Santals of Purulia and Bankura districts of West Bengal for long have been found to go southwards -to Burdwan,

Hooghly and Howrah districts to harvest the Boro paddy in winter. In Gujarat, Madhya Pradesh and Maharashtra the tribes are found to migrate for very long durations for harvesting sugarcane and cotton. Many of them have also been engulfed by the industrial sector mainly as unskilled labourers. The Warli and Konkna tribes near Mumbai work in the brick kilns in the agriculturally lean seasons. These certainly keep them away from the forest milieu for most parts of the year. Ultimately it may be stated that the tribes have often been found selectively to abuse the forest wealth both in the past and present.

Discussion

From the above descriptions, we get a glimpse of the tribe-forest interface and diverse scholarly viewpoints pertaining to non-forest occupations and engagements of the tribes of India. The general picture that emerges is approximately like this:

(1) Tribes, in many parts, have been living in harmonious relationship with the forests and pursue a healthy environment management, with concern for conservation;

(2) Tribes are in a way responsible for forest destructions;

(3) Tribes appear in the different historical crossing points, existing variously, and whereby they were exploited by outsiders,

(4) Tribes depended on forests variously in various historical times, and developed diverse economies;

(5) Today there exist a number of tribes in the fringes who do not depend upon forests directly and many of them earn cash through labour, indeed presently due to development projects and deforestation many tribes have turned into labour force.

(6) New writings suggest that under modern scenario, as the man-land ratio has changed, tribes may not be in same position to pursue conservation of the environment.

Here we need to emphasize that the onus of environment management cannot be put exclusively on the shoulders of the tribespeople, indeed once they did live in perfect harmony with the nature. Scholars (Baviskar and others) thus opine that "Portraying tribal communities as natural repositories of ecological wisdom may be politically correct, but it does a disservice to tribal people who are struggling to secure social justice through control over the natural resource base upon which they depend. The imagery of 'ecological stewardship' can be a powerful, confidence - giving cultural statement and an important input into forging a tribal identity. But this is a political exercise of symbols and should not be deployed to obscure present day contradictions in tribal life. While tribal access to and control over natural resources are crucial conditions for biodiversity conservation, they are not enough. As long as the larger contexts compel greater extraction and commercialization of' resources and the Adivasis remain vulnerable politically and economically, the pressure to destroy for short-term gain will prevail. In addition, it is crucial to recover or establish anew the value of conservation as an explicit ideology and not as something which occurs 'naturally' or which can be taken for granted" (Baviskar 1994: 267-268). Baviskar apparently supports the environment management role of the tribes. In fact, her position is amply clear as she categorically criticizes the present form of tribal development as a moribund affair, benefiting only the bureaucrats. She thus rightly suggested integrating tribal development programmes with environmental conservation, so that the tribes could have a chance to create sustainable (Baviskar 1994, 1998). Many academicians, such as Ghate (1992) have observed that a healthy progress can be achieved if the forestry development and tribal development are interlinked - they will reinforce each other. Ahmed ((2004: 148) states that if tribal economic development is to be a reality, then the forests have to be rejuvenated. The future of the tribal people is linked to restoring the degraded forestlands with appropriate technology and with participation of the tribals themselves. The restoration of the degraded forestland ensures sustained employment round the year and improve environment. The fact remains however that the 1988 Forest policy speaks of involving the local tribals in forestry activities as labourers instead of conferring territorial rights. It may argue that these suggested remedies, if not implemented properly, might turn out to be contradictory too.

There exist several over-passionate writings on tribe-forest issue. The fact remains that in many parts the tribes are faced with unanticipated intricacy, as in most of the tribal pockets forests have virtually vanished and besides in many of the traditional tribal areas they have (the tribes) turned to be hopeless minorities. B.K. Roy Burman has pointed out that of 236 districts in the nine states where the Fifth schedule of the Constitution has been in operation only 17 districts are fully covered by the Fifth Schedule. Another 52 districts are partly covered. Yet another problem is that in many forest-based tribal areas, affluent industrialists (Including multinationals) have taken up captive plantations in the tribal areas in the last decade (Sharma 1997: 56). Even the Left Front government in Tripura has taken up rubber plantations with international support in order to wean away the tribals from shifting cultivation. Who would reap the lion's share of the income is a foregone conclusion (Prasad 2005). Obviously the tribes-forest issue is quite complicated.

In the recent days, an influential body of policy makers is trying to evolve a national policy, which acknowledges the full right of the tribes over the forests. Discussions with some tribal leaders, however, brought to light the depressing fact that they are by and large opposed to the Tribes Forest BiII- 2005. They are against linking up encroachment issue with the tribal policy. To them, the tribal rights are much more important and the issue of right to self-determination and settlement of other political rights have to be given precedence. A few years ago at a seminar organized by WWF in Bhopal, a tribal group from Gujarat clearly stated that mining activities in a sanctuary couldn't be stalled in the name of saving 'Chincara' - impalas. They seriously pleaded that their right to self- determination is to be respected. They resented the benevolent dictatorial role of the urban elites and they demanded that the local tribes be permitted to carry out their mining activities as before. The tribal leaders from the North-East too have expressed their anguish over the Bill and have demanded settlement of the political issues at first (Right to self-determination being one of the foremost). According to some senior anthropologists and the present author more than land right or forest right, it is much more urgent to address the issue of territorial rights -of the tribes lost to the British. This would include not only the land and forest rights, but also, rights over natural resources, cultural rights and the right to self-determination (political right) - leading towards a political destiny of the tribes. Colchester (1994: 56) indicates that the ground for ensuring territorial rights of the indigenous peoples has gained momentum so as to ensure the customary rights over the use and exploitation of natural resources, which have become subject to hegemonic control exploitation. The importance of this is embodied in the status of stakeholders. Tribespeople indeed seek justice in terms not only of the legal provisions but also in terms of their participation relating to policies intended to allow people to participate in decisions made by the administration. There may not emerge sensible solution by mixing up tribal interests exclusively with the issues of forests and environment and vice versa, as is widely believed. This calls for serious policy attentiveness.

References

Ahmed, M. S. (2004), *Five Decades* of Planning and *Tribal Development*. Gyan Publishing House, New Delhi.

Arora, S. and A. K. Haldar (1994), Economy of the Nomadic Tribes. *Man in India* 74 (2): 181-191.

Baviskar, A. (1994), Fate of the Forest: Conservation & Tribal Rights. *Economic and Political Weekly* 17 September.

Baviskar, A. (1998), Tribal Communities and Conservation in India. In *Communities* and *Conservation: Natural Resource Management* in South and *Central Asia;* ed. by A Kothari *et al.* Sage. New Delhi.

Behera, S. (2000), Forest, Tribes and Resources. In Man in *the Forests.* Ed. by K. Seeland & F. Schmithllsen. D.K. Printworld. New Delhi.

Bhandari. J. S. & S. M. Channa (1992), Forests and Tribes: A Macro Level Perspective. *Mainstream.* September 26.

Singh, K. S. (2004), Rethinking Forest, Forest-dwellers and Ecological History. In *Tribes, Forest and Social Formation in Indian History* B. B. Chaudhri & A Bandopadhayay Eds. Manohar: New Delhi.

Colchester, M. (1994), Slave and Enclave: The Political Ecology of Equatorial Africa. Penang: World Rainforest.

Ghate, R. (2004), *Uncommons* in *the Commons:Community Initiated Forest Resource Management.* Concept: New Delhi.

Jewitt. S. (1998), Autonomous and Joint Forest Management in India's Jharkhand: Lessons for the Future? In *The Social Construction of Indian* Forests. ed. by R Jefferry. Manohar. New Delhi.

Mahapatra, L. K. (1997), Parameters of Forest Policy for Tribal Development. In P. M. Mahapatra & P. C. Mohapatro eds. Concept. New Delhi.

Mann, R. S. (1986), *The Ladakhi* Anthropological Survey of India. Calcutta.

Menon, G. (1988), Tribal Dependence on Forest Produce in India. In *Antiquity to Modernity in Tribal India* Inter-India, New Delhi.

Mitra, A. (2002), An Evaluation of Forestry Planning in Arunachal Pradesh.In *Forest Resource* in *North-East India.* ed. by B. Datta Ray & K. Alam.Omsons. New Delhi.

Munshi. I. (1995), Where Have the Forests Gone? An Exploration' into Thane District. In *Contradictions* in *Indian Society,* ed. by M. Savur and I. Munshi. Rawat. Jaipur.

Nongbri, T. (2006), Culture and Biodiversity: Myths, Legends and the Conservation of Nature in the Hills of North East India. In *Ordeals and Voices of Indigenous Tribal People of India;* ed. by J. Brara. Indian Confederation of Indigenous Peoples of India. Guwahati Branch. Guwahati.

Prabhu. P. (1986), Social Forestry: An Adivasi viewpoint. In *Towards a New Forest Policy,* ed. by Walter Fernandes and S. Kulkarni. Indian Social Institute. New Delhi.

Prasad, A. (2003), *Against Ecological Romanticism: Verrier Elwin and the Making of Anti-Modern Tribal Identity.* Three Essays Collective Publishers, New Delhi.

Prasad. A. (2005), *Environmentalism 'and the Left: Contemporary Debates and Future Agendas* in *Tribal Areas.* Left Word Books. New Delhi.

Rath, G. C. Ed. (2006), *Tribal Development* in *India.* Sage, New Delhi.

Roy, S. (1966), Aspects *of Pad am Minyong CuUure*. NEFA government. Shillong.

Roy Burman, B. K. (1982), *Tribes and Forest Commission Report*. Planning Commission. New Delhi.

Roy Burman, J. J. (2003), *Sacred Graves among Communities. Mittal* Publication. New Delhi.

Sharma, B. D. (1997), *The New Economic Policy and the Tribal People*. Paper presented In ICTP 3rd General Assembly Meet.

Shroff. J. (1997), Forest Development and Tribal Development. In Mohapatra, PM, Mohapatro, PC, (Eds) (1997): Forest Management in Tribal Areas: Forest Policy and Peoples' Participation. New Delhi: Concept Publishing Company.

Mohapatra, P. M., Mohapatro, P. C., (Eds) (1997), Forest Management in Tribal Areas: Forest Policy and Peoples' Participation. New Delhi: Concept Publishing Company.

INDIGENOUS KNOWLEDGE, POSTCOLONIALISM, AND INDIGENOUS EDUCATION POLITICS IN AFRICAN PERSPECTIVE

Ladislaus M. Semali*

The global proliferation of Intellectual Property Rights (IPRs) through the World Trade Organization's Trade Related Aspects of Intellectual Property Rights (TRIPS) Agreement, poses a grave threat for indigenous knowledge systems. There have been increasing amount of "piracy" of indigenous knowledge, whereby corporations and scientists from rich countries are claiming proprietary rights over knowledge that had belonged to cultures and people. Social and political structural problems emanating from the neglect of local communities and the devaluing of their knowledge are not in any way limited to the Africa region, but widespread, and found in a variety of situations within which poverty is rampant. The overarching aim of this paper is to discuss colonialism in its newest forms masked by educational goals that ignore years of research supporting the use of local languages, local epistemologies, and local ways of knowing. Author discusses how in new writings the meaning of indigeneity is emerging. New writings have introduced the critical ethnography, critical theory, historical materialism, Afrocentric frameworks of national development, African cultural epistemological constructs, and ecological feminist critique/analysis to critically examine contemporary meanings of development, relationships between indigenous and non-indigenous researchers, and the circumstances of the construction of ethnic and philosophical positions. Efforts of the Penn State's Interinstitutional Consortium for Indigenous Knowledge (ICIK) is crucial in this respect as it has coordinated several projects in Tanzania, Kenya and Namibia to meaningfully engage communities and transform the academy's strategy for development. This paper documents examples from East Africa to illustrate the dilemmas and contradictions that face communities in this region and their governments in the efforts to overcome poverty and implement the UN Millennium Development goals. Research on 'Politics of Knowledge' in recent years has yielded unrelenting efforts among scholars to study areas much neglected in the past. The challenges that face African governments in mitigating the barriers of development in many countries of Africa are perverse and they extend from education, ecology, social structure, poverty, and endemic tensions between customary law issues and traditional beliefs and practices.

* Pennsylvania State University, USA

Introduction

Rapid demographic and global technological transformations present universities, faculty members and students with enormous challenges for undertaking research and outreach enterprises that adequately respond to the needs and priorities of indigenous communities (Hrabowski III & Weidemann, 2004). Eager to assist with adult basic education (ABE) and establish a long-term working relationship with rural counterparts in Kenya, Tanzania and Uganda, Penn State University (PSU) faculty members are committed and constantly searching to finding appropriate methodologies to address local needs and priorities to achieve the United Nations Millennium Development Goals (MDGs), the internationally agreed-upon goals to reduce poverty, disease, hunger, gender inequality, and environmental degradation by the year 2015 (United Nations, 2005).

This paper documents examples from East Africa to illustrate the dilemmas and contradictions that face communities in this region and their governments in the efforts to overcome poverty and implement the UN Millennium Development goals. Goal four of the MDGs targets 2015 as the year that nations will achieve a 50 per cent improvement in levels of adult literacy by 2015, especially for women, and equitable access to basic and continuing education for all adults. This UN goal coincides with the World Bank's increased focus on helping African countries accelerate their progress towards "Education for All (UNESCO, 2004)." In fact, two goals of the Education for All (EFA) aim at Adult Basic Education – (a) to increase adult literacy by 50 per cent and (2) promote learning and life skills for young people and adults.

Most of the adult basic education (ABE) programs that target adults and out-of-school youth, have literacy and numeracy as a core, and include other elements defined by demand and the African context. Beyond equity, the overall objective of the World Bank's assistance strategy is poverty reduction, and literacy and basic education – key skills to help the poor extract themselves from the poverty trap and the conditions causing poverty. More than any other form of education, ABE is self-targeted on the poor. ABE programs also succeed better than most other forms of education in reaching women, which is assumed to be a pre-requisite to achieving the development goals of enhancing agricultural productivity, improving the health and nutrition status of the family, and reducing fertility (World Bank, 1989).

One of the challenges of conducting research in unfamiliar rural environments is avoiding the pitfalls of interpreting indigenous people's cultures and languages through the researcher's cultural and disciplinary lenses and values, resulting in inaccurate representations of cultures and misapplication of solutions to endemic problems (Semali, 2007). In the past three years, the Penn State's Interinstitutional Consortium for Indigenous Knowledge (ICIK) has coordinated several projects in Tanzania, Kenya and Namibia to engage communities and transform the academy's strategy for development. For example, in 2007 nine university faculty members took part in an ICIK organized workshop conducted in collaboration with Tumaini University in Arusha, Tanzania. In 2008, two groups of Penn State faculty conducted collaborative projects in Tanzania that were initiated during the 2007 workshop. In 2009, an ICIK Workshop was held in Nyeri, Kenya to highlight the work of Penn State students and faculty engaged with communities and involved with the Children and Youth Empowerment Center in Nyeri, Kenya. Students and faculty working with Khanjan Mehta, an Engineering Design faculty member, have been piloting *Mashavu*, a networked health care system aimed at poor communities and prototyping *Wishvast*, a cell phone-based social networking system that targets youth and adults.

These projects illustrate the situatedness of local development and the complexity of postcolonial legacies. As students, faculty and local Non-governmental organizations (NGOs) engage these projects, there is a constant tension between academic and non-academic approaches to development and well-being. Through ICIK, faculty, staff, and students find opportunities to network with others who share a vision of the academy as a place where multiple ways of knowing are valued and respected. Three questions have dominated the transformation agenda: (a) how do communities negotiate and connect various knowledge systems in order to address local/global concerns? (b) What can the global community and academic institutions learn from indigenous knowledge innovations? (c) How do we integrate and internalize a local knowledge orientation within academic institutions? Together, these three concerns hone in the politics of knowing, knowledge production and validation that educators have intensely debated since the UN conference on Environment and Development (Rio De Jeneiro, 1992)[1]. Institutionalization of knowledge production, validation, and distribution in universities and research laboratories characterizes the academy. This academic way of knowing contrasts with non-academic indigenous knowledge that resides in a particular locality. Indigenous knowledge is derived from many years of experience, and is usually communicated orally through family members' social networks and across generations.

Research on the politics of knowing in recent years has yielded unrelenting efforts among scholars to study areas much neglected in the past. As current economic global forces take a toll on the most vulnerable people of the African populations, academicians and researchers are pushed to find new practical solutions that are innovative, entrepreneurial, and sustainable in addressing such endemic problems. The challenges that face African governments in mitigating the barriers of development in many countries of Africa are perverse and they extend from education, ecology, social structure, poverty, and endemic tensions between customary law issues and traditional beliefs and practices.

Over the past decade, however, besides the World Bank efforts, there has been a growing interest among social scientists, activists and NGOs in understanding ecological knowledge, the environment (also referred to as wealth of nature), and global knowledges, and how these concepts interface with indigenous education at the local level. Significant spaces have been opened up within the academy and within some disciplines to talk more critically about research with particular groups and communities – women, the economically oppressed, ethnic minorities and indigenous peoples. In the attempt to rethink indigenous education in the context of ABE, for example, education anthropologists, sociologists of education, and curriculum theorists have openly challenged the research community about issues such as racist practices and attitudes, ethnocentric assumptions and exploitative research, sounding warning bells that research can no longer be conducted with indigenous communities as if their views did not count or their lives did not matter (Smith, 1999; World Bank, 2004).

In present times, even though many of us live in high-tech surroundings and make use of the most up-to-date information and communication techniques, little or no recognition is given to the well-being of people that is very much connected with the "wealth of nature." Nature's wealth continues to be inspiring of research, economic activities and political action, but it also leads to conflict and even war. Nature's wealth is a place-based ecological resource that encompasses both the tangible and intangible assets of a community including the wealth of knowledge resident there. Valuing nature's wealth is necessary for any adult basic education (ABE) to sustainably take place in the African context.

Another area of scholarship that has not impacted heath and social development programs in Africa in significant ways is locality studies.[2] This area of studies has opened up important new avenues of research but also provoked as yet measured questions (Cox, 1998; Wilkinson, 1970; Halfacree, 1993). One of these concerns is precisely the specificity of locality as distinct from its generic formation by larger social forces. Local social structures, the territorialization of politics and the appeal of community are important elements in seeking to pin down the nature of the tension between indigenous education, adult basic education and local specificity (Cox, 1998).

Locality studies are critical in the African context because the continent presents quite serious concrete problems: in particular, the problem of local economies undergoing contraction and debates as to how they might be revived – biodiversity vs. genetically modified varieties; extraction of bio-medicinal properties from native lands and patenting; changing pastoral lands to agricultural lands (e.g., case of the Maasai of Kenya); ecological conservation, parks and people, (e.g., the case of Ngorongoro Crater (Tanzania), Mozambique, and Namibia); welfare of local communities and small scale mining (e.g., in Tanzania, Ghana, etc); small scale vs. large scale commercial farming; and land re-distribution (to redress past injustices , e.g., the case of Zimbabwe).

Clearly, in locality studies, these cases expose a bias towards political economy that makes the politics of restructuring an important object of interest. In Africa, politics evidently has quite strong territorial aspects and effects on adult basic education, indigenous education, survival, subsistence and relationship to the current forces of globalization and the lingering legacies of postcolonialism. Locality studies provide important intervention that serves to engender awareness that raises once more the questions of the geographical specificity of social life. Locality is said to have effects specific to it; most of which are not reducible to the generic categories of class, gender, and ethnicity, to examine poverty.

It is important to note however, that social and political structural problems emanating from the neglect of local communities and the devaluing of their knowledge are not in any way limited to the Africa region, but widespread, and found in a variety of situations within which poverty is rampant. For example, the global proliferation of intellectual property rights (IPRs), most recently through the World Trade Organization's Trade Related Aspects of Intellectual Property Rights (TRIPS) Agreement, poses a grave threat for indigenous knowledge systems. There are reports of an increasing amount of "piracy" of indigenous knowledge, whereby corporations and scientists from rich countries are claiming proprietary rights over knowledge that has belonged to cultures and people for hundreds of years. From the *hoodia cactus* and the Mexican *yellow bean*, to the use of *neem* and *turmeric* in India, IPRs have been inappropriately utilized to promote growth for the rich while hindering development and perpetuating poverty within many indigenous knowledge-holding communities (Srikantaiah, 2008). The separation of humans from culture, culture from ecology, and ecology from economics has caused severe ecological exploitation and subsequent degradation and tightened the poverty trap.

Despite the many positive impacts of adult basic education, and the hope it inspires to alleviate poverty, support for ABE programs (including support from the World Bank) has been relatively modest over the last two decades. The reasons for this are the concerns about the content and relevance of many past programs and the degree to which the participants retained their newly won literacy skills (Semali, 1995). There were also questions about the cost-effectiveness of such programs when local knowledge is ignored or devalued.

Postcolonialism, Globalization, and the Subjugation of Indigenous Knowing in ABE

The overarching aim of this paper is to discuss colonialism in its newest forms masked by educational goals that ignore years of research supporting the use of local languages, local epistemologies, and local ways of knowing. The thesis of this article is simple: To bring about social and educational changes in ABE among indigenous communities, we must recognize that indigenous peoples have knowledge systems of theorizing and conceptualizing their social and natural worlds.

The suggestion, that indigenous languages are valid vehicles of teaching in ABE and also as the dominant dialogue is madly contested. Indigenous African language education and knowledge have generally been understood and reckoned as a simplistic process of socialization involving the preparation of children for work in the home, the village and within a select ethnic domain. Thus, most contemporary discussions on indigenous African education rest in the shadow of Western globalization ideas about structural adjustment, development, etc.; and congruently it is projected as a stagnant, limited, and inoperative paradigm which pushes some people to conclude that any serious discussion about the indigenous transmission of values and its accumulated knowledge in Africa is a waste of time (Itabari 2006).

In this paper postcolonial theory refers to the critical inquiry that investigates, rediscovers, and reclaims subjugated knowledge systems, cultures, and traditions. In such inquiry, indigenous knowledge becomes a way to recover from the artificial split between mind and body brought on by the theorizing of the Western European Enlightenment and a challenge to the ways in which Western knowledge have become hegemonic and globalized (Dei, 2000). In this debate, many indigenous intellectuals actively resist participating in any discussion within the discourses of postcoloniality. This is understandable because postcolonialism is viewed as the convenient invention of Western intellectuals that reinscribes their power to define the world. Most notably perhaps, postcolonial criticism has helped to undermine the traditional conception of disciplinary boundaries (Memmi, 1965, p. 2, 79). Postcolonial criticism was first used in the early 1970s in political theory to describe the predicament of nations that had thrown off the yoke of European Empires after World War II. Later in the 1980s, the term was being used to describe "all cultures" affected by the (European) imperial process from the moment of colonization to the present day. Colonial discourse analysis" now operates across an ever-broader range of fields, including the history of law, anthropology, political economy, philosophy, historiography, and psychoanalysis, including the sociology of knowledge.

Revival of Indigenous Education

The dilemmas and contradictions found in the revival of indigenous education are borne out of a social movement of indigenous peoples at both national and international levels. The movement developed simultaneously out of the survival strategies and cultural systems that nurtured people, their values, and their beliefs within their own communities and nations for over 500 years. This movement is often referred to as cultural revitalization but that term has been criticized because it tends to imply that cultures need rescuing. This is an important element but it is not the only one. In Africa, for example, the movement has been explained as one of Africanization or African renaissance (Ssekamwa, 1997). By and large, the movement is borne out of the frustrations of colonization, urbanization, traditional revivalism, or out of the grassroots cultural dynamics.

A critical examination of the competing readings of the world found in academic texts about indigenous peoples, and the theories supporting the examination of the power dynamics that underlie the politics of knowing, and notions of equity and justice, can be seen as part of this renaissance which has spurred research privileging indigenous concerns that are framed beyond the decolonization aspirations of a particular indigenous community. In the context of this paper, rethinking indigenous education means that scholars and curriculum theorists must ask hard questions beyond the decolonization project—questions about intelligence, discipline-related subject matter, or about cultural factors that contribute to academic achievement and transition to work. Using a postcolonial theoretical lens, this essay explores the notion of indigeneity as applied to the politics of knowing and schooling. The analysis focuses on the disciplinary and ideological problems inherent in the decolonization of indigenous education and the overall ABE project.

In the sense used here, indigeneity is a construct that points to the notion of specific locality that identifies peoples with their environment. Such identity gives adults and youth in ABE programs a consciousness or awareness to perceive themselves and their local-level understandings of how things are and done, including perceptions of problems and strategies to solve them. Adult and young people's consciousness of indigeneity also includes a sense of pride in owning their past, culture and traditions. A sense of pride motivates local peoples and their children to be able to critically use knowledges about their histories, cultures, and traditions as a basis for contributing to global knowledge systems about their social development, welfare and survival. In short, the movement of indigenous peoples aims at survival of indigenous peoples everywhere—survival from the effects of a sustained war with colonizers, from the devastation of diseases, from the dislocation from lands and territories, from the oppression of living under unjust regimes, or the survival at sheer basic physical level as peoples with their own distinctive languages and cultures.

ABE (Adult Basic Education) Curriculum Issues

As I have defined it elsewhere, a curriculum immersed in indigenous pedagogies involves epistemological questions relating to both the production and consumption of knowledge, the relationship between culture and what is defined as successful learning, the contestation of all forms of knowledge production and the purposes of ABE itself (Semali, 2007). More recent attempts to decolonize curriculum and the research methodologies employed to study indigenous and rural peoples have energized scholars to make advances in understanding culturalism, postcolonialism, and the politics of knowing, including contexts around issues of race, gender, class, sexual orientation and so forth. Publications by Linda Tuhiwai Smith (1999), *Decolonizing Methodologies: Research and Indigenous Peoples,* and by George Dei (2000), *Indigenous Knowledges in Global Contexts* collectively shed new light on indigeneity. They introduce critical ethnography, critical theory, historical materialism, Afrocentric frameworks of national development, African cultural epistemological constructs, and ecological feminist critique/analysis to critically examine contemporary meanings of development, relationships between indigenous and non-indigenous researchers, and the circumstances of the construction of ethnic and philosophical positions.

It is important to note that in our work in Kenya, Tanzania and Namibia, we engage adults and the youth in ABE to offer a new approach, which is informed by transformative learning theory and cross-cultural engagement. This approach aims to create a unique learning environment with local leaders as the principal teachers. We believe that this approach can go a long way to engage communities in meaningful and sustainable ways when participatory research and collaboration with traditional African cultural groups is used to address issues of intellectual property, rights of indigenous groups, respect for cultural traditions, religious beliefs and knowledge systems of groups whose "ways of knowing" are not exclusively based upon the Western model of theory-based experimental research design.

In contrast, the World Bank, for example, describes basic education as a "supplement," not a "rival" to the formal system. Playing a supplementary role, basic education is thus "intended to provide a functional, flexible and low-cost education for those whom the formal system cannot yet reach or has already bypassed" (World Bank, 1988). Thus, for the World Bank, basic education and literacy aim to do the same thing, namely to supplement in out-of-school contexts whenever basic education is missing in non-literate adults. This approach views basic education as a second change or supplement to what schools failed to provide at one stage.

Such an approach to adult learning is problematic on two grounds. First, such 'deficit" tendencies lean towards blaming the victims of illiteracy, underscoring the individual qualities of the illiterate person as being incompetent and underachieving. It is assumed therefore that the presence of illiteracy in society and particularly among indigenous peoples is related to the presence of individuals who are incompetent or underachieving in the school system. Second, this perspective produces very different kinds of intervention programs geared toward supplementing what is lacking instead of directing attention to practical or entrepreneurial applications of literacy.

This deficit approach also helps to explain the proliferation of literacy programs that tend to emphasize only the technical aspects of learning (Semali, 1995) from textbooks, reading materials, primers, and picture books to classroom practice. Literacy programs in Southern Africa include pedagogical styles that stress memorization of question-and-answer schemes, word drills, and testing on vocabulary instead of emphasizing practical and entrepreneurial applications. Measures and evaluation methods of classroom reading and writing processes frequently used in reading research have been introduced to adult literacy programs. This has been done partly because of assumptions made about non-literate populations. Insofar as many low literates come from poor rural communities, the assumption is often made that they are helpless and come to adult literacy classes as blank slates ready to be filled. For this reason, they are thought to require basic education skills, as do school-age children in formal education. The confluence of these factors has precipitated a climate within which the goals of adult basic education and formal classroom teaching have not been clearly defined. As a result, some countries have developed policies of literacy education that fail to distinguish between adult literacy and basic education. Consequently, it is a poor strategy to separate adult literacy from formal schooling, relegating it to the secondary importance in the educational system.

By the same token, adult learners' motivation is likely to be sustained only if literacy education aims to teach individuals to think, to communicate their thoughts to others, and to understand and evaluate the communication to others. Adults will learn these skills in so far as they are relevant to their community, workplace, and current situation, It is only as the adult literates use these skills that the need and desire to learn the specific skills of effective listening , speaking, reading writing, and locating information will be attained. Within this view, literacy is a product of social interaction. Thus, the need to continue to read and write is explained by social relationships, and the transactions thereof, whether occupational, educational, social or economic.

The curriculum development we propose aims to critique the process of the generation and validation of curricular content, and the ways that groups of people benefit from the 'certification' of some forms of knowledge while other groups do not. A radical curriculum theory prompts us to ask critical questions: How is knowledge defined, legitimated, and tested? What constitutes official knowledge? Whose knowledge is of most worth? Whose interests are served by particular approaches to psychological and educational perspectives? How do students and ABE teachers construct meanings? Why do students frequently resist the imposition of meanings that are foreign or degrading to them and reject schooling practices that belittle them and devalue their culture? How can teachers and parents ensure that learners are informed by the complete history of ideas and events that have shaped and continue to shape human growth and social development?

These questions sum up politics and the complexity of efforts of trying to decolonize ABE. The organization of school knowledge, the hidden curriculum and the representation of difference in academic texts and school practices all contain discourses that have serious implications for indigenous students as well as other minority ethnic groups. This essay was conceptualized with a focus on the use of indigenous or local languages as a strategy to uncover the subjugation of knowledges in educational contexts. The process of decolonization explored in indigenous languages, for example, maps out the discursive terrain of indigeneity, histories, cultures, and traditions, and how collectively they impact common folk in indigenous communities in their ways of being, doing, and thinking. This process of decolonization requires indigenous peoples everywhere to confront the insulting idea that others know and understand them better than they understand themselves.

Local Language Issues

In the summer of 1988 I visited several schools in remote areas in Tanzania, Kenya, Botswana, and Zimbabwe. I met with children from different village communities. My intention was to gain first hand information from these children what the school experience meant for them. These children had one thing in common. They came from indigenous communities, far removed from cities and metropolitan areas. For them, the school experience meant walking long distances everyday—an average of two to three hours to reach the schoolhouse in search for education. The language they spoke at home was not the language spoken at school. At home they spoke "Kimbulu (Irawq)", "Kimaasai", "Sseswana", and "Ndebele" respectively. Though mutually intelligible with their national African languages, the local languages spoken by these children were soon to be ignored when they were thrown into a total immersion environment where the language of instruction was "English". These children had to abandon their home languages, images, history, and metaphors as soon as they entered the gates of the schools. They had to give up the metaphors, images, riddles and stories that describe their out-of-school experiences and begin to learn the new language of school—English and the Western ways of knowing.

In Tanzania, for example, where the author attended early education and where he was able to return as an adult to examine the culture of classrooms, African languages at the time of his elementary school days were suppressed and made illegal to be spoken on the school grounds. In the 1950s, at the height of the colonial rule, indigenous knowledge and local language literacy had no place in the school experience. For many students, as well as for adult education programs, indigenous knowledge was the unofficial knowledge that was essentially anecdotal memories of customary law, inheritance rights, and beliefs about witchcraft, taboos, and rituals.

This body of knowledge formed the wisdom of how things were done in the villages where the majority of students came from. Such indigenous knowledge—the local knowledge that is unique to a given culture or society—contrasts with the knowledge of other nations or international systems, which is generated through the global network of universities, research laboratories and institutes. Contrary to today's expectations, this body of knowledge was not part of what students ordinarily learned at school. The distinction between indigenous/African and Western / European education and the attendant languages was clear. The dichotomy between these knowledge systems did not glorify the similarities. Instead, Africans had to find a way to accommodate and make sense of both systems and, as a result the two systems competed for attention.

Even though indigenous or community languages formed the primary means of communication and discourse that was vital in the socialization of children and crucial to the survival of a cultural community, it was muted or relegated to second place at school. English, as a foreign language was believed without question to be superior and more efficient in academic work. What was quickly forgotten, though temporarily, was that within the community's native language was contained "the codification of lived experiences that provided the avenues for adults and children to express their own realities and to question the wider social order" (Darder, 1991, p. 37).

Although some parents and teachers were willing to accept the apparent repression or language domination exercised during the pre-independence era in return for a "good" education, they became ambivalent when it came to the psychological damage manifested by students (Semali, 2009). It was acknowledged and widely known that colonial education silenced student voices and seriously curtailed their active participation in school life. There was little to comment about Shakespearean language or the metaphors used in these works of literature. With few opportunities to enter into dialogue and reflect on their reality and lived experiences in terms of political and historical contexts, many students who spoke indigenous languages (or non-European languages) were caught between two worlds: Swahili versus English, local versus global (foreign) language. To master schoolwork and pass the national examinations, many students had to use rote memorization and reproduction techniques that they had learned to value and were good at doing. After taking the examinations, whatever materials were learned soon got forgotten. Little knowledge that was garnered applied to their local reality. Students quickly returned to speak indigenous languages and to do things the way their community has always done them.

This phenomenon of repression of local language literacy represents a systematic process of colonizing the curriculum. However, individuals had to find ways to mediate or address the different strategies of survival in response to the dynamics of living in constant tension between conflicting cultural values and conditions of cultural subordination between the dominant discourse of educational institutions and the realities that students must face as members of indigenous or remote area cultures. When colonialism is examined in the broader contest of cultural domination, it is significant to note that cultural invasion through the repression of indigenous languages was spread throughout the world during the European colonization period before World War II.

The legacies of this period remain in many countries until today, particularly in former colonies in Africa, Asia and Latin America. For example, there are over eight thousand African languages spoken on the continent. In general terms, you would find no single ethnic group is large enough to constitute a significant section of the population. So there is no concentration of power in the hands of any particular group to exert a continental language. These African languages are distinguished from the colonial European languages that were imposed on Africans in the colonial period by the British, French, Spanish, and Portuguese governments. As colonial languages, these tongues were introduced to schools and have been constitutionally recognized either as official languages or national languages. Often times, the distinction between official and national languages is not clear. In this confusion, however, lie the contradictions, politics, and ideologies that surround native or indigenous languages in many of the 52 countries of Africa. In South Africa, for instance, after the fall of Apartheid, 12 languages were selected among the many indigenous languages found in the country to become official languages and languages of instruction in lower primary grades.

The politics of language bias—Swahili versus English, Bambara versus French, indigenous versus European languages—foment much of the dilemmas and contradictions underlying local language literacy and cultural invasion legacies. For many politicians in African countries both in English-speaking East Africa and French-speaking West Africa, the questions of local language literacy and the case of repressed indigenous languages are better left alone than addressed. Nevertheless, within the national language politics lies the tension between assumptions of being "educated," "literate or civilized" and the impetus for promoting local language literacy, dialects and indigenous languages rather than English or French.

Conclusion

This essay exposes the faultlines and contradictions inherent in knowledge production debates and illustrates the challenges of subjugation that oppressive situation presents, particularly the continued absence, erasure, and subordination of local people's knowledge, history, and experience from academic texts, discourses and materials, social and political practices found in curricula and texts in Northern societies. I suggested in this paper that we conceptualize African adult basic education broadly to encompass the reality of Africa. Instead of promoting ABE exclusively as adult learning based on formal schooling pedagogy, jobs, employment, and workplace productivity, I propose we talk about ABE as a way of knowing, thinking and doing that enables indigenous innovation to build the capacities of farmers, farmers' groups, women's groups, youth and communities to identify their needs, their community assets, the collective capacity for innovation and for creating new alternatives for resource-poor farmers, especially women. Building on farmer innovation implies a fundamental change in the roles of extension agents and health educators, from transmitters of technical messages to facilitators of knowledge exchange between farmers and other farmers, and between farmers and extension officers themselves. Such a shift in ABE curriculum approach offers a different outlook where locality becomes central in the conceptualization of ABE and where farmers, adults and youth become ethnographers of their territory and cultural environments, poised to discover knowledge rather than become depositories of extension education, innovators rather than beggars for hand-outs and job creators rather than job seekers.

Notes

1. Emerging from this conference was **Agenda 21 (Agenda for the 21st Century)**, a global program that committed 118 countries to environmental restoration, preservation and social development. Their aims are to meet the challenge of global warming, pollution, biodiversity and the inter-related social problems of poverty, health and population.
2. Some of the assumptions of development insist that the development process is a cultural activity with embedded power asymmetry and that cultural perspectives are discourses supportive of power relations and material effects.

Essentially, development is a concept, an idea, a discourse, a construction with different meanings to different people. Consequently, to begin activities aimed at development, we must first critique our own culture and ideas about development, our own preferences and capabilities, values, and assumptions, ends and means.

References

Darder, A. (1991), *Culture and Power in the Classroom. A Critical Foundation for Bicultural Education* Westport, CT: Bergin & Garvey.

Dei, G. (2000), "African Development: The Relevance and Implications of 'Indigenousness,'" In *Indigenous Knowledges in Global Contexts: Multiple Readings of Our World*, Ed. G. Dei, B. Hall, & D. Rosenberg pp-70-86.Toronto: University of Toronto Press, Halfacree, K. H. (1993). Locality and Social Representation: Space, Discourse and Alternative Definitions of the Rural. *Journal of Rural Studies*, Vol. 9, No. 1, pp. 23-37.

Hrabwski III, R. & Wiedemann, C. (2004), University Outreach and Engagement: Responding to a Changing World. *Journal of Higher Education Outreach and Engagement*, 10(1), pp. 15-28.

Itabari, Z. (2006), Critical Indigenous African Education and Knowledge. *The Journal of Pan African Studies*, Vol. 1, No. 3, 32-49.

Memmi, A. (1965), Th*e Colonizer and the Colonized*. Boston: Beacon Press.

Semali, L. (1995), Postliteracy in the Age of Democracy. Bethsda, MD: Astin and Winfield.

Semali, L. (2007), Challenges of Rebuilding Education in Crisis: Access to Universal Primary Education in Africa. In Baker, D, and Alexander-Wiseman, *Education for all: Global Promises, National Challenges*. pp. 395-425. New York: Elsevier.

Semali, L. (2009), Indigenous Pedagogies and Languages for Peace and Development. In Brock-Utne, B. and Gunnar Garbo, *Language and Power: Implications of language for peace and development*. Dar es Salaam: Mkuki na Nyota.

Smith, Linda Tuhiwai (1999), *Decolonizing Methodologies: Research and Indigenous Peoples*. New York: Zed Books.

Srikantaiah, D. (2008), Indigenous Knowledge and Intellectual Property Rights: Confronting Modern Norms to Promote Sustainability. *Diaspora, Indigenous, and Minority Education*, Vol. 2: 4 October 2008, pp. 276–294.

Ssekamwa, J. C. (1997), *History and Development of Education in Uganda*. Kampala, Uganda.

UNESCO (2004), Education for All: The quality imperative. EFA Global Monitoring Report. Paris: UNESCO.

United Nations (2005), *The Millennium Development Goals Report*. New York: United Nations.

Wilkinson, Kenneth (1970), *The Community as a Social Field.* Social Forces, 48: 3; pp. 311-322.

World Bank (1988), World Development Report 1988. New York: Oxford University Press.

World Bank (1989), Sub-Sahara Africa: From Crisis to Sustainable Growth. Washington, D.C.: World Bank.

World Bank (2004), *Indigenous Knowledge: Local Pathways to Global Development.* Washington, D.C.: The World Bank–Knowledge and Learning Group, Africa Region.

Worster, David (1994), *The Wealth of Nature: The Environmental History and the Ecological Imagination.* London: Oxford University Press.

DIVERSITY, PLURALISM AND CONVERGENCE
South Asia and India in Perspective

N. K. Das

"Cultural-Diversity" is a multifaceted concept. It includes several representations and perceptions. It includes a variety of race, ethnicity, language, tradition, culture, morality and religion. In order to quantify or estimate cultural diversity we need to count the number of cultures being practiced and the variety of languages spoken regionally or globally. However, in any attempt at measuring the diversity of cultures, the essence and frontier of culture has to be identified. Here lies the value of the expertise of and the professional role of the anthropologists. The approval of the UNESCO Convention on the Protection and Promotion of the Diversity of Cultural Expressions (20 October 2005) has led to considering a solid framework for policies in favour of the diversity of cultural expressions and to define both cultural diversity and the diversity of cultural expressions as objectively as possible. "Cultural-Diversity" includes several perceptions. At present, people's values, customs, beliefs and traditional knowledge systems that collectively shape the 'culture' are increasingly recognized as vital sources for grassroots development. Former anthropological theories of culture defined culture as coherent, integrated, ordered, and stable. Today, however, the issues of cultural differences, identity and 'ethnicity', which have emerged as a political factors, are witnessed globally. Globalisation and localization are simultaneously operating today. Today we live in a new geo-religious reality. One of the decisive facts of these days from a global perspective has been the tremendous migration of peoples from one nation to another, both as immigrants and as refugees. People in every part of the world today confront and they frequently endure the plurality of religious traditions and cultures. Indeed, increasing competitions for scarce resources and increasing movements of peoples and their increasing culture contacts have made the terms ethnicity and syncretism as leading concepts. At one level ethnicity also represents common and shared culture. These concepts have generally outdated the concepts of acculturation and assimilation. Indeed, instead of any real 'clash of civilizations', the world is heading for convergence. In this milieu it is all the more fundamental to discuss the theme of community in Indian perspective, mainly in the framework of pluralism in the wider perspective of state. This paper aims to deal with the three interconnected conceptions of Cultural-Diversity,

* Superintending Anthropologist (C), Anthropological Survey of India, 27 Jawaharlal Nehru Road, Kolkata-700 016

Cultural Pluralism and Cultural Convergence, with reference to above-mentioned wider theoretical prelude, particularly in the south Asian/ Indian contexts.

"Cultural-Diversity" is a multifaceted concept. It includes several representations and perceptions. It includes a variety of race, ethnicity, language, tradition, culture, morality and religion. In order to quantify or estimate cultural diversity we need to count the number of cultures being practiced and the variety of languages spoken regionally or globally. Decline in any of these elements may indicate a decline in the world's cultural diversity. Cultural diversity refers to the differences that exist among people as a function of characteristics such as race, cultural and ethnic background, socio-economic status, and sexual orientation. The status of cultural diversity needs to be explored in an effort to accommodate needs for changes in policies on both federal and state levels, regarding economic and educational issues.

The approval of the UNESCO Convention on the Protection and Promotion of the Diversity of Cultural Expressions (20 October 2005) has led to considering a solid framework for policies in favour of the diversity of cultural expressions and to define both cultural diversity and the diversity of cultural expressions as objectively as possible. A precise definition of cultural diversity is therefore needed. As in the case of biodiversity, this is clearly 'more than matters for semantic wrangling' (McIntosh, 1967, p.392). Definitions of biodiversity have enabled researchers to discuss this concept in a way that is neither ambiguous nor arbitrary (Sugihara, 1982). In any attempt at measuring the diversity of cultures, the essence and frontier of culture has to be identified.

Today, people's value systems, customs, beliefs and traditional knowledge systems that collectively shape the 'culture' are increasingly recognized as vital sources, particularly for grassroots development. We need to learn from local communities to enrich the development process". Unfortunately, indigenous knowledge and folklores, based on the sustainable use of environmental resources, are dying a slow death; the most visible factor in this is of course, the usurping by market forces of resources and knowledge in the public realm and placing into the profit-oriented market. Unless these resources are documented, the indigenous peoples have no means of fighting back, which makes the effort to involve school children and their teachers in this project to record traditional knowledge all the more path breaking. There is another dimension to culture concept, also discussed in contemporary anthropological literature. Here we are dealing with the issue of cultural differences, wherein 'culture' is seen as provoking the identity and in consequence 'ethnicity' emerges as a political factor. Earlier anthropological theories of culture defined culture as coherent, integrated, ordered, and stable. In the works of contemporary anthropology, borders between 'cultures' are seen as incidental. Hence we are faced with situations of overlapping, differentiation, creolization and hybridization (Borofsky 1994 b: 3 13, 3 18). Indeed, increasing competitions for scarce resources and increasing movements of peoples and their increasing culture contacts have made the terms ethnicity and syncretism as leading concepts. At one level ethnicity also represents common and shared culture These concepts have generally outdated the concepts of acculturation and assimilation that were prevalent terms earlier in anthropology/ sociology (Barth 1969: 10-11; Roosens 1989: 12; Eriksen 1992: 3-15, 28-30; Verdery 1994: 40-41; Banks 1996. 11-13, Eriksen 1992: 2, 3; Eriksen 1993 a: 3, 4; Roosens 1989: 11; Williams 1989: 401, 402). Today we live in a new geo-religious reality. One of the decisive facts of these days from a global perspective has been the tremendous migration of peoples from one nation to another, both as immigrants and as refugees. People in every part of the world today confront and they frequently endure the plurality of religious traditions and cultures. Indeed on account of long persistence but now redundant notions of "melting-pot", 'assimilation" and "acculturation" theories, there appeared oversimplification and vague pronouncements in much of the early anthropological-sociological writings, which need to be quashed. Instead of any real 'clash of civilizations', the world is heading for convergence. In this milieu it is all the more fundamental to discuss the themes of identity by placing in the framework of pluralism in the wider perspective of state. Ethnic identity is a dynamic, multidimensional construct that refers to fluid and dynamic understanding of self and ethnic background.

The idea and the concept of multiple identities are now becoming crucial in post-modern states (Anderson 1991: 16 - 17; Verdery 1994: 3-7). Ethnicity is seen as an instrument for competition for scarce resources and it is used to obtain certain privileges. Roosens (198 9: 13) has remarked that many people would even change their ethnic identity if they could gain by doing so. The instrumentalist view, in its strictest sense, has been criticized for not paying any attention to the symbolic aspects of ethnicity, and the emotional meanings of ethnic identity (Eriksen 1993 a: 45, 47, 73, 74). In ethno- politics, ethnicity becomes a relevant political factor. Cultural differences and 'possessing culture' becomes the 'politics of culture'. Becoming extremely politicised, it also leads to violent conflict. This is why it is important to study how the concept of culture is used for political, ethnic and nationalistic purposes (Ehn 1992: 3, 4; Borofsky 1994 b: 3 18). In this theoretical backdrop here our concern is with the three conceptions of Cultural-Diversity, Cultural Pluralism and Cultural Convergence, particularly in the south Asian/ Indian perspectives.

Cultural pluralism and multiculturalism, despite their differing perspectives, are regarded as synonymous (The Columbia Electronic Encyclopaedia, 6th ed. 2007). By making the broadest range of human differences acceptable to the largest number of people, multiculturalism seeks to overcome racism, sexism, and other forms of discrimination. Cultural pluralism is rather a term unfolding the coexistence of many cultures in a locality, without 'any single culture dominating' the region. It also signifies as a national policy favouring the coexistence of a variety of cultural, ethnic, or religious groups. Scholars, such as Diana L. Eck, have pointed to the fact that:

> *Diversity is just plurality, plain and simple. Pluralism is the engagement that creates a common society. Indeed pluralism that would engage people of different faiths and cultures in the creation of a common society is not a "given," but an achievement. Pluralism does not require relinquishing the distinctiveness of one's own tradition of faith. Pluralism invites people of every faith to maintain all their particularities, and yet to be engaged in creating a civil society, through the critical and self-critical encounter with one another. Pluralism is a process of creating a society by acknowledging, rather than hiding, its deepest differences.*
>
> **(Diana L. Eck 2006).**

The new paradigm of pluralism does not require us to leave our identities and our commitments behind, for pluralism is the encounter of commitments. It means holding our deepest differences, even our religious differences, not in isolation, but in relationship to one another. The language of pluralism is that of dialogue and encounter -give and take, criticism and self-criticism (Eck, 1993, 1996). Many scholars attribute the success of the state in part to pluralism's effect on conflict resolution. Pluralism and federalism now appear as the two essential principles for organizing heterogeneous societies into a viable pattern of political sharing of power, by reconciling the twin processes of political unification and social diversity; of commonality for certain purposes and specificities for others. In its praxis, federalism builds and sustains the unity of polity and simultaneously preserves and promotes the plurality of society. It is from this perspective, and ideological premises of federal nation, participatory democracy, secularism and social justice that we should re-examine federal polity and plural society. Culture has two reference points, one external and the other internal. The external reference is to other cultures, nations and nation-states. The internal dimension of the culture power fusion is what constitutes the specifically modern element in the notion of nation (Erja Marjut Hänninen 2002).

Ethnicity and ethnic group are generally defined as a common identity based on characteristics acquired either at birth or through cultural experience (language, religion, caste, sense of regional identity etc.). Ethnicity and nation are multivocal words: their meanings depend upon who uses the word and in which context. The primordialist approach to the study of nationalism bases its image of identity on ethnicity, whereas Max Weber has noted that nation has notions with the sentiment of solidarity of ethnic communities, but the sentiment of ethnic solidarity does not by itself make a nation (Erja Marjut Hänninen 2002). Nationalism is perceived in terms of notions of primordialism, instrumentalism and constructivism. It is seen that there has been much denunciation of the primordialist conviction that every person belongs to a community (place of birth, kinship relations, religion, language and social practices). Thus, the current debate about nation and nationalism raises several questions. This has led to bewilderment between citizenship and nationality in modern States, the dissolution of nationalism as a result of multiple factors acting now, the elevation of the status of national minorities, and the idea of supposed "national culture" as a personal and collective good. Appadurai stresses that the simultaneous process of 'global homogenisation' and 'heterogenisation' has necessitated the conceptualisation of a different kind of locality that addresses the aspirations of a globalising population everywhere. South Asia is no exception. If anything, the need for re-conceptualising an inclusive identity is even stronger in this region, as nation-states here are younger, though ethnic identities deeper and competing population groups denser. But a fear of 'Indianisation' indeed remains rampant all over the neighbourhood (C. K. Lal 2003).

South Asia: Doomed States/ Minority Victimisation

If a nation is to be perceived as a political and cultural identity then South Asia has two major nations with religion as their defining feature - Hindu and Muslim (C. K. Lal 2003). Even though these identities overlap all the time, Pakistan is homeland for Muslims, Sri Lanka for Sinhalas, Bangladesh for Bengali-speaking Muslims, Nepal for the HANS (Hindu, Aryan Nepali-speakers), and India remains a predominantly Hindu entity. There is another South Asian identity. Whether one is dismissed as a 'Paki' or ridiculed as Indian, people from all over South Asia have come to be identified with curry, quawalli, cricket, Hindi films, and a distinct variety of South Asian English. In an age when boundaries are blurred by globalisation and geographical markers are becoming fluid there is need to contemplate a distinct South Asian identity, on account of several internal and external factors.

Despite democratic institutions having been enshrined prominently in the constitutions of South Asian countries, large sections of the people of South Asian countries are mostly powerless, vulnerable and poor. In South Asia, there are two broad categories in which democratic parliamentary institutions can be seen. One: where parliamentary democracy has taken considerable roots and another, where this system is under stress and still evolving. In the first category, India, Sri Lanka and Bangladesh may be included. The remaining four countries, Pakistan, Nepal, Bhutan and Maldives fall into the second category of pseudo- quasi- or slowly evolving democratic systems. Little regard is shown to local government institutions here. Bhutan has gracefully introduced the electoral democracy recently. India has articulated an elaborate framework of constitutional guarantees for minority rights protection and asymmetric federal structures for devolving power, in Pakistan and Bangladesh; the constitutions are less activated to stop discrimination and victimization. Bangladesh does not recognise that it has explicit linguistic, religious, and ethnic minorities; it styles itself as mono-ethnic, mono-linguistic, and mono-religious, thus excluding non-Bengali Chakmas, Marmar Tripuris, and plains tribes/ ethnic communities. Pakistan's constitution does not recognise the 'multinational' character of the state. Minorities are brutally ill-treated. "Islamism" has been used to suppress the claims of the nationality/ minority/ethnic question, but 'it remains a flashpoint and is intensifying' (Human Rights Commission of Pakistan [HRCP] 2001 and 2003).

Pakistan's women and Christian, Hindu, and Ahmadi communities are victimised by a constitutionally sanctioned legal and juridical regime that promotes a culture of discrimination, intolerance, and extremism. Pakistan does not recognise its Sindhi, Balochi, or Pashto nationalities. In Nepal too, exclusion is deeply institutionalised. In Nepal, the caste Hindu hill elites make up 16 percent of the population and dominate political economic and sociocultural life, while 85 percent of the population, including women, are marginalised and excluded. Nepal's constitution however recognizes the country's multilingual character. Sri Lanka's minority rights discourse does not include recognition of social /ethnic minorities. Sri Lanka has sought to evolve a constitutional and legal regime of protection against the backdrop of an ethicised conflict with no success. Ethnic polarization has generally reinforced the state's Unitarian ideology and centralized structure, as well as Sinhala-Buddhist hegemony. In many South Asian states parliamentary democracy is already a farce; though theoretically the 'elections' remain the only bridge between the state and individuals (Simi Kamal, 2000).

The critical links between identity, cultural pluralism and the State in the South Asian context are neither comprehensively articulated nor portrayed meaningfully, particularly in social anthropological writings. This has left a lacuna in South Asian literature. There are some publications, which address such issues (Simi Kamal, 2000, Malik 2005). Kamal looks at major issues of citizenship, democracy, cultural diversity, pluralism, ethnic strife, civil society and minority issue in theoretical and empirical terms and within the context of South Asia. Kamal (2000) says that the end of the British Raj and the events surrounding the partition of British India made the main countries of what is now South Asia (India, Pakistan, Bangladesh, Sri Lanka, Nepal, Bhutan and Maldives), very sensitive to 'unity', 'security' and 'integrity'. There are good numbers of scholars who are writing on the issue of fundamentalist approaches to the religion in South Asia. In his latest research effort "Jihad, Hindutva and the Taliban: South Asia at the Crossroads", Iftikhar H. Malik, has provided comparative perspectives on the fundamentalist approaches to the religion in South Asia. This Book addresses a changed regional and global political context. Iftikhar H. Malik (2005) has provided comparative analysis of the Taliban, Hindutva ideology, Jihadi outfits that are the proponents of various politico-religious concepts. Malik argues that the proponents of ethno-political majoritarianism draw their support from history and yet achieve their ends through modern means. To substantiate his thesis, he indicates that the proponents of political Islam, despite wearing a traditional look, use modern strategies, slogans and symbolisms. So much so, the concepts of secularism and gender equality, primarily espoused by Western political outlooks, were also supported by Muslim scholars, though in minority, including the towering Allama Iqbal, Sir Syed Ahmed Khan and Muhammad Abduh. Malik therefore, suggests that political Islam, with all its fundamentalist undercurrents, need to be understood in a democratic framework. (Malik: 2005: 298). Malik suggests that the modern dimensions of political Islam need to be explored more closely, rather than just affiliating it with Jihad. On Jihad, the author states "jihad is still operating as a major source of massive political mobilisation in North Africa, the Middle East, South Asia and the Caucasus" (Malik: 2005: 46). Malik, while reviewing the issues concerning the Indian polity, questions the political prospects of the Nehruvian model of secularism and pluralism by pointing to the rise of saffronists (Radical Hindus) and the growing polarisation of Indian society. He goes on to illustrate the widening cleavages in the Indian society by quoting the demolition of the Babri mosque; state-sponsored 'Muslim pogrom' in Gujarat; Sikh 'genocide'; recurring communal riots and several secessionist movements across India; the plight of ethnic and religious minorities; and growing economic disparities (Malik: 2005: 85-88). On Pakistan the author ascribes the extending role of the state and minimising character of the civil society for most of the political and social misfortunes of the country. According to him, the Pakistani state, synonymous with corruption, inefficiency and coercion, has been resistant to substantive restructuring, devolution and democratisation. He lambastes several state institutions especially the army and intelligence agencies for the criminalisation of the state structures and the marginalisation of the civil society forces. The writer notes that despite their diverse ideological trajectories, all the South Asian states are confronted with similar problems of internal dissensions augmented by external tensions. He argues that South Asia with its rich heritage can reinvent itself as a bastion of peace, pluralism, tolerance and democracy by reviving the prowess of their civil society. In a current analysis, Selig S Harrison ('A Pakistani federation', Times of India 2 Feb 2008), has argued that 'Whatever the outcome of the Pakistani elections (February 2008) the existing multi-ethnic Pakistani state is not likely to survive for long unless it is radically restructured. Pakistan is headed for a bloody confrontation with the country's Pashtun, Baluch and Sindhi minorities that could well lead to the break-up of Pakistan into three sovereign entities. In historical context, such a break-up would not be surprising. There had never been a national entity encompassing the areas now constituting Pakistan, an ethnic melange thrown together hastily by the British for strategic reasons when they partitioned the subcontinent in 1947. Reinstating and liberalising the defunct 1973 constitution, which has been shelved by successive military rulers, could still preserve Pakistan.

In the post-colonial world, the countries of South Asia have evolved politically in different ways, amidst internal and regional conflicts, but retained some commonality of institutions and cultures. Since the 1990s, the promise of market-led development and the growth of a middle class, especially in India, have reshaped expectations, with common aspirations and achievement of economic well-being - what might be a new "idea of South Asia." In that case, a new idea of South Asia will require building social capital in ways that will challenge all of the region's societies. Effective collective action across, but first within, the nations of South Asia will be the true test of whether this potential South Asian identity emerges (Nirvikar Singh 2005).

The increasing infringement of the rights of minorities in the countries of South Asia during the last few decades has been a matter of considerable concern. Several commentators feel that the momentum acquired by 'fundamentalism' during the last two decades has worsened the situation (K. N. Panikkar, Minorities in south Asia, 2005). Some states have introduced laws, from time to time, which are particularly 'repressive for the minorities'. For instance, Pakistan in 1986 provided for punishing those who offend the Koran. The fundamentalists in pursuit of their conservative agenda often invoked the law. In India too the majority of those who had been arrested and jailed under TADA, 1985 and POTA, 2001 belonged to minorities. Bangladesh and Sri Lanka have continuously witnessed maltreatment of minority segments. K. N. Panikkar has rightly observed that the consciousness of the civil society is a crucial factor in the well being of the minorities (K.N.Panikkar, 2005, Minorities in South Asia, Keynote address delivered to the workshop on the Condition of Minorities in South Asia held at Delhi from 16 to 19 September 2005).

Regionalism and Communalism: Indian Brand

After a long struggle, the Indian subcontinent was divided into two states, India and Pakistan, in 1947. Pakistan portrayed itself as a state of a homogenous people whereas India was proclaimed a pluralistic nation that welcomed religious and cultural diversity. India opted for secularism, as it was considered vital for the existence of the Indian state. The principle of non-discrimination in the Indian constitution recognised on grounds of caste, place of birth, sex, residence and religion guarantees equal citizenship. The framers of India's Constitution sought to shape an overarching Indian distinctiveness even as they acknowledged the reality of cultural pluralism by guaranteeing fundamental rights to all, with specific provisions for the protection of Minorities. These include freedom of religion (Articles 25-28); the right of any section of citizens to use and conserve their "distinct language, script or culture" (Article 29); and the right of "all minorities, whether based on religion or language," to establish and administer educational institutions of their choice (Article 30). State autonomy and statehood for territorially based regional/linguistic identities remains the most comprehensive method of political recognition of identity in India, and key to India's plural-cultural federalization. India's centre-state/ province/union territory framework provides an institutional framework of autonomy and decentralization, which manages the need for development and identity. Linguistic identity movements in various parts of the country had threatened India's unity. This was seen as genuine demand. Hence there was necessity to undertake the division-reorganisation of 'states' and 'provinces'. In the post - 1980s era India witnessed a series of protests, often based on ethnic, linguistic and regional issues. Spheres of social inequalities, cultural differences and conflicts came to be perceived also in terms of the 'majority-minority' issues. According to Zoya Hasan, the 28 states of India's federal system have played a more prominent role in India's public life. There have been demands for creation of new smaller states by breaking the bigger ones. Demand for state is based on ethnicity in most cases. However beneath such demand we may see the urge for political autonomy for power sharing and governance at each appropriate level.

Regionalism is rooted in India's manifold diversity of languages, cultures, tribes, communities, religions and so on, and encouraged by the regional concentration of those identity markers, and fuelled by a sense of regional deprivation. India's broad regions, socio-culturally speaking, are distinct from one another. For instance, southern India (the home of Dravidian cultures), which is itself a region of many regions, is evidently different from the north, the west, the central and the northeast. The British colonial division of the Indian Territory broadly between the directly ruled provinces, and some 560 (indirectly-ruled) despotic princely kingdoms of many sizes, religions, tribes, and languages added complexity to regionalism in India. Even after various phases of territorial reorganization since 1950, most regions of India contain many sub-regions marked by some social and cultural identity symbols (Harihar Bhattacharyya, Federalism and Regionalism in India: Institutional Strategies and Political Accommodation of Identity). The first States Reorganisation Commission (SRC) in 1953 faced a difficult task of reconciling multitude of interests. The 14 states created by the SRC have now doubled. Indeed there are some very genuine cases seeking the constitutional rectification. Thus, the demands of the Telangana, Vidarbha, Harit Pradesh and Darjeeling have been mentioned in the present context in the face of other demands such as Leh, Bundelkhand (UP), Kosal (Orissa), Delhi, Karbi Anglong (Meghalaya), Bodoland (Assam) and a few others in the north-east, indicates the political turmoil that the SRC would generate. According to Ajay K Mehra (2008) the first SRC appeared to be influenced by several considerations of 'redistribution of provinces' - "partly geographical and partly economic and financial, but the main considerations being the wishes of the people and the linguistic unity of the area concerned". No doubt originally the state reorganisation based itself on linguistic majoritarianism. Today however, beyond linguistic considerations, development deficit has been the underlying politics for other subsequent aspirations, each of which was organised around ethno-regional identity. There is greater need to develop a consensus on issues of autonomy, power sharing and an agreeable basis for creation of states for good governance (Bring out the maps, Times of India 18 Jan 2008, Ajay K. Mehra).

In India there has been long tradition of angry outburst of communalism. Erja uses the word 'communalist' to refer to communalism as ideology and movement and word 'communal' to refer to a feeling based on the togetherness of a community, which may or may not be related to communalism. Communalism aims to improve the social, economic or political position of a community based on religion, language or common descent/ethnicity within a state. Communalisation takes place when some issue is being used to promote the social, economic and political position of the community. An important aspect of communalism is collective antagonism (Erja Marjut Hänninen 2002). Nationalism and communalism are both based on a group of people connected by common ethnic cultural features. However, whereas communalism aims at political power and social and economic benefits, nationalism aims at creating a state for a nation. In India, Erja feels, communalism supposes that Hindus, Sikhs and Muslims form separate communities that oppose each other. These communities can then imagine themselves as nations through their communal feeling, which is created, for example, by emphasizing the periods of history when the community was the one that ruled in India (Erja Marjut Hänninen 2002). Bipan Chandra asserts that there is a difference between communalist parties, which are structured along communalist ideologies, and secular, even weakly secular, parties taking an opportunistic stand towards communalism. Communalist forces have contested Indian secularism essentially. Communalist incidents, according to Erja Marjut Hänninen (2002), have increased in India since the 1960s. It has led to the decay of secularism. Indian society is very complex. Indian social scientists such as Ashis Nandy, T. N. Madan and K. N. Panikkar have very different ways to explain and interpret the history of India and issues of nationalism and secularism. Erja finds P. Chatterjee's historical time not suitable in such review. Erja is close to estimation of T. N. Madan ('Locked Minds, Modern Myths') particularly when Madan sees religious behaviour as a reason for the rise of fundamentalism, which has then caused the decline of secularism. Several scholars indeed see Hindu nationalism more in religious terms: they emphasize the historical roots of Hinduism and the central role of the Hindus in Indian nationalism (Erja Marjut Hänninen 2002). Hindutva, or Hindu nationalism, in the early twentieth century was a philosophy premised on exclusivist notions of "nation-ness" and "nation-state-ness." India is regarded as the pitrubhumi and the punyabhumi of "Hindus," the fatherland and holy land. This ideal realm is alleged to have been corrupted by Muslim and Christian "invaders," foreigners who defiled and split asunder "Akhandbharat," the one-India of Hindus. These scholars maintain that ssecularism and nationalism are of Western origin and therefore it is hard to apply them to the Indian context.

Greater India/ South Asia: Colonial "Oriental" Misconstruction: Colonial and Post-Colonial Narratives

India Defined-The 'Image', The 'Idea' and The Model of "Unity in Diversity"

The issue of defining India - culturally or politically-is problematic. Jawaharlal Nehru, more than anyone else, sought to create a popular version of "national" identity and articulated it expressively. In the Discovery of India, written on the edge of country's independence, Jawaharlal Nehru sought to create a collective discourse through which Indians could express themselves as Indians through the medium of a shared past. The key terms through which Nehru attempted to reconcile the demands of diversity are: internalising and Indianhood and "unity in diversity." Nehru often said India's strength is "the unity in diversity". India's leaders were thus unanimous in choosing an anthem, which emphasized diversity in a fabulous manner. The first verse in anthem glorifies names of different geographic regions, ethnicities and cultures. India is hailed as Punjab, Sindh, Gujarat, Maratha, Dravida, Utkala, and Banga in the same verse. India's 687.6 million Hindus of innumerable sects, 101.6 million Muslims (making India the third largest Muslim-populated country), 19.6 million Christians, 6.3 million Buddhists, 3.3 million Jains and 3.1 million people of other persuasions (1991 census) shape the cultural diversity of the country. Heinz Werner Wessler says India's traditional multicultural society that came into being in the pre-modern context is probably the most important resource for a political and cultural vision of "Unity and Diversity". An authentic documentation of this cultural diversity, focusing on communities, languages and hundreds of culture/ecology traits is accomplished in the Anthropological Survey of India's the People of India (PoI) project. The diversity of Indian culture and society is seen in its ethnic / linguistic composition, religions, customs, attitudes, practices, food habits, dress, art, music, theatre and the regions. Each group, each region has its own set of identities. Divided in distinct communities, the people of India regard themselves as belonging to the land -mass of *Jambu-Dwipa* - a geographical area comprising India and other parts of the world. India, called *Bharata Varsha, is* situated to the north of the ocean and to the south of the *Himadri*, the snowy mountains. Rig Veda mentions *Bharatas* ruled the land that spread over the banks of the rivers *Parushni* (Ravi) and *Vipasa*

(Beas). Kautilya (c. 350-283 BC) regards *Bharata Varsha* as the land stretched from Himalaya to Kanyakumari; and the epigraph of emperor Kharavela (209-179 B. C) created in Hathigumpha (Bhubaneshwar) mentions the nomenclature *Bharata Varsha.* Cultural influences that engulfed different countries of south Asia in different historical periods, largely originated from Indian region. India can therefore be placed in the centre of the south Asian identity complex, historically if not otherwise today. However, there are several distinguishing features that set them apart from the rest of Asia. The dominant cultures of the south Asian people are Indo - Aryan, Dravidian, and the Mongoloid populations (in north-east India, Bhutan, Nepal and Tibet). A critical review of cultural studies literature of Bhutan, Nepal, Tibet, and northeast India including Sikkim shows great linguistic -cultural syncretic connectedness (Das 2006). Persian, Arab and Turkish cultural traditions originated in the west also form an integral part of Islamic South Asian culture. Belief in Sufism, pilgrimage to dargahs and Quawalli singing form a typical South Asian Muslim cultural tradition.

Whatever may be the debate about political unity and cultural diversity in India, the fact is that the diverse peoples of India developed a peculiar type of culture far different from any other type in the world and they have learned to live together as one people. This unity transcends the countless diversity of religion, customs, language, dress, manners and sect etcetera. In popular perceptions, many inferences are illustrated for the unity of Indian culture. Thus, in the main India chapter on culture the Encyclopaedia-Wikipedia focused attention to the syncretic tradition of India, in following citation:

> *"India's culture is marked by a high degree of syncretism. The pan-Indian, civilizational dimension of cultural pluralism and syncretism encompasses ethnic diversity and admixture, linguistic heterogeneity as well as fusion, and variations as well as synthesis in customs, behavioural patterns, beliefs and rituals in India" ("Cultural Diversity, Religious Syncretism and People of India: An Anthropological Interpretation" by Das, N.K. Bangladesh e-Journal of Sociology, July 2006 3- 2-Encyclopaedia-Wikipedia).*

Today India is the world's largest emerging potential market. India is also the world's largest potential democracy. Indian state, which cherishes modern, liberal and humanistic values, is confronted with its staggering diversity. Despite enormous pressures, India has been remarkably successful in accommodating cultural diversity and managing ethnic conflict through democratic institutions. This success has been the product of India's federal system, which has succeeded to keep cultural and ethnic peace.

Colonial Image of India

The colonial power produced an image of India as a geographic and demographic entity, made up of diverse religious groupings. The British also 'created' the Indian peasantry by forming a new type of property right on land by welding together existing forms of proprietary domination with the obligation to pay the land revenue. Beginning with 1872 the colonial census of India introduced the notions of religion, caste and race. Religion was used as a fundamental category in census tabulations. The colonial census adopted the following homogeneous and mutually exclusive categories of classification:

I Indo-Aryan,

(A) Hindu:

- (a) Hindu Brahmanic,
- (b) Hindu (Arya-Vedic Theists), and
- (c) Hindu (Brahmo-Eclectic Theists)

(B) Sikh,

(C) Jain,

(D) Buddhist,

(E) Iranian,

(F) Zoroastrian, (Parsi)

(G) Semitic,

(H) Musalmans,

(I) Christians,

(J) Jews,

(K) Primitive, Animistic, Miscellaneous

In this colonial scheme of social categorisation, the people living in India were identified basically in terms of their individual religious leanings. In this design, the Hindus were defined as, "a native of India". Bhagat says, the census had not only tried to define Hindus but it had gone further to identify 'genuine Hindus' (Bhagat 2001). It is widely asserted that the colonial census played an important role in identity formation in whole of south Asia. Some scholars argue that modern politicised identities in India derive their definite geographical and social boundaries through census enumeration initiated during British rule [Bernard Cohn (1987) Anderson 1991; Appaduarai 1996]. Indeed the early practice of use of the identification terms was full of faults. Thus, we see that, in early writings, for example, jats and Rajputs were often treated as tribes [Baines 1893]. On the other hand, the concept of race was introduced to differentiate between the natives of Indian origin and those coming from the western countries. The population was divided into races such as Indo-Aryan, Iranian, Semitic and primitive race followed by categories of religious groups within each of them, as mentioned above. The British understanding of caste was based on their reading of oriental literature as well as their reliance on local scholars of Hindu scriptures. Their sources of knowledge about caste remained based on religious texts, which presented a model of caste system primarily based on varna and it did not present the way caste was actually practised in different parts of India. It has been stressed both by colonial and Indian scholars that historically Indian communities cannot be bounded in rigid categories – their boundaries have remained fluid, fuzzy and dynamic [Dirk 2001; see "People of India" K S Singh 1991, 2001].

In contrast to Census of India, a few contemporary social anthropological studies have taken note of the variety of social groupings, economic pursuits, ecological adaptations, new sects and traditional modes of veneration, as well as diverse linguistic traits of the people. There has been remarkable denunciation of terms such as 'caste' and 'tribe' including the term 'primitive-tribe', still used at official level in India. There is now greater craving for calling the 'Castes' and 'Tribes' as the 'Communities', using insider's perspectives. This approach has been initiated with greater rigour in publications of the People of India project. For the first time we get through these publications the insider's view with regard to articulation of identity, including religious identity, of all people of India (K.S.Singh 1985, 1994, 1996, 1992[2002]).

Indian Communities

The People of India (PoI) Study of the ASI

The People of India project of the Anthropological Survey of India (ASI) estimated that there are 4,599 separate communities in India with as many as 325 languages and dialects in 12 distinct language families and some 24 scripts. These are called unique entities. Indians are all immigrants; most people have come to a particular part from another part. If considered in terms of all India spread these unique communities makeup 4635 communities from entire India, amongst whom, a high correlation of cultural-linguistic traits is reported between different cultural regions.

Ethnic identities and culture traits of Indian people have never been frozen in time or in space. They have been in state of flux. This may be determined by re-interpreting the data of People of India (PoI) project (1985-1995) of the Anthropological Survey of India. The ASI had compiled initially a list of 6748 communities. After checking them in field, finally 4635 communities were accepted for study. 500 scholars in 3581 villages and 1011 towns, spread in 421 districts and 91 cultural regions, studied these communities. Information was collected for 775 cultural traits. For comparison, data gathered under another project of the Survey, Material Traits Survey (1959-61) was used, as far as possible. As regards ethnic/cultural/linguistic identity, PoI data revealed that people perceive their distribution at regional (state), inter-regional and national level. More than one hundred communities, including Nagas, Mizos and many others, perceive their distribution across international borders. We found that among all People of India, 16.2 per cent are S.C.s, 13.7 per cent S.T.s and about 70.1 per cent other communities, which included OBCs, and minorities. Nine religious categories (Hinduism, Islam, Christianity, Jainism, Sikhism, Buddhism, Judaism, Zoroastrianism and Tribal Religions) are the faiths proclaimed by Indian people.

The people of India identify themselves through various markers. The major markers are male dress, female dress, male shawl, female shawl, turban, male headgear, female headgear, male ornaments, female ornaments, male body marking, female body marking, male tattooing, female tattooing, flag and emblem. Every second community identifies itself as such. A flag is the identification marker for 41 communities spread over 17 states. North-east India has a large number of the communities with female dress as the identification marker. Central India uses tattooing more frequently as a marker. Ornaments used by females as identification markers occur sporadically in most parts of India. Significantly, turban and female headgear in Jammu and Kashmir and male and female shawls in Manipur and Nagaland are important identification markers (Nagaland-People of India, Das and Imchen 1994). India's population is largely concentrated along the major rivers or in the coastal belts. Parts of the hilly terrain of the north-eastern states, Jammu and Kashmir, Himachal Pradesh and northern parts of Uttar Pradesh have a thin population density. In the coastal area a large number of communities have fishing as their primary occupation. The Jains, Buddhists and Sikhs are markedly absent in coastal areas. A few communities live in the high rainfall and low rainfall zone. Agriculture flourishes in this zone. The snowfall zone of the north-western Himalayas is mainly inhabited by Buddhists, and by Hindu and Muslim communities which comprise pastoral nomads. It is in this entire belt that we witness strong processes of syncretism. The Arabian Sea group of islands has Muslim populations such as Manikfan, Thakurfan, Koya, Malmi, Melacheri, Raveri and Thakru, while the islands in the Bay of Bengal have Negrito and Mongoloid components in their tribal populations, such as Jarwa, Onge, Sentinelese, Shompen, Nicobarese and others-besides a very large population of immigrants (Singh 1996).

Tribes of India: Native Beliefs vis-à-vis Folk Hinduism

The colonial construction of former India, the region then coinciding with Greater India/ South Asia, was intensely religious: thus grew the oriental misconstruction of people and religiosity of diverse sections of Indian people. Gradually alien terms were imported to designate the segments of people. Caste and tribe were two major artificial and fallacious categorizations. The colonial ethnographers differentiated tribes from non-tribes on the basis of religion alone. A large number of anthropological works, unfortunately even in the post-colonial era tried to see the cultural contexts using the colonial vocabulary. Thus many colleagues pointed to trends such as tribes being absorbed or assimilated into Hindu society or tribes becoming castes. In fact, much of the social anthropological discourse on tribes has been primarily couched in terms of tribes being transformed into castes. There has been much inquiry in anthropology with regard to the extent to which tribal people in India can be regarded as peasants.

In tribal societies religion does not emerge as an independent phenomenon. Indeed it is closely tied with social structure in tribal societies. Often it is the tribal headmen who perform certain priestly functions and the political, economic and religious ties reinforce one another in tribal societies (Das, 1983, 1988, 1989, 1993: 128 -132, 2003). The chief /headmen ensure the mystical welfare of tribe. Through access to spirits and/or medicine the chief /headmen emerge as rainmaker or medicine man also, but they can all be different people as well. The tribal religions tend to be less systematized and less specialized than Hinduism, Christianity or Buddhism. The religion of the tribal people is generally defined in terms of animatism or animism. It is conceived that everything in this world has life and is animate whether plants, minerals, animals or the natural phenomena or there are a number of souls sneaking around which are intangible and non-material spiritual beings which can influence and interfere in the life of the living persons. Belief in a high god or a Supreme Being is present in most tribal societies. Moral issues are not inherent in tribal societies, though moral behaviour is mandatory. There is hardly any temple of tribal god and no formal worship. Shrines are few and priesthood is informal. The spirits are distinguished according to domains such as earth, sky, water and forest. There are many systems of divination and oracles that are consulted. Ancestor cults occupy important place in tribal religious life. Immense attention is given to funeral. At family, lineage and clan level congregations, headmen/ elders function as religious specialists. In Naga society one elder holds multiple positions. Among the Nagas the will of the ancestors is made known through dreams and misfortunes (Das 1993).

However, the tribespeople perpetually adhered to many aspects of native belief even after their close contact and 'adoption' / 'conversion' of new religion. As our studies show pre-conversion native religious specialists also continued to operate in such societies. There are many similarities in belief and practices of the 'Hindu' and tribe 'worship' systems. This similarity is often regarded as result of the 'conversion'. This is a fallacy. From the third century B.C. there are references to tribes in the edict of Ashoka (Basham 1954: 53). The tribes of Gangetic Plains, according to D.D. Kosambi, were "conquered by and assimilated" into the kingdoms of Koshala and Magadha beginning in the sixth century B.C. (Kosambi 1965:120). H. H. Risley noted in 1873 that the tribes all over India are gradually being transformed into 'castes'. J. H. Hutton was only colonial ethnographer who realised the inadequacy of the term 'animism'. He is said to have reconstructed tribal religion as an independent system (Singh: 2003). He is credited rightly with having rescued tribal religion from the waste paper basket of animism, identified the parameters of its autonomy and the range of its linkages with Hinduism (Singh: 2003). However, like other census officials he too was prone to describe tribal religion as the "surplus material not yet built into the temple of Hinduism". In 1931, of the total number of tribes estimated at 24.6 million, about one third was returned as adhering to tribal religions. According to Singh (2003) Hinduisation of tribes was ascribed to three factors namely (a) the energetic propaganda by the Hindu Mahasabha to return as Hindu every person whose religion could not be found to have originated outside India, that is practically everyone except Muslims, Christians, Parsis and Jews, (b) agitations by such tribes as Gonds and Oraons to be returned as Hindu and (c) action of the overzealous census enumerators mostly Hindus. W. G. Archer also held responsible the Hindu enumerators for returning tribes as Hindus.

There are many facets of the affiliation of popular Hindu mythologies with folk/ tribal traditions. Popular Puranic traditions, which have diffused throughout India and beyond, provide one best example. We observe that even when the tribes have come in little contact with Hindus they have adopted and internalised elements of popular versions of mythical Ramayana/Ram-Katha/Mahabharata in their folk tales, as per their own interpretations.

Tribes of India have an enduring heritage of connections with the natural world. No distinction is made between the spiritual and the 'secular' because it is a holistic. Cultures of Indian tribes are coherent belief systems that include cosmologies - creation myths, transmitted orally, which explain the origins of the people and their relationship to the wider natural world. Some tribespeople worship an all-powerful, Creator. Members of most tribes of India believe in the immortality of the human soul and an afterlife. Tribespeople call upon the Shaman or spiritual specialists, whom they believed to have acquired supernatural powers through visions. The Shaman carried out special ceremonies, songs and dances. Tribal religion indeed remained indissoluble elements of Hinduism in the writings of American and Indian anthropologists associated with the Redfield School. Scholars subsumed within widespread "Hinduism" many beliefs and practices observed among tribal people, including the worship of numerous godlings, animal sacrifice, witchcraft and magic (Singer 1972: 45). Several studies have revealed that tribal people in many parts of India closely resemble peasant societies. In fact the tribal people often mix up the beliefs without drawing boundaries. Hence we see syncretistic religiousness (for critical analyses see Singh 2003, Madhav Menon 2003, Das 2003, 2004, 2005, 2006). In fact branding variously pre-existing religions of tribal communities, as "essential ingredients of Hinduism" will be a serious negation of empirical findings. Several studies have revealed that tribespeople in many parts of India closely resemble peasant societies; even though they exist outside Hindu social order. Continually pre-existing multi-religious, multi-linguistic and multi-ethnic situations in India demand more value-free conceptualisations and objective models. Old theories of acculturation or even 'little' and 'great' tradition indeed seem to serve limited purpose in our understanding of plural-cultural Indian situation today. What indeed lie behind India's multitudinous-ness are a variously and continuously interactive process of discoverable interculturalism and a vibrant process of syncretism (Das 2003).

Results of new works (Das 2003) show that tribal religions have not lost their distinct identities in spite of their prolonged interaction with Hinduism and Christianity. There are traditions within Hinduism, which do not stand apart from various magical-religious practices of the tribespeople. At rural-folk level in rural India popular Hinduism is closely tied to basic religious practices of the local tribespeople. This is possible essentially through the pluralism witnessed within the Hinduism, which can never be identified as a religion of sort in anthropological jargon. Tribespeople have preserved their systems of beliefs and practices including propitiation of deities, observance of magic and witchcraft, tribal priesthood and tribal calendar of fairs and festivals, which reinforce the tribes' sense of autonomy (Das, 1989, 1983, 2003, 2006, 2009).

Anthropology of Religion vis-à-vis Syncretism: Indian 'Composite Culture' and Syncretic Tradition

Theoretical and Empirical Domains

Despite an enduring interest in religion, there is no standardized anthropological theory of religion or a common methodology for the study of religion. Anthropologists do not agree as to exactly how "religion" should be defined or what the term religion should encompass. Efforts at defining religion—ranging from Tylor's 1871 definition of religion as "the belief in spirit beings" to the more intricate definitions offered by Clifford Geertz and Melford E. Spiro—have met with considerable resistance (Morris 1987, Klass 1995, Saler 1993). Geertz's definition however remains the most influential anthropological definition of religion. Geertz has met with disapproval nevertheless for failing to explain specifically how to identify religion. According to Stephen D. Glazier, a major stumbling block to all definitions of religion, of course, is that religion is not a "thing" but an abstraction. Indeed, functional, cognitive, and symbolic approaches have dominated the anthropological study of religion as researchers have become increasingly concerned with the concept of meaning. Earlier views centred on beliefs versus practices, character of religious entities or forces and the spiritual or supernatural realm. Even Durkheim's claim that religion has to do with the "sacred" came to be challenged by scholars, as such terms coming from 'Western context" are not applicable to non-western societies. Goody found that no distinction is made between sacred and profane in a West African society (Goody, 1961). The terms sacred and profane were found to be meaningless in the Azande society (Evans Pritchard, 1937). Anthropologists eventually turned from 'origin issue' to seeking explanations of religion within its 'social context' (Hendry, 1999: 119-120). Hence multiple approaches emerged in terms of "reflection of social organization" and as a "conceptual system". The anthropological definition of religion came to over-generalize the presumed "unvarying' character of religious allegiance of people concerned; ignoring the veiled side of synthesized and syncretistic religious domain.

With almost paradigm shift experienced in the contemporary contexts of the globalisation, cosmopolitanism and the advent of "deconstructionist strategy", there has been a reappraisal of existing knowledge related to culture, identity and religious domain. Gupta and Ferguson (1992) set out to challenge the classical anthropological assumption that cultural identity is coherent with space/place. In today's multiculturalists world the archetypal borders of cultural identity are easily crossed. This emergent phenomenon is related with what anthropologist Clifford Greetz refers to as "cultural-syncretism", a useful answer to misconceptions about essentialised identities and 'enclosed cultures. Having survived peripherally in anthropology, "syncretism" has resurfaced as a valuable tool for understanding the complex dynamics of identity, interconnectedness and pluralism. Syncretism was erroneously included within "the study of acculturation" (Kottak 1991: 407). Syncretism tends to facilitate coexistence and constructive interaction between cultures. Syncretism refers to the mixing of different cultural traditions whether as active, ongoing process or as historical fact. Terms such as "eclecticism" and "cosmopolitanism" have also been used to discuss 'harmonious' ethnic diversity. Clifford regards syncretism as the rule rather than the exception in modern world, where everyone's "roots" are in some degree cut, and therefore it has become "increasingly difficult to attach human identity and meaning to a coherent 'culture'" (Clifford, 1988: 95). In post-modern anthropology syncretic processes are considered basic not only to religion and ritual but also to culture (Shaw and Stewart: 1994). Clifford argues, "Identities no longer presuppose continuous cultures or traditions" (Clifford 1988: 14-15). Within anthropology, where notions of the 'purity' of traditions have not had much credibility, anthropologists have ascribed increasingly a neutral, and often positive, significance to syncretism. Alongside syncretism the issue of hybridity is also brought in to centre of discourse. Hybridity as understood in this way is not only a social or a genetic hybridity but also an individual choice to cross the borders of a constituted identity. Cultural hybridity thus implies a personal strategy. In this post-colonial era the rhetoric of hybridity, is fundamentally associated with the emergence of postcolonial discourse and its critiques of cultural imperialism. This development focuses on the effects of mixture upon identity and culture. Key theorists in this realm are Homi Bhabha, Stuart Hall, Gayatri Spivak, and Paul Gilroy. A key text in the development of hybridity theory is Homi Bhabha's *the location of culture* (1994), which analyses the liminality of hybridity as a paradigm of colonial anxiety.

One important dimension of Indian brand of cultural syncretism, witnessed through prolonged discourse of intermingling of linguistic and religious groups, is that it corresponds closely with the notion of Indian cultural pluralism. In many parts of India, several Hindu communities have both Hindu and non-Hindu customs for different spheres of life, and see nothing wrong in describing themselves as Muslim Hindus or Christian Hindus. Most Salam Girasia Rajputs traditionally had two names for every member of the community, one Hindu and one Muslim. Some Hindu temples have shrines of both a Hindu God or goddess and a Muslim saint. Hindus widely worship Sai Baba, who was a Muslim saint. The moral worldviews of the Bhakti saints suggest high degree of coming together , 'co-mingling' and 'fusion' of thoughts and living.

Hinduism is the largest pluralistic religion in the world. It teaches that there are many paths, many sages, and many holy books and that no religion can claim any exclusive or final representation of truth. Hinduism recognizes a total and profound unity but one that is broad enough to allow for diversity and to integrate multiplicity, like the many leaves on a great banyan tree. Hinduism is built upon diversity and holds within itself an amazing, even bewildering, variety of teachers and teachings from what appear to be the most primitive forms to the most abstract spiritual philosophies and yogic practices. One could say that there are more religions inside of Hinduism than outside of it. Hinduism has more Gods and Goddesses, more scriptures, more saints, sages and avatars, than any other religion in the world, perhaps more than all the other major religions put together. This is because Hinduism has sought to preserve all the main spiritual practices that developed in India over the past five thousand years. What Hinduism really teaches is religious pluralism (David Frawley – 'A Hindu Call for Religious Pluralism'). Hindu pluralism therefore is not the denial of unity but the affirmation of real unity, which transcends outer differences. True unity is built upon freedom, not conformity, and is a state of the heart or inner consciousness, not an outer condition of labels and slogans.

Anthropological Survey of India and Indira Gandhi Rashtriya Manav Sangrahalaya and many Indian anthropologists and historians have contributed towards the growth of the study of syncretism in India. Indeed the greater applicability of syncretism concept has been highlighted in India only recently (K.S.Singh 2003, N.K. Das 2003a, 2003b, 2005, 2006a, 2006b). Syncretism as this author has elucidated elsewhere is a matter of degree, - some societies have blended prominent aspects of two religious dogmas, in others only certain aspects of the original or adopted religion/sect has been retained and internalized. It is seen that syncretism pertains to a commingled religious sequence whose ill-defined frontier shapes its fundamental collective character (Das 2003a, 2003b, 2005, 2006a, 2006b). In his compiled book -"Culture, Religion and Philosophy: Critical Studies in Syncretism and Inter-Faith Harmony", this author has presented over twenty case- studies examining thereby the varied manifestations of syncretism in religious experiences of diverse people of India. In this pioneering work syncretism emerges not only as a viable way of, life but also as a vigorous theoretical category (Das, 2003). Essay of K.S.Singh in this volume has highlighted that tribal religion retains a great deal of internal autonomy in spite of tribals having embraced Hinduism or Christianity. There are many aspects of the relationship of tribes with the Hindu Shrines, with Jagannath or Danteshwari cults, of various modes of worship and perceptions, shamanism and interaction of male and female spirits. Many of the elements described as tribal or aboriginal, particularly those belonging to the Tantra traditions had already been absorbed into the great traditions, both Buddhist and Bramanical. Not only had the Tantra works been written down in Sanskrit language but also the Tantra deities, icons, symbols and rituals had become part of the great traditions. This process was probably complete by the early medieval period. The ferocious tribal deities had been tamed. The Mundas' Sing-Bonga or the Oraons' Dharmesh or the Gonds' Burha Deo remain as tribal as ever, in spite of valiant attempts being made to link them to sun worship or some gods of Hindu pantheon (Singh, 2003). Syncretism, as such is an in-built feature of Indian society and is expressed everywhere passing through cultural interaction over time (Das 2003 (Das 2003, 2006, 2007, 2009)).

Cultural-Integration and more particularly inter-culturalism has been an ancient phenomenon. People visited sacred centres all over the country and thus a process of continuous interaction operated continually at the grass roots level in all historical phases. Regular exchange and sharing of cultural and religious traits, thoughts and ethos contributed to cultural synthesis. One scholar has perceived Indian society as a "honeycomb" in which communities are engaged in vibrant interaction, sharing space, ethos, and cultural traits (Singh 1992 (2002): III). Between themselves the communities look more at commonalties than differences and they easily establish rapport. While reviewing the data set of the People of India project of ASI, we observed that there exists a high correlation between different religious groups, and that people in religious sphere mutually share a high percentage of traits at the levels of Hindu-Muslim (97.7%), Hindu-Buddhist (91 %), Hindu-Sikh (88.99%) and Hindu-Jain (77.46%). Such sharing included performing actual roles in religious ceremonies of 'other' communities, visiting shrines of 'other' religious groups in big numbers. Over 15-22 per cent of people perform specific roles in festivals of other religions such as making image, dress, and ornaments for deities, organizing worship and processions. At the same time we noticed increased linguistic syncretism too. There is a phenomenal growth in bilingualism in India during last two decades (1961 census-9.7 per cent, 1971-13.4 and according to PoI survey done in 1985 = 64.2 per cent bilingualism). It signifies expansive syncretistic growth in cultural interaction (Das 2003). Y. Singh has reviewed the POI data. He says "the fact that the local cultures of castes, ethnicity and communities dispersed into over four thousand entities (4635 communities) lend itself to rationalization of culture zones into 91 configurations and affirms the presence of linkage and interaction between the local and trans-local cultural manifestations (Yogendra Singh 2000: 46-47), (Also see K. S. Singh 1992 (2002); 112-113, Also see "People of India and Indian Anthropology", by N. K.Das in Economic and Political Weekly, July 22, 2006).

India's syncretic tradition, which is often portrayed as 'Composite Culture', has been a principal feature of Indian civilisation. Indian statesmen and scholars have perceived this concept differently. Thus, in the words of Tara Chand a co-mingling and a 'sense of larger allegiance', and according to Humayun Kabir a 'fusion of mentalities' came about in the encounter of Hinduism and Islam and in the argument of Nurul Hasan, there was 'the development of a composite culture tradition'. Nehru's "The Discovery of India" written on the eve of India's independence, applauds India's composite culture. Undeniably, in multiple spheres, right from the plane of philosophical thought, architectural styles, and musical composition to modes of thinking, styles of living, moral outlook, could be advanced, to strengthen this argument. However, the curious feature of synthesis survived, according to Javed Alam, as long as they were left alone; in other words, as long as there was no intervention from above. Once the intervention began (through the dominant versions of the orthodoxy, by the elite or by the state) the common features or compositeness begin to dissolve into the parallel neo-orthodoxies. However the fact remains that unlike the perception of Javed Alam, the nature of the Indian composite culture or syntheses is not so fragile which may not withstand the interventions from above. It is here that we find the slippery ground on which the ethnography as well the historiography of contemporary genre stands. Anthropologists and historians need to portray critically the composite culture, mainly by probing the foundational basis of our composite culture.

Numerous scholars believe that India's historical identity and unity have always been derived mainly from its culture, not from politics or economics, and that this culture is inherently, inalienably, and anciently pluralistic, syncretistic, and tolerant, in other words, perfectly compatible with and supportive of the liberal and secular nationalism of modern India (Robert Eric Frykenberg, Yogendra K. Malik, Dhirendra K. Vajpeyi, and Rajni Kothari).

Bhikhu Parekh reaches out to define Mahatma Gandhi's position:

> *'For Gandhi, Indian civilization was not only plural but pluralist, that is committed to plurality as a desirable end'. --- Hinduism itself 'included all that is known to be best in Islam, Christianity, Buddhism, and Zoroastrianism' and more from India's folk culture, where he witnessed Indians of all communities ready to share in each other's cultural and religious life. The challenge to the Gandhi-Nehru secular state and to India's tolerant pluralistic culture came from 'communal formations', in different phases. Cleavages within Hindu society are seen mainly in the attempts at the construction of a "homogenized" and supralocal "Hindu identity".*

Indeed ever since the late medieval period India witnessed a creative synthesis of Hindu and Islamic cultures and thus grew a composite tradition, a pluralistic synthesis of the Indo-Islamic tradition including inter-faith convergence (Das 2003, 2006). India's multifarious syncretic phenomenon is epitomized in the rich data, which are appearing now. Anthropological findings, from the People of India study, recent anthropological writings, and the findings of the 'Syncretism project' of the ASI reveal any "homogenized" cultural identity was hardly ever observable across the landscape of India. The sharing of space, regional ethos and cultural traits cut across religions and linguistic differences and bind the people together. There are numerous minor religions such as adivasi religions and reformist sects, which have adopted elements from major/dominant cultures and religions around them. However, in doing so they have not diluted their identities, nor have they ignored their basic culture traits/ religious beliefs and practices (K. S. Singh 1985, 1996, 1992 [2002], 2003, Yogendra Singh 2000, N.K.Das 2003, 2003a and b, 2006, 2006a and b).

Innumerable features contribute towards the cultural unity of India. One of the important features is the sacred geography of India. In fact whole of India is said to be one single sacred zone, symbolised in four major shrines-tirthas- and countless temples, shrines, monasteries and river sites regarded as sacred. Classical and popular /folk versions of the Indic religions and beliefs survive. Priestly class pursue the classical version, while the common masses are often tied up with more popular variety of the religious practices. The mystic-devotional traditions such as Sufism and Bhakti sects broadly shaped the popular beliefs of India and beyond. In popular Hinduism the images of Hinduism as well as its contents and values are derived from the compositions of saint-poets. In the Hindi-speaking regions, the Ramacharit Manas, the Padas of Surdas, the Sakhis of Kabir, and the Bhajans of Mira have shaped popular Hindu religious orientations. Muslim poets like Rahim and Raskhan, besides Kabir, who contributed to bhakti literature in the dialects of Hindi. Other Indian languages too have had a galaxy of saint-poets who enriched Indian culture and philosophy, reinterpreted tradition, and introduced reform, often in the shape of protest against the caste tyranny. One of the dominant features of the popular Hinduism is Kirtan or community singing of devotional songs. The Qawwali, often regarded as Sufi style of devotional singing, has been inspired mainly by Islam, but it does incorporate the work of non-Muslim mystics and saints. Rajinder Puri has observed that Farid and Chishti were Muslim saints, Sarmad was a Jew; Nanak, Tukaram, Namdev were Hindus; Ravidas was a Chamar, and Kabir a Muslim weaver. They attracted disciples from all faiths, communities, and all regions. They never sought their religious conversion. Hindu society would have been fractured and ultimately disintegrated had it not been for the traditions of dissent, protest, and reform which acted as safety valves and were instrumental in bringing about adaptations in society to keep it united, said S. C. Dube. However very often such sectarian orders and traditions surrendered to pressures of the regional caste based norms and values, and ended up as varieties of the popular Hindu-centric sects. In India religion is both a way of life as well as an integral part of Indian tradition. Many dances, theatrics and folklore are religious and based on Indian mythology and folk legends. There are many who stress that Hinduism forms the core of Indian tradition. Hinduism, a polytheistic and ritualistic system comprising numerous cults and sects, is the oldest of several religions that originated in South Asia. It remains broadly the unifying force of Indian culture. The epistemological pluralism, in which the Hindu theory of tolerance is embedded and which gives it its distinct identity and appeal, breeds humility and open-mindedness and creates a climate conducive to inter-religious tolerance.

The scholars of the Anthropological Survey of India recently presented several case studies. These studies explain that despite contradictions and diversities, there exists vibrant sharing of cultural and religious traits amongst the Indian communities and a basic sense of regional cultural harmony prevails. The scholars conducted fieldworks in various parts of India. This author was involved in fieldworks in Jharkhand, Orissa and Sikkim to gather data pertaining to syncretic situations. It was seen that in

Jharkhand the Santal had long resisted the process of Hinduisation historically. They were more influenced by the reform movement, launched in the area by the Santal elders in colonial era originally. While holding on to their religion and beliefs, they even ignored the powerful 'Sarana' politico-cultural mobilisation, which was seen as part of the Jharkhand movement. Under the garb of reform the new religion of Safa Hor, have however allowed recently slow penetration of the Hindu cultural traditions and symbols, in Santal area. This inclination for the Hindu-centric ideologies is indeed result of the new demands of political aggregation, initiated by the local variants of the national Bharatiya Janta Party. In early 19th century the Santals were affected by the maltreatments and the economic exploitation by Hindu moneylenders and land grabbing by members of Hindu castes who were called Dikus. Insider's perspective became so intense that they opted for the newly introduced Safa Hor religious movement, which had certain political overtones, as it was the by-product of the larger Kharwar movement. An unconscious aversion for the symbols of Hinduism, led to check the Santals from sliding towards Hinduism. By joining the post -colonial Jharkhand movement the Santals again re-assessed and reviewed their status vis-à-vis non-Santal tribes and Hindus. Jharkhand movement introduced the notion of a common tribal religion to be called Sarna. Santal, Munda and Oraon showed inter-tribe solidarity by associating their respective religions with the term "Sarna". They together returned their religion as Sarna Religion in 1951 Census. Tribespeople emphasised the retention of tribal traits in "witchcraft", which was almost legitimised as a tribal trait, which removed "sin" from public sphere. Thus a morality - religion connection was emphasised as an ideological force. Though the term Sarna is known to Santals of studied villages but they look at Sarna homogenisation process in much of Jharkhand rather as a political attempt to consolidate tribal following. Indeed, in the studied are we found no traces of Sarna homogenisation. Even today they get sustenance from the Santal insurrection of 1855-57, which is regarded as the most important event of Santal history. The Kharwar movement was originally launched as a cultural revivalist movement (to re-establish their "Golden Era") that was aimed at worship of Ram-Chando, a syncretistic formation combining a Hindu deity Ram and a tribal deity Chando (morning sun). By 1880 one Kharwar leader Dubia Gosain adopted the model of Hindu Sadhu by smearing his body with ashes, though political protest also remained part of the objectives. Slowly the movement split into Safa, Samra and Babajiu sects with greater religious overtone. The respective gurus stopped the devotees from worshipping Santal Bongas. These three religious sects emerged with varied influences.

In Pakur district where we conducted our study the Safa Hor sect has a strong presence. The Santal intellectuals like Vasudev Besra whom we interviewed at Dumka argued that Safa Hor is essentially a Hindu sect, which has in more recent years assimilated both Sakta and Vaishnav elements. However, there were also some who rationalised the 'new' developments as demands of political mobilisation.

In our anthropological study also we made a statistical opinion assessment to get into the intensity of Safa Hor sect and also to determine the knowledge about Hinduism among the 'Bonga Hors', follower of 'old Santal Religion'. The fact that several Hindu deities, often with new names, have been 'internalised' and worshipped through tribal procedures helped us to conclude that the 'sanskritisation' is reversed, and even if there is recognition of Hindu elements today it is operating in a politico-secularist mode, because of need for political affiliation. In the last analysis then what survives is more of a syncretistic phenomenon. We can expand this argument. The Santal prefer to 'identify' them as 'Hor', the people. Thus when they are adherents of tribal religion they identify themselves as Bonga Hor, and adherents of Safa sect call them Safa Hor (and Christians are called Esai Hor). Our data revealed that the use of Sindur, an important icon of a married Hindu woman is used by 57% Safa Hor married women, compared to 26% Bonga Hor married women who used Sindur. Tulsi plant or Tulsi pind is available in 57% Safa Hor houses and 4% Bonga Hor houses. Photos of Hindu deities (including calendars) adorn the walls of 62% Safa Hors and 7% Bonga Hors. Duriyo is a typical tribal straw structure hanged on a corner of roof of Santal houses to ward off evil influences of witches and the effects of evil eye. It is common sight in the houses of Safa Hors (76%), Bonga Hors (67%) and even Esai Hors (83%). Though the Santals of all categories recognize the relatively higher/distinct ritual status of the Safa Hors in actual practice the inter-group behaviour patterns are more guided by tribal values. Thus while rice beer has been abandoned by Safa Hors a good number of them (38%) consume it on regular basis. The Hindus funeral rites demand cremation of a dead body but a large number of Safa Hors go for burial. Visits to Hindu religious shrines and river Ganga for holy dip are again a regular affair. Amazingly over 25% Bonga Hors regularly go to Azamganj for holy dip at Ganga River and actual worship, while 100% Safa Hors do so.

Frankly for us, "Sanskitization" and "spread in Hinduism" and "acculturation" theoretical models ill-served in describing the Santal tribal situation where tribal ethos, tribal values and tribal religious traits bounce back following adoption of Hindu elements, some of which are slowly internalized, absorbed and put behind the tribal mask. Thus , a visible binary principle of pure-impure, notions of Aakash (Sermapuri) - Patal (Patalpuri), terms such as Thakur for tribal deity, basil plant, use of vermillion (which is said to be a Mundari gift to Hindu civilization) even Ojhaism with its Hindu-centric magical spells have become essential parts of "Tribal" collective religious existence. The ethos and style of Santal movements were shaped by the characteristics of the society. The wider developments entangled the reform movement with wider current of Gandhian freedom movement. The birth of Jharkhand parties in 1940s led to the prolonged processes which may be variously called de-Hinduization/re-tribalization and indigenization processes. Indeed the various stages of the movements may be seen in the perspectives of dissent, ethnicization and reform. Today it is the reformist/sectarian character of Safa Hor which characterises and shapes a significant segment of the Santal life, even though cultural resiliencies shown by the Santals are part of a unique phenomenon. We see the events here in terms of adoptions and resiliencies observed in a village having dominant Santal presence. A good number of Muslims made no cultural impact though they participated actively in oprganisation of village level collective Hindu pujas such as Saraswati puja. In the ultimate analysis than the Santals indeed give shape to a composite culture buttressed by a vibrant syncretistic religion, if we are to regard Safa Hor as a Hindu sect which it is. Syncretism that thrives in two sections of the Santals emerges as a dynamic two-way process, whereby both sides tend to imbibe and supplement each other continuously.

We also studied the Binjhals of Orissa. The Binjhals are followers of 'tribal' religion, but their long contact with the 'dominant' caste populations, often prompted them to 'identify' themselves with Hindus, even though they agree that Brahmans never served them and majority of their religious festivals are essentially 'tribal', which are managed by their tribal priests. However, in the vast 'tribal' areas of Orissa state we witness penetration of lord Jagannatha, a Hindu deity having a 'tribal' antecedent. Indeed as in most parts of India, so in Orissa folk popularity of Vaishnavisam, which in western Orissa gradually assumed a syncretistic shape as it assimilated dogmas from other faiths. The western Orissa tribes express their identity and distinctiveness also through the veneration of Mother Cults of Samalesari and Patnesari, belonging to tribal religious order, and which also display certain Tantric and Buddhist elements. Within this complex religious synthesis we also witness the place of Jagannath, which is also known to have a syncretic character, which is little known.

Conclusion

In this critique we reflected upon the issues of cultural diversity, cultural pluralism and cultural convergence among the peoples of South Asia in general and the people of India more specifically. Cultural diversity and cultural pluralism are allied concepts, though they differ on their basic inclinations. Concepts of cultural pluralism, multiculturalism, ethnicity, culture, identity and nation-state are most discussed themes of today even though they do not appear as fully justified and pragmatic constructs in today's era. The concept of pluralism implies not only the condition of existence of cultural diversity in any society but signifies a concrete vision, and perspective of promoting, and maintaining the separate identities of the constituent groups on the basis of equality, equal rights and cultural dialogue. The concept of pluralism authenticates and substantiates the social reality of languages, religions, ethnic memberships, and cultural traditions and implies control of institutions by members of the constituent groups. 'Pluralism' also includes the toleration as also acceptance of diversity of opinions, values, and theories. In so doing cultural pluralism seeks to overcome all forms of discrimination. Cultural pluralism is too often now defined in terms of the power relation since it looks at how power and resources are distributed amongst cultural groups.

The South Asian peoples and their cultures illustrate several distinguishing features that set them apart from the rest of Asia. One witnesses in this region characteristic linguistic-cultural convergence. On one hand the Persian, Arab and Turkish cultural traditions from the west form an integral core of Islamic South Asian culture. Thus, belief in Sufism, pilgrimage to Dargahs and Quawalli singing are the typical cultural traditions among South Asian Muslims. On the other hand the Buddhism, having spread in vast Himalayan regions, as also in distant Southeast Asia countries, has many sects and diverse practices variously incorporating pre-existing indigenous religious beliefs in these countries, in syncretistic manner. In south Asian countries , however, there is definite abuse of the democratic norms, as the minorities continue to suffer and there is no respect for human rights in most states. In the debate on India, the nature and functioning of the 'federal' power structure occupies an important place. The foundations of federalism were laid down on the grounds of concern for the uniqueness of culturally diverse groups; eve though Indian constitution does not talk of 'federalism'. No specific provisions for religious or cultural minorities were incorporated, except that they were given equal rights. The principle of "special economic inducements" applied in the case of scheduled castes and scheduled tribes, was designed more to undo their social and economic backwardness. However, in more recent years the steps are initiated variously to preserve and promote their cultural distinctiveness. The Indian state has also commenced a number of measures to preserve the cultural heritages, tangible and intangible, including minority languages and cultures. India is a democratic and federal state, which cherishes modern, liberal and humanistic values. In view of the staggering diversity, the framers of India's Constitution acknowledged the reality of pluralism by guaranteeing fundamental rights to all people of India, and more specifically, through precise provisions, the protection of minorities. Despite enormous pressures, India has been remarkably successful in accommodating cultural diversity and managing ethnic conflict through democratic institutions. In the post - 1980s era India witnessed a series of protests, often based on ethnic, linguistic and regional issues. However, India has succeeded mainly on account of India's federal system, its vibrant democratic institutions which have ensured cultural and ethnic peace.

In the ultimate analysis then it is clear that both integrative and disruptive forces have been simultaneously operating. Indeed, the battle for preserving and promoting "unity in diversity" in India and in wider South Asian region is not lost. It must be recognized that the south Asian people are strongly rooted in their composite culture and secular commitments, evolved over centuries of cultural synthesis. Despite emerging issues of ethnic/ tribal/ minority rights and claims of linguistic and religious identities in countries of south Asia, long traditions of composite culture, which shape the south Asian consciousness, may provide the comfort. South Asia and its people have enough inherent strength and resilience. There is greater need today to reinforce pre-existing cultural interconnectedness of peoples to achieve harmony. It must be recognized that the people of south Asian region are strongly rooted in their composite culture and secular commitments, evolved over centuries of cultural synthesis. There is greater need today to reinforce the pre-existing cultural interconnectedness to achieve a meaningful balance between syncretistic traditions and cultural pluralism.

References

Anderson, Benedict (1991), *Imagined Communities. Reflections on the Origin and Spread of Nationalism.* London-New York: Verso.

Appaduarai, Arjun (1996, 1997), In Modernity at Large. New Delhi: Oxford University Press.

Appadurai, A. (1990), 'Disjuncture and difference in the global cultural economy' in M. Featherstone, ed. *Global Culture*, London: Sage.

Arcia, E., Skinner, M., Bailey, D., & Correa, V. (2001), Models of Acculturation and Health Behaviours among Latino Immigrants to the US. *Social Science & Medicine, 53*, 41-53.

Ashis Nandy (1993), "The Politics of Secularism and the Recovery of Religious Tolerance," in Mirrors of Violence: Communities, Riots and Survivors in South Asia, ed. Veena Das, (Delhi: Oxford University Press, 1990), 69-93.Ashutosh Varshney, "Contested Meanings: India's National Identity, Hindu Nationalism, and the Politics of Anxiety" Daedalus, 122:3.

B. Morris (1987), *Anthropological Studies of Religion* (New York: Cambridge University Press.

B. Saler (1993), *Conceptualizing Religion* (Leiden, Neth.: Brill).

Banks, Marcus (1996), Ethnicity; Anthropological Constructions. London and New York: Routledge.

Barth, Fredrik (1969), Introduction — Fredrik Barth (ed.), *Ethnic Groups and Boundaries. The Social Organization of Culture Difference*. Oslo-Bergen-Tromsø: Universitetsforlaget, 9 — 38.

Barth, Fredrik (1994), Enduring and Emerging Issues in the Analysis of Ethnicity. — Hans Vermeulen & Cora Govers (eds.), *The Anthropology of Ethnicity. Beyond 'Ethnic Groups and Boundaries'*. Amsterdam: Het Spinhuis, 11 — 32.

Bernstein, Richard (1994), *Dictactorship of Virtue: Multiculturalism and the Battle for America's Future*, New York, Knopf, 367 p.

Bhabha, H. (1987), 'Interrogating Identity' in L. Appignanesi, ed. *Postmodernism and the Question of Identity*, London: Institute of Contemporary Arts.

Bhagat, R. B. (2001), Census and the Construction of Communalism in India in *Economic and Political Weekly*, Vol. 36 No. 46 and 47 November 24 - November 30, 2001

Bhikhu Parekh (1989), Colonialism, Tradition, and Reform. An analysis of Gandhi's political discourse (New Delhi: Sage Publications,).

Bjørklund, Ivar (1982), Hvem var kvenene? Keitä kveenit olivat? — Maija-Liisa Kaihania (toim.), Suomalaiset Jaameren rannoilla. Finnene ved Nordishavets strender. Kveeniseminaari 9. — 10.6.1980 Rovaniemellä. Turku: Siirtolaisuusinstituutti, 212 — 218.

Borofsky, R. (1994), On the Knowledge and Knowing of Cultural Activities. In: Borofsky, R. (ed). *Assessing Cultural Anthropology*. pp. 331-347. Pacific University, Hawaii

Borofsky, Robert (1994a), Rethinking the Cultural. — Robert Borofsky (ed.), Assessing Cultural Anthropology. New York: McGraw-Hill, 243 — 249.

Borofsky, Robert (1994b), The Cultural in Motion. — Robert Borofsky (ed.), *Assessing Cultural Anthropology*. New York: McGraw-Hill, 313 — 3 19.

BOURQUE, Gilles, DUCHASTEL, Jules et PINEAULT, Éric, (1999), 'L' incorporation de la citoyenneté', *Sociologie et Sociétés* vol. XXXI, no 2, 41-64. BOWEN, William

G. and BOK, Derek, 1998, *The Shape of the River: Long-Term Consequences of Considering Race in College and University Institutions*, Princeton, N.J., Princeton University Press, 472 p.

Clifford, J. (1988), The Predicament of Culture: Twentieth Century Ethnography, Literature and Art, Cambridge, MA: Harvard University Press.

Cohn, B. S. (1987), The Census, Social Structure and Objectification in South Asia. In An Anthropologist among the Historians and Other Essays. Delhi and London: Oxford University Press.

Czarnitzki, Dirk (2001), Die Auswirkungen der Forschungs- und Technologiepolitik auf die Innovationsaktivitäten ostdeutscher Unternehmen, Schmollers Jahrbuch - Zeitschrift für Wirtschafts- und Sozialwissenschaften (Journal of Applied Social Science Studies) 121(4), 539-560.

Das N. K. (2003a), "Introduction: An outline of Syncretism" In Culture, Religion and Philosophy: Critical Studies in Syncretism and Inter-Faith Harmony. Ed. N. K. Das. pp. 11-36, Jaipur: Rawat Publications.

Das N. K. (2003b), "Religious Syncretism and Cultural Homonization in North East India" In Culture, Religion and Philosophy: Critical Studies in Syncretism and Inter-Faith Harmony. Ed. N. K. Das. pp 295 - 324, Jaipur: Rawat Publications.

Das N. K. (2006), Cultural Diversity, Religious Syncretism and People of India: An Anthropological Interpretation. Bangladesh e-Journal of Sociology. Volume 3. Number 2. July 2006.

Das N. K. (2003a), "Introduction: An Outline of Syncretism" In Culture, Religion and Philosophy: Critical Studies in Syncretism and Inter-Faith Harmony.Ed.N.K.Das. pp 11-36, Jaipur: Rawat Publications.

Das N. K. (2003b), "Religious Syncretism and Cultural Homonization in North East India" In Culture, Religion and Philosophy: Critical Studies in Syncretism and Inter-Faith Harmony. Ed. N. K. Das. pp 295 - 324, Jaipur: Rawat Publications.

Das N. K. (2003a), "Introduction: An outline of Syncretism" In Culture, Religion and Philosophy: Critical Studies in Syncretism and Inter-Faith Harmony.Ed.N.K.Das. pp 11-36, Jaipur: Rawat Publications.

Das N. K. (2003b), "Religious Syncretism and Cultural Homonization in North East India" In Culture, Religion and Philosophy: Critical Studies in Syncretism and Inter-Faith Harmony. Ed. N. K. Das. pp. 295 - 324, Jaipur: Rawat Publications.

Das N. K. (2006), Cultural Diversity, Religious Syncretism and People of India: An Anthropological Interpretation. Bangladesh e-Journal of Sociology. Volume 3. Number 2. July 2006.

Das N. K. (2006), "People of India and Indian Anthropology", in *Economic and Political Weekly*, July 22, 2006.

Das N. K. (Ed.) (2003), Culture, Religion and Philosophy: Critical Studies in Syncretism and Inter-Faith Harmony. Jaipur: Rawat Publications.

Das, N. K and C. L. Imchen, Eds. (1994), *Nagaland, People of India*. Calcutta: Anthropological Survey of India.

Das, N. K. (1988), Tribal Priesthood and Shamanism in Chhattisgarh, *Journal of Indian Anthropological Society*. 23: 223-231.

Das, N. K. (1989), *Ethnic Identity, Ethnicity and Social Stratification in North East India.* New Delhi: Inter-India Publication.

Das, N. K. (1993), Kinship Politics and Law in Naga Society. Calcutta: ASI.

Das, N. K. (1988), Tribal Priesthood and Shamanism in Chhattisgarh, *Journal of Indian Anthropological Society*. 23: 223-231.

Das, N. K. (2006a), Perspectives on Religious Syncretism: A Critique of Conceptions of Culture: Humankind, Vol. 2.

Das, N. K. (2006b), Cultural Diversity, Religious Syncretism and People of India: An Anthropological Interpretation: *http://www.bangladeshsociology.org*

Das, N. K. (1989), Ethnic Identity, Ethnicity and Social Stratification in North East India. New Delhi: Inter-India Publication.

Das, N. K. (1993), Kinship Politics and Law in Naga society. Calcutta: ASI.

Das, N. K. (2001), Ethnic Character and Regional Identity of Chhattisgarh. *The Journal of the Anthropological Survey of India* (2001) 50: 45-55.

Das, N. K. (2005), Divergent Traditions and Converging Faiths: Perspectives on Religious Syncretism: *Journal of Social Anthropology*, Vol. 2, No. 1, June 2005.

Das, N. K and C. L. Imchen, Eds. (1994), *Nagaland, People of India*. Calcutta: Anthropological Survey of India.

Das, N. K. (2001), Ethnic Character and Regional Identity of Chhattisgarh. *The Journal of the Anthropological Survey of India* (2001) 50: 45-55.

Datta, B. (1993), Rama Katha among the Tribal Communities of the North East in Rama - Katha in Tribal and Folk Traditions of India. Eds Singh and B. Datta. Calcutta: Seagull Books.

Diana L. Eck (2006), On Common Ground: World Religions in America, by *Diana L. Eck* published by Columbia University Press (1-800-944-8648). Revised 2006).

Diana L. Eck, (1996), "The Mosque Next Door: Neighboring Faiths," *Harvard Magazine* (September-October 1996): 38-44.

Eck, Diana L. (2006), On Common Ground: World Religions in America Columbia University Press USA.

Eck, Diana L. (1993), Encountering God: A Spiritual Journey from Bozeman to Banaras. 2nd edition 2003: Beacon Press.

Ehn, Billy (1992), Kulturalisering pa gott och ont. Kulturella perspektiv 1(1): 3 – 7.

Eisenberg, Avigail I. (2000), (1995) Reconstructing Political Pluralism, Albany, New York: SUNY, 1995, pp. ix, 211.

Eriksen, Hans Kristian (1982), Kveenikulttuuri tänään j huomenna. – Maija-Liisa Kalhama (ed.), Suomalaiset Jaameren rannoilla. Finnene ved Nordisha vets strender. Kveeniseminaari 9. – 10.6.1980 Rovaniemellä. Turku: Siirtolaisuusinstituutti, 130 – 145.

Eriksen, Knut Einar & Einar Niemi (1982), "Suomalainen vaara" — Pohjoisen rajaongelniia ja vahemmistOpolitlikkaa (1870—1940). — Maija-Liisa Kaihama (ed.), Suomalaiset Jaameren rannoila. Finnene ved Nordishavets strender. Kveeniseminaari 9.—10.6.1980 Rovaniemella. Turku: Siirtolaisuusinstituutti, 79_10g•

Eriksen, Thomas Hylland (1992), Us and Them in Modem Societies. Ethnicity and Nationalism in Mauritius, Trinidad and Beyond. Oslo: Scandinavian University Press.

Eriksen, Thomas Hylland (1993a), Ethnicity & Nationalisn. Anthropological Perspectives. London-Boulder, Colorado: Pluto Press.

Eriksen, Thomas Hylland (1993b), Smd steder—store spørsmål. Inføiing I sosialantropologi. Oslo: Universitetsforlaget.

Eriksen, Thomas Hylland (1996k), Kampen om fortiden. Et essay om myter, identitet og politikk. Oslo: Aschehoug & Co.

Evans-Pritchard, E. E. (1937), *Witchcraft, Oracles and Magic among the Azande*. Oxford: Clarendon.

Friedman, Jonathan (1994), Cultural Identity and Global Process. London: Sage.

Gadgil, M. and Guha, R. (1992), *This Fissured Land: An Ecological History of India*. Oxford University Press, New Delhi and University of California Press, Berkeley.

Goody, Jack (1961) (1967), *The Social Organization of the Lo Willi*. Second Edition. 1967. London: Oxford University Press.

Gupta, A., and J. Ferguson (1992), Beyond "Culture": Space, Identity and the Politics of Difference, Cultural Anthropology 7: 6-23.

Hannerz, U. (1987), The World in Creolisation, *Africa* 57: 546-59

Hannerz, U. (1992), *Cultural Complexity: Studies in the Social Organisation of Meaning*. New York: Columbia University Press.

Hannerz, Ulf (1993), When Culture is Everywhere: Reflections on a Favourite Concept. — Ethnos, volume 58:1—11. Stockholm: The National Museum of Ethnography, 95—111.

Hänninen, Erja Marjut (2002), The Contest of Indian Secularism Master's thesis, University of Helsinki Faculty of Social Sciences Political History, 2002).

Helly, Denise (2002), Cultural Pluralism: An Overview of the Debate since the 60's Published in Ethnopolitics, Studies in Ethnicity and Nationalism (Grande Bretagne), 2002, 30 September.

Hendry, Joy (1999), *An Introduction to Social Anthropology*. London: Macmillan Press.

K. S. Singh (1994), Towards a Documentary History of Anthropological Survey of India, Vol. I, Anthropological Survey of India, New Delhi, (mimeo).

K. S. Singh (ed) (1991), *The History of Anthropological Survey of India - Proceedings of a Seminar*, Seagull Books, Calcutta.

Kamal, Simi (2000), Democratization and Poverty Alleviation in South Asia, Paper Presented at Democracy Forum 2000 "Democracy and Poverty: A Missing Link?" South Asian Regional Workshop, Katmandu, Nepal April 10 - 11, 2000;

Keesing Roger M. (1994), Theories of Culture Revisited. — Robert Borofsky (ed.), Assessing Cultural Anthropology. New York: McGraw-Hill, 301—310.

Kosambi D. D. (1965), The Culture and Civilization of Ancient India in Historical Outline. London: Routledge and Kegan Paul.

Kottak, Conrad Phillip (1991), Anthropology The exploration of Human Diversity. New York: McGraw Hill.

Kymlicka and Norman. (2000), Citizenship in Diverse Societies. New Delhi and London: Oxford University Press.

Lal, C. K. (2003), "The Necessary Manufacture of South Asia" Himal, January.

M. Klass, (1995), *Ordered Universes* (Boulder, Colo.: Westview.

Madan T. N. (1997), Locked Minds, Modern Myths. Oxford University Press. Delhi.

Madan, T. N. (1987), "Secularism in Its Place," The Journal of Asian Studies 46:4 (November 1987): 747-59.

Malik, Iftikhar H. (2005), Jihad, Hindutva and the Taliban: South Asia at the Crossroads Karachi: Oxford University Press.

Menon, T. Madhava (2003), Tribal Religion and Hindu Cults: Case Studies from South India. In Culture, Religion and Philosophy: Critical Studies in Syncretism and Inter-Faith Harmony. Ed. N. K. Das. pp 11-36, Jaipur: Rawat Publications.

Nandy, Ashis (1985), An Anti-secularist Manifesto. Seminar 314. Delhi: Oxford University Press.

Nandy, Ashis (1990), The Politics of secularism and the recovery of religious tolerance. In Veena Das, ed., Mirrors of Violence: Communities, riots and survivors in South Asia, pp. 69-93. Delhi: Oxford University Press.

Nathan Glazer (1975), Affirmative Discrimination: Ethnic Inequality and Public. Policy,. New York: Basic Books,

Ohnuki-Tierney, Emiko (1984), Illness and Culture in Contemporary Japan. London: Cambridge University Press.

Panikkar, K. N. (2005), Minorities in South Asia, Keynote address delivered to the workshop on the Condition of Minorities in South Asia held at Delhi from 16 to 19 September 2005.

Panikkar, K. N. (1991), *"Communalism in India"*, People's Publishing House, New Delhi.

Roosens, Eugeen E. (1989), *Creating Ethnicity. The Process of Ethnogenesis*. Newbury Park, Calif.: Sage.

Roy Burman, B. K. (1958), The Ramayana as Related by a Mech Elder. Folklore October-December 1958.

S. D. Glazier (ed.) (1997), *Anthropology of Religion* (Westport, Conn.: Greenwood).

Sanjek R. (1991), *American Popular Music* .New York Oxford University press.

Shaw, Rosalind and Charles Stewart, (Ed.) (1994), Introduction: Problematizing Syncretism. *Syncretism? Anti-Syncretism: The Politics of Religious Synthesis* London: Rutledge.

Singer M. (1980 [1972]), *When a Great Tradition Modernizes: An Anthropological Approach to Indian civilization*. New York: Praeger.

Singh K. S. (1985), *Tribal Society in India*. New Delhi: Manohar.

Singh K. S. (1992 [2002]), *People of India: Introduction*. Calcutta: Anthropological Survey of India.

Singh K. S. (1995), *The Scheduled Castes*, Calcutta: ASI.

Singh K. S. (1992 [2002]), *People of India: Introduction*. Calcutta: Anthropological Survey of India.

Singh K. S. (1996), *Identity, Ecology, Social Organisatrion, Economy, Linkages and Development Process: A Quantitative Profile*. New Delhi: Oxford University Press and ASI.

Singh, K. S. (2003), Hinduism and Tribal Religion In *Culture, Religion and Philosophy: Critical Studies in Syncretism and Inter-Faith Harmony*. Ed. N. K. Das. Jaipur: Rawat Publications.

Singh, K. S. (1993), Introduction, *Rama-Katha in Tribal and Folk traditions of India*. Eds. K.S.Singh and B. Datta. Calcutta: Seagull Books.

Singh, Nirvikar (2005), The Idea of South Asia and the Role of the Middle Class. Univ. California SCCIE Working Paper No. 05-08 University of California, Santa Cruz - Department of Economics).

Singh, Yoendra (2000), *Culture Change in India: Identity and Globalization*. Jaipur: Rawat Publication.

Sinha, Surajit (1959), 'Tribal Cultures of Peninsular India as a dimension of Little Tradition in the Study of Indian civilization: A Preliminary Statement' in Milton Singer (ed.), *Traditional India: Structure and Change*. Philadelphia: The American folklore society, 298-312.

Srinivas, M. N. (1952), *Religion and Society among the Coorgs of South India*. Oxford: Clarendon Press.

Verdery, Katherine (1994), Ethnicity, Nationalism, and State-making.—Hans Vermeulen and Cora Covers (eds.), *The Anthropology of Ethnicity. Beyond 'Ethnic Groups and Boundaries'*. Amsterdam: Het Spinhuis, 33—58.

Williams, Brackette F. (1989), A Class Act: Anthropology and the Race to Nation Across Ethnic Terrain. *Annual Review of Anthropology*. 18, 401-444.

Wolf, Eric R. (1994), Perilous Ideas. Race, Culture, People. — Current Anthropology 35(1): 1—12.

Worsley, Peter M. (1990), "Cargo Cults" in *Anthropology: Contemporary Perspective* Ed. Whitten, P. and D.E.K Hunter, New York .USA: Harper Collins Publication.

Wright, Susan (1998), The Politicization of 'Culture'. – Anthropology Today 14(1): 7–15.

Sugihara, George (1982), 'Diversity as a Concept and its Measurement: Comment', *Journal of the American Statistical Association*, 77:379, Sep., 564-565.

McIntosh, Robert P. (1967), 'An Index of Diversity and the Relation of Certain Concepts to Diversity', *Ecology*, 48:3, May, 392-404.